GROWING UP WILD:
A Mountain Ranch Childhood

Also by Paul Willard Richard

COLORADO'S NORTH PARK:
History, Wildlife, and Ranching

Walden Press

GROWING UP WILD:
A Mountain Ranch Childhood

Paul Willard Richard

Order this book online at www.trafford.com
or email orders@trafford.com

Most Trafford titles are also available at major online book retailers.

© Copyright 2010 Paul Willard Richard.
All rights reserved. No part of this publication may be reproduced, stored in a retrieval system, or transmitted, in any form or by any means, electronic, mechanical, photocopying, recording, or otherwise, without the written prior permission of the author.

Printed in Victoria, BC, Canada.

ISBN: 978-1-4269-3302-8 (soft)
ISBN: 978-1-4269-3303-5 (hard)

Library of Congress Control Number: 2010906200

Our mission is to efficiently provide the world's finest, most comprehensive book publishing service, enabling every author to experience success. To find out how to publish your book, your way, and have it available worldwide, visit us online at www.trafford.com

Trafford rev. 5/27/2010

 www.trafford.com

North America & international
toll-free: 1 888 232 4444 (USA & Canada)
phone: 250 383 6864 ♦ fax: 812 355 4082

DEDICATION

To the Monroes who made it possible for we Richard boys to grow up on a mountain ranch, and to my parents, Edith and Willard, who had the patience and love to let us live wild and free.

And, to my brothers Jay, Bob, Larry, and Jimmy who lived the Two-Bar days with me.

"Every kid deserves an adventure-filled childhood with many freedoms."

--Paul Willard Richard

Preface

My sharing of the glorious fun, wonderful freedoms, and deeply satisfying adventures while growing up on a great Colorado mountain cattle ranch, motivated my doing this book.

Over many adult years, I had seldom swapped stories with anyone who wouldn't have traded their childhood adventures for mine. Why had growing up on this particular ranch made my experiences richer than those of my peers? Why had I been able to get away with more than other kids while roaming the Two-Bar? Why were the unique opportunities I experienced not the same for other North Park ranch kids? Why had all of these wonderful facets of childhood come together for me and my brothers? Trying to answer these questions is a part of sharing the adventures in this down to earth story.

Going back, many years had slipped by before I was able to make any headway on the actual writing. For, even then, others had to shove me into doing what I feared I could never properly do. My high school English teacher and mentor, Bill Porterfield, after listening to another session of my growing up stories, suggested I get busy and actually write about my wonderful life while growing up in North Park, pushing me into working instead of telling the stories over and over.

I strongly felt that people who never roamed freely in the great outdoors or had the chance to be wild and ornery on a ranch would find my growing up deeds and follies gripping, interesting, or at least entertaining. So, I did write. Driving me was how my grand Two-Bar Ranch had been the sacred site of wild kid days. My plan was to relive those years myself as I enjoyed writing for others whose growing up had been far different and probably much more tame.

After having such a grand love affair with our home ranch while growing up, I wanted to tell how it was to be a real kid doing real ranch activities. Could a slim middle child, overshadowed by towering older handsome brothers, survive and ever become anything in a working ranch paradise? This story is about whether those efforts came to fruition.

During this maturing, I also had to come to terms with changes in my ranch life. Like my brothers, in my bliss, I had always taken much for granted while adventuring amid mountain beauty. How could I stop or fight the emancipation and grim growing up changes suddenly coming my way? Such is the ride through this book's adventures, with the reader wondering how it all works out for a Two-Bar kid.

GROWING UP WILD: A Mountain Ranch Childhood is based on authentic ranch life. The place names are factual. However, nearly all the names of people mentioned have been changed with the exception of family and people no longer living. Otherwise the story is true.

To my dearest old friend, baseball coach, and English teacher, Bill Porterfield, "I finally finished it and am deeply saddened that you are not here to grade my last assignment."

I want to acknowledge and thank the fine people who worked on the manuscript, made suggestions, and helped the final product read as it does. Novelist, Elaine Long, of Buena Vista, Colorado, edited the early work, providing vast improvements. Karen Miller, an artist and author of Cowdrey, Colorado gave great feedback. Dr. Robert King, a creative writing professor of UNC in Greeley and North Dakota, was a mainstay of sound advice, inspiration, and essential wisdom. Helen Williams, of the *Jackson County Star* in North Park, helped during the ups and downs over many years never giving up on the effort. Ken Whitney and Linde Thompson of Greeley both added helpful insight and direction to the work.

My heartfelt thanks goes to David Hartman for his unique illustrations throughout the book, showing drawings that refresh this author's soul.

North Parkers Marian Schmidt Turpen, Luella Shillings Lindquist, Jean Hanson, and Bill Porterfield all read the manuscript and provided some locally slanted comments on the final product.

And most importantly, I'm indebted to my mother, Edith Richard, who thought the story should be told and that I was the one to do so.

Introduction

In Paul Richard's previous book, *Colorado's North Park: History, Wildlife, and Ranching,* he recounted his family's five-generation history in a remote northern Colorado valley. Here he focuses on the vivid memories of growing up in that landscape, the true story of the adventures of a young boy in the 1940's and '50s on a beautiful and expansive mountain ranch.

He can remember himself as a poor example of a cowboy--a small, blond, glasses-wearing, buck-toothed middle child--but the reader will watch this skinny ranch kid explore what seemed to him the paradise of a working ranch with the ingenuity of a Tom Sawyer, the wild-loving ways of a Huckleberry Finn, and the resonance with nature of a future biologist.

Richard's story of growing up is familiar in its outlines as he tries to earn the respect of his stoic father, live up to his mother's big expectations, win the companionship of his difficult older brother, and be the leader of his younger brothers. What will be unfamiliar to many these days is the environment in which these adventures take place.

Richard lived in the West many of us never realized was still going on at that time. The West of hard work, of haying and cattle-drives and taking care of the stock, of surviving the summers of grown-up work and the isolated winters of intense cold and bitter winds. The West of ranch-hands and cowboys and drovers, the experts and heroes along with the drifters and bums. And the West of a child's individual freedom almost unimaginable to us now.

Imagine your childhood backyard as a 40-mile wide valley of fields and pastures with two winding streams and an abundance of sloughs and ponds all there for you to explore. Imagine major stands of alders and willows, perfect for treehouses or primitive camping or just youthful wandering. Imagine being able to watch first hand, and for years, the interplay of predator and prey with an abundance of rabbits, hawks, coyotes, foxes, owls, gophers and sage grouse. Imagine having a child's responsibilities in a ranching family but also imagine having the freedom to make solitary journeys of discovery wherever you could.

And there is more. The offspring of a stable and somewhat stern family, Paul and his brothers push the limits of youthful exploration. It may sound romantic for a future biologist to be living that close to nature, but we can't forget he was a growing child. These were not all days of a child's exploration of nature, but hand-fishing, horse-stealing, magpie-catching, woodchuck-raising, river-rafting, fist-fighting, flaming-arrow-shooting, rock-throwing "wild kid days," as Richard admits.

Several of the youngsters' exploits made me wince. Richard and his brothers were, in effect, young lords of their large land, and brooked little interference from "outside". Both the exploits of the boys and some of the members of the isolated community may shock the reader who prefers to think of only the gentle side of childhood, the other side accounting for the title: *Growing Up Wild*.

The book opens with an older Paul returning to the Two-Bar and the scenery of his childhood days on the occasion of its being sold. He is losing his vital connection to the pristine land he grew up in, causing a struggle against change in both his mind and heart. Holding off going inside his childhood home, Richard details the currents of his childhood in chapters with colloquial titles for the major activities such as ridin', riverin', hayin', helpin', schoolin' and winterin'. This book invites you to the heart of a childhood with large responsibilities and a large personal freedom through vivid details and evocative images.

But things are now different and Richard realizes those carefree days are gone and that what he took for granted, a young boy's adventures amid the mountain beauty, has passed. He would like, at the end, to stop or fight the changes suddenly coming his way, but facts are facts. The Two-Bar must be sold, the strenuous necessities of summer work and the bitter winters of the valley too much, finally, for his aging parents. In a brief coda at the end, Richard reads pages from the journal his mother has given him, discovering for the first time what life on the mountain ranch looked like from her point of view.

This book contains the treasures and losses of a Western boyhood and we savor the intensity of his experiences as we mourn their passing. It is clear that Richard will never forget these childhood memories and, after reading his book, neither will we.

Robert W. King

Contents

Chapter One: Returnin'................................. 1
Chapter Two: Ridin'.................................. 21
Chapter Three: Pettin'................................ 51
Chapter Four: Springin'............................... 73
Chapter Five: Movin'.................................. 93
Chapter Six: Riverin'................................ 119
Chapter Seven: Protectin'............................ 143
Chapter Eight: Roamin'............................... 165
Chapter Nine: Raidin'................................ 191
Chapter Ten: Hayin'.................................. 211
Chapter Eleven: Doin'................................ 239
Chapter Twelve: Helpin'.............................. 261
Chapter Thirteen: Gettin'............................ 281
Chapter Fourteen: Schoolin'.......................... 309
Chapter Fifteen: Exertin'............................ 329
Chapter Sixteen: Winterin'........................... 347
Chapter Seventeen: Changin'.......................... 369
Chapter Eighteen: Realizin'.......................... 389

Illustrations

Map of the Two-Bar Richard Ranch where boys roamed .. 10
Buildings on the ranch in the 1920s. 19
Willard Richard horseback in the 1950s 45
Our Magpie who talked 56
Larry Richard 87
Map of Colorado locations 94
Willard, Edith, and Richard boys during the Depression .. 98
Richard range cattle 135
Edith Richard in 1926 146
Map of North Park Richard/Monroe ranches 155
Smokey the wonder dog 187
Richard boys rocking the train 195
Stacking wild hay at the Richards 213
Walden, Colorado viewed from the Two-Bar Ranch 239
Jay Richard 277
The willowed Illinois River bottom 286
Jimmy Richard 292
Early Richard learners at Hopewell school 311
Paul Richard 333
Croppie, the boys first horse 353
Bob Richard 386
Two-Bar Ranch gate 407

Chapter 1

RETURNIN'

"This isn't just a ranch."

Snowcapped mountain peaks surrounded me in all directions as I skirted sleepy Walden, Colorado, on the rutted dirt road and turned into the lane toward the Two-Bar Ranch. Everything in my heart seemed to be falling apart. Come hell or high water, I didn't want to give up the past by losing the ranch. As I had driven back to our home ranch, I had overwhelming thoughts of my boyhood, pondering why everything had to now suddenly change.

I stopped the car just inside the big square gate that framed the buildings and captured the looming snowy mountains sixteen miles beyond.

"Oh my God in heaven, I thought it would never happen," I muttered aloud, as I stepped from the rusty Plymouth and stared at the ranch buildings across the barren dirt yard. For years my folks had talked of selling. Dad had often said, "When someone comes along that wants to pay more than this place is worth, then we'll sell." I thought it had just been talk.

This isn't just a ranch. It holds my life, and childhood, the bones of our great Smokey, and a thousand memories of brave deeds along its pristine rivers, bluffs, and willowed meadows. We Richard boys explored every inch of the 2,029 acres of the Two-Bar and found mysteries and adventure in our realm. Now it's to belong to someone else, just for money?

I gazed at the huge old barn where the thick logs had been cut in the settlement days of hardships. Each section of fence at the pole corrals surrounding it was burned into my brain with events from fence walking on rainy evenings to a mad cow's escaping. Who I was and what I believed were tied up here.

"We have to be off the Two-Bar in thirty days," Mom had said on the phone to me yesterday in Greeley, where I was attending college. She seemed so calm about it, adding, "Your Dad is happy with the deal." How could that be, and how could she allow such a black deed to happen? The Two-Bar had been in the family since my great grandparents (the Monroes) had purchased it during World War One.

I had always assumed that the Two-Bar would remain in the family with one of us boys taking over in a deal of some kind as ranch people usually arrange. But no! It was to be sold to strangers from Nebraska, who didn't know the secrets of its haunts or truly appreciate our history and who probably didn't even care about those things. We were to be estranged from our home, probably even have to ask permission to visit it in the future, good God in heaven!

A walk after the long drive from Greeley would loosen my legs and help my mind clear before I faced them in the big log house. Maybe I could come up with some great reasons for them to back out of the deal and to keep the Two-Bar. Somehow this place, which had shaped my life, had to be held onto.

For decades my parents had struggled to build what was here. They overcame the Great Depression, the dirty thirties, family financial disasters, deaths, and even stolen ranches. Everything they had worked for all of their lives was tied up in the cattle, in the horses, and in this fertile land. I trodded on. I crossed the yard and moved by the towering red barn and acres of gray wooden poled corrals that were surrounded by wind-breaking high-board fences.

I had never swapped stories with anyone who wouldn't have traded his boyhood for mine. Why had growing up on this particular ranch made my experiences more unique and richer than that of my peers?

....

I thought back with fondness on one of the many solo river quests of my boyhood. Seeking the unexpected, I often spent my spare non-school September time along those willow-lined river bottoms. Although on such wanderings I usually carried my bow and arrows, as if hunting, I had no set boundaries or goals. Sometimes my brothers were along, but not this time. They were hard asleep under wool blankets made from our own flock in the big ranch house. Always, Smokey, my "god" spelled backwards, was at my heels.

Prior to sunrise the river was pure, peaceful, and new. Steam in a waist-high cloud rose above it, showing that its water was warmer than the hovering air. The rippling of the stream sent reassuring messages to me and my dog.

As I scurried along in the frosty pre-dawn light, excitement welled up in me. My sacred river was untouched and pristine. The ice was frozen in the back eddies and outward from the shore in uneven toothed plates, and broken only by the slow moving black water slipping by in dank silence. Black tangled and twisted willows lined the creek shores.

I had entered a golden era of childhood when we exchanged our prairie ranch for one in the towering Rocky Mountains of Colorado. Two willowed rivers rich in trout ran through our new place. Lush hay meadows spread on each side of our house, a slow train snaked across the Two-Bar, and a small town of 500 souls bordered our ranch to the south. Opportunities abounded for a kid.

Moving along the river, I felt kin to a Ute brave. I absorbed all the sounds and scenes as Smokey, my dog, explored with me. As the welcome sun brightened the sky above the mountains, magpies squawked in many voices, gadwall quacks echoed up the river, and crow calls could be heard far across the damp meadows. Five times in the early day mist the river bottom resounded with the thumping hollow jug sounds of a bittern's mournful voice somewhere far down the river. That morning I saw a mule deer in the meadow, black crows on the wing, a sneaking badger on a nearby ridge, and a lone red fox. In the early dawn, I loved to move in close before these wary animals bolted or flew.

What to expect on such mornings was as difficult to know as was the future. The thrill was in the surprise of what was around the next river bend. When I was alone in these wilds of our meadows with Smokey, I felt unequaled. I was born under the water sign of the Pisces fish, feeling strong in the wilds with the rivers and Smokey at my side.

Because I was also small for my age, this confidence seemed to collapse when I was with people. Not knowing about my life, my future seemed more of a threat than a thrill. I questioned who I was, how I fit in, and what I was going to become. I worried about making a living someday for I knew full well that there wasn't room on our Two-Bar for five ranching sons, and I had two older bigger brothers.

Now I walked on and reminisced. To the left of the barn, a sagebrush flat extended to the west edge of Walden's shanty fringe of tiny low-roofed houses. Walden's courthouse towered, as if it were the cathedral above a tiny Mexican village. Far beyond, mountains of the Never No Summer and Rabbit Ear Ranges dwarfed the courthouse. Gray-topped sagebrush leading to the town's edge rekindled a memory of a spring long ago with my two younger brothers, Larry and Jimmy.

Between the slumbering town and the stately set of ranch buildings, we three crouched in the blackish sagebrush between low scattered islands of the winter's half-melted snowdrifts. Cattle were bawling beyond the buildings, and a lone coyote yapped in the far distance as night lifted slowly. None of these had to fear boys hunting birds before sunrise.

"Are we close enough to shoot yet?" whispered energetic Larry, who, two years my junior, was always impatient. At ten he was unafraid, bold, and totally stubborn.

"Not quite," I replied, as I looked ahead at the dozen dark figures moving across a rocky hillcrest into the gray-green sagebrush.

"I think we can crawl across that little clearing and head them off," said Jimmy, keeping his head low to avoid detection. Jimmy, an eager, action lad, had a zest for adventure far beyond his eight years. Always chattering with enthusiasm, he was as difficult to hold back as a young Cheyenne warrior.

"Yes, if we do'er fast and keep down, we can blast those leaders when they hit the next open place," whispered Larry breathlessly as he checked the arrow notched to his taut bowstring. I could see his nearly solid freckled cheeks and dark hair even in the pale light and knew his sense of determination.

The three of us crawled on wet knees through icy standing water, mud, patches of crusted snow, and beds of rocks. After about fifty yards we stopped against a bunch of giant sagebrush. Rising to the kneeling position, we readied our arrows. Our position was perfect. Straining our eyes, we waited. For weeks we had been shooting arrows at them at dawn and dusk, but we had never been this close.

As the first one walked silently into the opening ahead of us Larry murmured, "You say when, Paul."

I whispered, "Wait until at least five are in the open. Don't move."

With numb fingers, in the early morning light we held our arrows as the two leaders strolled into the opening.

Like a flash, a huge dark object swooped in from our right. It plucked the leader from the clearing amid the wing beats of the other rising birds. We rose to our feet and loosed our arrows in vain at the airborne golden eagle that was clutching one of the sage grouse.

"Stupid eagle!" yelled Jimmy, after the vanishing giant as it gained altitude and banked southeast toward sleepy Walden.

We stood silent in the small clearing and watched the eagle climb skyward over the town's square courthouse and disappear. The eleven sage grouse had flown eastward over Walden's north edge and headed across the Hanson Place toward the Woolover Ranch beyond.

"That was really something," I said. "Never knew an eagle could just grab one like that."

"Sure spoiled our shootin'. We had 'em perfect," grunted a dejected Larry. He never wanted to lose at anything.

"Let's find our arrows and get home. I'm hungry" said Jimmy. "Huntin's over for today."

"We'll get those sage hens tomorrow if you guys want," replied Larry as he searched for his arrow.

"You bet," I said.

Discouraged, we returned to the big ranch house to tell our tale of the morning's hunt. Jay, our oldest brother, listened attentively, even though he didn't have a lot of interest in hunting with bows and arrows. Our parents just listened.

Across the table Bob, black-haired and handsome, expressed disinterest. He made fun of our failed efforts and doubted that it was an eagle. He was the self-centered brother who was interested in his own doings. Two years my senior, he was my rival who sometimes sought to influence our younger brothers and to pull them into doing his bidding.

Larry was as stubborn as he was tough and independent. He vacillated between "bein' " with Bob or with me. He was four years younger than Bob.

Jimmy sported sandy hair and flashing dark eyes. He was the youngest of the tribe. He had enthusiasm to burn and was easy to influence. Full of life and burning with energy, he had an inborn yearning for adventure. Jimmy was ready to happily do anything at the drop of a hat.

As an older brother, I worked hard to lead and boss my little brothers around and to do my bidding during our ranch quests, just as my older brothers worked me. Yet when I pressed too hard for my own way, Larry and Jimmy would walk away and do something else. On a big ranch, I couldn't be a total tyrant.

Way back in 1936 when I was born, Joseph Stalin had started the Great Purges in Russia and killed millions he considered different. On this side of the Atlantic, economic pressures were denying those Americans who lacked wealth the basics of life. In Colorado, however, even in the darkest of times there was no denying life itself the right to come forth naturally.

My dynamic mother told and re-told the story of my birth. On the evening when I was born, a gray-brown dust blizzard had departed. The night cleared as the choking powder settled on the barren short grass prairie that surrounded Genoa, Colorado, a tiny town along lonely railroad tracks.

"It's about time you got back here; this baby is half born now," snapped Mrs. Jones at Doctor Kessinger across the room dimly lit with a coal oil lamp. He tossed his black coat onto a chair and quickly washed his dusty hands in a waiting basin of steamy water.

"Guess I shouldn't have gone back home to Limon."

"Things happened real fast after you left, and I've almost got this kid delivered. Get over here and finish!"

"OK, for heaven's sakes keep your shirt on."

"My job is taking care of Edith and this baby after birth, not during."

"You're right. Looks like its a boy, and not a membrane or sack is broken. Never had one of these before, Mrs. Richard. He is extremely rare, a Caul Child." He held the baby aloft and inspected it, then caused its first cries of life.

"My God, you've got an easy delivery here, Doc. You're not going to charge her much for this are you?"

My mother, Edith, interrupted, "Holy cow, I'm just glad it's here; we wanted a girl so bad, and the bill is already paid." Edith was on snow-white sheets in an otherwise dusty room where she had sweated and groaned a new son into the world.

"This child came easier than any I've seen in all my years as a nurse," said Mrs. Jones in a low and serious tone.

"What is this, your fifth, Edith?" asked Doctor Kessinger.

"Heavens to Pete, no! The fourth son. We lost the second one to dust pneumonia, so this makes three boys and no girls yet," whispered Edith from the bed where she would be confined for ten days of recovery while Mrs. Jones cared for me.

"Maybe the next one will be the girl you want."

"For heaven sakes, let's hope so. Who needs all boys? But they run in Willard's side of the family."

My birth, much like that of my four brothers, was on the flat shortgrass prairie east of Denver. I was thus born the middle son in a poverty-stricken ranch family struggling to survive during the depths of the Great Depression on the flat and barren plains of dust-bowl eastern Colorado. I was the great-grandson of a Son-of-the-Confederacy speculator, the grandson of a cattle-speculating millionaire, and the son of a destitute working rancher.

From my earliest recollection Mother always had great expectations. "Paul, you can do better than that," she'd say. It was as if I had to behave better, think more, and help more around the house than the others. I often thought that I was supposed to have been the daughter she and Dad sought.

A small kid, I was also the only blond in the family. From the age of five, I wore glasses because of my poor eyesight and roving left eye. I seemed to be out of place with my darker complexioned parents. My tall, handsome, older brothers, Jay and Bob, often said, "Paul isn't part of the family because he's a blond tow-head" or " He's adopted" or "They found you under a big rock someplace." How could I ever compete with them, let alone excel or do something special?

My father, Willard, a good and quiet man, never took time to play with me nor with any of my brothers. His father and grandfather hadn't played with him either. They assumed no major roles in child raising. Dad's grandfather, Ben, was a proud member of the Sons of the Confederacy since his father, Henry, had been involved in the Civil War. Ben Richard, who had been a terrible penny-pinching tyrant in Virginia, had directly clouded his son Charlie's skills as a parent. Dad also grew up not really knowing his father or feeling close to him. Charlie, too, had taken a distant hands-off approach with my dad. No man on the Richard side of the family, in the straight-laced Victorian Age when the man brought home the bacon and left the kids to his wife, had known how to be a good father. A father was called on to deal with a kid mostly when discipline was needed. Then the fathers, down through the generations, were quick with the stick.

Mother, Edith, an outspoken, frank woman with a soft and caring heart, had been an only child. Unwanted by her own mother, Evelyn, she grew up as a semi-orphan cast about between boarding schools in Denver and Fort Collins. She stayed with other people during most of her growing years. She survived because her father, Jay, and her grandmother, Lindy, helped at critical times in her wretched growing years and saved her from becoming a street urchin or even worse.

Paul Willard Richard

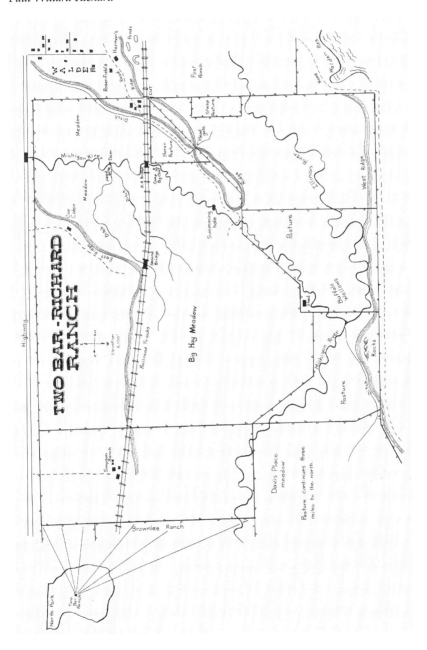

Two-Bar Ranch map showing where Richard kids roamed.
Illustration by David Hartman

Even earlier, Mom's great-grandfather, Daniel Brush Monroe, a Yankee captain, had been gunned down in Zanesville, Ohio by one of his own drunken Union troopers during the War Between the States. Her grandfather, Jap, was left without a father while growing up. The past was littered with tragedy. A sense of security and confidence were lacking in kids with no father or with a father whose main face-to-face interactions were at whipping time.

Out of Victorian family disorder in horrible Great Depression times stumbled my parents, Edith Monroe and Willard Richard, who did a unique job in the way they let me grow up.

There, in the thin mountain air, I was raised in a way most kids only dream about--free, wild, and with four brothers at 8,100 feet elevation on a beautiful mountain ranch, surrounded by animals, wildlife, and lofty mountain ranges on all sides. There was continually something worth doing, as my brothers and I manufactured our own fun and folly during all of those formative years of childhood and youth.

....

I recalled how we ranch boys had conflicts with people who did something wrong to us. Fishermen would sneak onto our place without permission and catch our beautiful, river trout.

My dad allowed almost anyone, who asked permission, to fish on our ranch streams. He would never refuse native North Parkers, either. In fact, he was generous with our rivers, and he set aside a half-mile stretch of stream from the railroad bridge to the highway bridge for kids under fifteen to fish. Dad, however, frowned upon people who fished on his land without permission. When he spotted them on the river, he often sent his boys to run them off.

Jay would ride his saddle horse up real close, within three feet or so, to crowd the trespassing fisherman. Then Jay would ask him to leave. Often times the fisherman refused for, after all,

Jay wasn't an adult. So Jay would ride his horse up and down the middle of the stream to scare the fish until the man left.

Swinging his rope round and round, Bob would threaten to rope a fisherman and drag him across the meadow if he didn't depart. Other times he would ride his horse right into the river where one was fishing, turn toward him in his saddle, and innocently ask, "Are you having any luck?" Then Bob would say, "Get the hell off this ranch." Saying "hell" was a strong message in my boyhood days.

Larry, Jimmy, the hired man's kids, and I raided fishermen. Because they were violating the law by trespassing and doing us an injustice, I felt brave and cocky while running them off. What kind of people were they anyway, not asking permission to fish and just sneaking onto our private land?

Usually Larry or I would tell them to leave. Since they seldom paid much attention we'd cuss them out, telling them they'd be sorry and that we'd get the law on them.

First we heaved rocks into the water near the fisherman, doing what we called "rockin'" the water. He would usually swear at us, reel in his line, and move around a bend to fish in undisturbed water. We'd sneak Indian style in the willows to his new spot. In the tall grass, and from behind high riverbanks we rocked the water again. We raiders usually stayed across the river from our adversary. If we ran out of rocks, we'd yell war whoops and heave willow sticks into the stream.

One guy flogged the river with his fly line and wouldn't leave. Scary and nasty talking, he threatened us when we rocked his fishing spots. Because he doubted such ruffians could be the owners of a ranch, he wanted us to prove our identities. After having climbed trees to get magpie eggs, we sneaked across the river to the fisherman's side, made a running surprise attack on him and from close range showered him with magpie eggs. He immediately gave chase but our knowledge of the willow trails enabled us to dart away from him. Slowed by his heavy fishing boots, he soon gave up the chase. With great satisfaction we watched the egg splattered jerk collect his fishing pole and head across our meadow.

Sometimes when we shot arrows close to fisherman, they broke them over their knees. Then we'd threaten to shoot them with arrows by drawing our bows and aiming at them. Since we couldn't really shoot them and if our bluff didn't work, we'd heave rocks and spears at the stubborn intruders.

Larry had style in dealing with these unauthorized fishermen. After having tried unsuccessfully to run off a fisherman, Larry would pretend to give up and depart. Later, he would sneak in the tall grass behind the intently fishing trespasser. With a sudden lunge Larry would send the man sprawling into the river. Then Larry would run. By the time the fisherman pulled himself out of the water, Larry was nowhere to be seen. It was a proud hit-and-run.

After one of our big raids on five fishermen, they went to the house to complain. Really mad, they told Dad all the things, attack by attack, that we'd done. One even said that we were the meanest bunch of kids he'd ever seen. Dad listened and finally told them that they were still trespassing and that they had gotten what they deserved. He told them to get off his ranch. What encouragement for us--having Dad's total support! I planned with Larry and Jimmy to do even worse things to the next bunch!

That evening at the supper table, however, Dad, unsmiling, turned to me and said, "I hadn't better hear of you drawing your bow at a fisherman and threatening to shoot a hunting arrow into his guts. If you do that again, I'll take that bow and break it."

Then he looked at Larry. "Larry, don't you ever hit a man across the knees with a club again."

Finally his eyes fell on Jimmy. "If you hit a man in the right spot on his head with a rock like you hit that one today, you can kill him. Stop this throwing rocks at people! Understand?"

Much later, a trespasser who had parked his car on the edge of the ridge several hundred feet above him, was fishing directly below the high ridge at the Point of Rocks.

Larry yelled down to him, "Get the hell up here fast. If you don't, we'll take your car out of gear and let it roll down where you are."

In a few minutes, a heavy-set man with sweat streaming down his face and puffing like a steam engine topped the two hundred-foot steep rocky ridge. He was fighting for breath so badly he couldn't talk. He opened his car door and sat gasping for awhile. When he had recovered enough to speak, he told us who he was and explained that Dad had given him permission. We quickly apologized and never mentioned the incident to Dad.

If we could get into trespassers' parked cars, we would. Once we loaded up on cigars we found in a car and smoked them in the willows--an experience we never repeated. Food was a far better item to snitch.

For sure, we weren't the only people in Jackson County who ran fishermen off their ranches. Only our methods may have differed. I often wanted to grow up, get real big, and beat them up. But I stayed ninety-eight pounds and under five-and-a-half feet tall.

....

My mind next wandered to a typical supper in the big ranch house with its pointed cupola on the south end. Willard Richard would raise his eyebrows and give a stern glance at any of us five sons who got out of line. Boys were to be seen and not heard most of the time, especially if there was company. Mom chattered and Dad led the topics at the table.

After we had eaten, we'd move to our spacious living room where soft throw rugs covered glistening hardwood floors. Sunday evenings, Dad turned on the radio and everyone listened intently to the Jack Benny Show. Occasional laughter broke out at Rochester and Benny exchanges. Little talk took place among us boys. We knew Dad and Mom wanted to hear the entire program.

When there were heavyweight champ fights on the radio, we had to be stone silent, too. Dad rooted against Joe Lewis in all his fights because he thought a white man like Billy Conn could whip him. None ever could.

Using a large orange as a darning egg, Mom's busy hands darned socks whose jagged holes were caused by active boy feet. Near the end of the Benny program, she would move to the kitchen and pop corn and prepare cocoa. A big treat.

"Mom, do you think it's fair for Larry to help me with the two town kids who gang up on me after school?" asked Jimmy, who sprawled flat on the floor, was kicking his feet back and forth while stuffing popcorn into his mouth.

"Well, I don't know, Jimmy. Isn't Larry bigger?"

"Sure! But there are two of 'em and they rock and chase me."

"Two against one is bad. I think Larry should clean up on 'em," said Bob as he stroked Smokey's long blue hair. The dog rolled over to have his belly rubbed.

"I know I can lick 'em both," said Larry.

Jay looked up from the *Batman Comic* and said, "I don't think it's smart having Larry clean up on smaller kids. They have brothers. I'm not crazy about fighting 'cuz of Jimmy."

"Are you chicken?" probed Larry.

"No, stupid," retorted Jay.

"Now just a minute, you two! For heavens sakes, Jimmy, why don't you talk with the teacher or principal?"

"Oh, Mom!"

"What do you mean 'Oh Mom'?"

"I just can't be a tattle-tale. That makes it worse."

Dad lowered the *Denver Post*. "Why don't you get Larry or Paul to walk home with you?"

"Guess I could," replied Jimmy. "But what do I do when they can't?"

"Run real fast," Jay laughed.

"Real funny, Jay," countered Jimmy.

Bob looked up from petting Smokey and said, "I was reading this book about outlaws attacking this guy to steal his herd of horses. There were five of 'em, and they expected him to run. Instead, he got a gun in each hand and charged them at full gallop, shootin' like mad. They scattered."

"You're a good rocker, Jimmy. Just load up and attack 'em like mad," said Jay.

"You bet, get some guts and go after 'em, Jimmy," ordered Bob.

Dad changed the conversation asking, "Paul, do you think there's any chance of getting that cow up you guys found on the Illinois?"

"I don't think so. All of us tried to lift her at once. We even used poles to pry her up. Even when she almost made it to her feet, she'd just fall."

"I think she's too far gone," said Larry.

"Good Lord, someone should take a gun down there and shoot her. She's suffered enough losing her calf and should be put out of her misery," replied Mom emphatically.

"Dad, if you want me to, I'll do it in the morning when I run the sheep out," said Jay.

"Go ahead. She's done for," answered Dad. He always hated giving up on a downed cow.

"I'll go with you, Jay. Maybe we can get a shot at that fox," said Bob.

"It had the biggest tail you ever saw," said Jimmy, "I'd love to hang it in our room."

"Why don't you just leave it alone? It's not hurting us any," said Mom as she set up the card table and dumped a puzzle.

Dad replied, "You know, Edith, they do eat a lot of duck eggs and small sage hens."

"Yes, Willard, but we have lots of ducks and sage hens. I just think foxes are beautiful. Shoot at 'em if you wish, but I think they're not hurting us any."

"If that fox saw us today, there won't be hide nor hair of 'em around tomorrow. They are really savvy," added Dad who never put restrictions on our going after wildlife on the ranch.

Teasingly, Bob said, "That fox would be as bad eating as those gophers Paul, Larry, and Jimmy keep chasing down the ridge."

"Bob, we're not trying to kill them. It's just givin' target practice so we can get ready for summer huntin'," responded Larry.

"You'll like it when our hunting arrows get a bunch of meat this summer on the Illinois. You're just jealous 'cause you can't hit anything with a bow," said Jimmy.

....

Clearing my mind again and viewing the buildings, I well remembered my first sighting of our town and ranch when I had just finished the second grade. It was 1943 and we were moving to the Two-Bar from the flat prairie. We had sped across the open expanses of North Park sagebrush until the road suddenly dropped down a bluff to the Michigan River. Walden covered the southern horizon above a beautiful green meadow and rested on a long sagebrush ridge. Its courthouse high on the hill towered above all other structures. It appeared to be a more worthy building than any other in the small town. Mom turned the car westward, and we passed a few scattered houses on the sagebrush flats. Barking dogs ran out and chased the car. Our wheels sprayed water when we hit the many shallow mud holes in the wide dirt road.

Resting a quarter-mile northwest of town, the treeless ranch buildings appeared tall, stark, and stately. As we passed under the big square gate, the enormity of the buildings shocked me. A giant red barn, a square two story log barn, a squatty log shop/coal house, a large "T" shaped log cook house with a dinner bell, a big ranch house with a three-windowed sun room topped with a cupola, a two story bunkhouse, plus chicken houses, many pole corrals, a windmill, and assorted buildings clustered together. I had never seen such grandeur.

The ranch buildings rested on a rather barren and narrow sage-covered ridge that extended northwest from tiny Walden. This small rocky ridge disappeared as it blended into meadows half a mile north down the valley. There was a broad flood plain and a river on each side of the ranch buildings. On the far side of each flood plain rose a tall ridge covered by rocky outcrops and sage that spread east and west. The ranch was actually the flood plains of two rivers, the Michigan and Illinois. A mile northward the rivers met to become the Michigan. Both flood plains joined into a wider valley that extended to join the North Platte on to the north and flow into Wyoming.

As an adult looking back today on my first viewing of the home ranch, I was too young then to realize what potential this place held for a young boy to grow up wild and free in his own empire of rivers and meadows.

I continued my mind-clearing walk before having to face the folks in the big house. As I tramped beyond the corrals to the north, I saw the place anew with far more appreciative eyes.

I could see the green meadows that extended from the bottom of the sage-covered ridge to the winding silver rivers. The sun reflected from hundreds of ponds and sloughs in the distance. Willows, alders, and a few cottonwoods bordered the two streams.

The Two-Bar, which had been built as a showplace ranch for North Park, had been in Mom's Monroe family for many years. Its magnificent buildings with a huge sixteen-stall horse barn and a ranch house, which displayed seven wooden columns on its long east side porch facing Walden, testified to its luxury. Mom had often told me of many happy times she spent on the Two-Bar with her pioneer grandparents, Jap and Lindy.

Buildings of the ranch in the 1920s.
Illustration by David Hartman

As a boy, my North Park ranch time was worthy of remembering, too. In my heart, I always knew that because the ranch had been in our family for so long, it just had to be the best one around. Being a kid way back then, I had great feelings about my Two-Bar, but I had had questions about myself as a boy. In the mirror, I had always seen a runt with blond hair, weird eyes, and thick glasses--the bane for any ranch kid. Looking back on my childhood, I now knew how little my appearance had to do with what was ahead for me.

I sat down against the gray high-board fence in the thin mountain air and thought for a long time while my eyes scanned the ranch for my haunts of the good old kid days. My memory revisited in great detail many highlights of my Two-Bar adventuring years that were locked into my mind as if they had been carved there on hard granite.

Chapter 2

RIDIN'

"The son-of-a-gun doesn't live who can get away from me and this little brown horse."

As I looked west to the Illinois River valley beyond the corral pole fences, my eyes fell on a lone brown saddle horse grazing on fresh spring pasture grass. It reminded me of my youthful riding days helping work cattle from horseback.

One of my earliest childhood memories on the ranch was gazing out an ice bordered kitchen window to see Dad riding his saddle horse totally plastered with snow in a whirling world of white. The horse's black tail was whipped against its side. The tip of the red scarf around Dad's face and neck and the horse's mane stood out straight in the howling wind. I just knew then my Dad was a tough cowboy, but I learned later he'd rather be known as a rider. How I yearned to ride a horse as he did, with dignity and such calm confidence.

I spent years hanging around the barns watching but staying out of the way. I hid in the stalls, grain room, tack room, and our hayloft watching horses being talked to, curried, and sometimes cussed. In no case dared I spook a horse being harnessed or saddled. It might have gotten someone hurt and would bring a hard spanking on the spot from my dad.

There was work to be done on our Two-Bar from the back of a horse. Our horses were essential working animals, not pets, according to my dad. To him a horse was a way of getting someplace or doing something that couldn't be accomplished otherwise. Riding a fine animal and doing so was a pleasure, but the enterprise had to have purpose. He was a determined livestock man.

As a ranch boy I was soon involved in the horse-cattle relationships under the watchful eye of my no-nonsense father. I was free to like or dislike the riding duties of ranching, but I had to be in on some of it to help make our ranch work. I wanted the most wonderfully sound horse as my very own, as did my brothers. Yet such dreams weren't always realized. We had to make do with whatever kind of horse was available.

Dad said, "A good horse doesn't eat any more than some counterfeit one." However, he never spent much money providing his kids terrific mounts. He wanted safe ones for his boys, often meaning what we called "plugs."

He disapproved of hurried efforts in working cattle, believing a slow calm approach was in everyone's long-term best interest. Never were we boys to run cattle. A racing, fast-riding cowboy pace spooked cattle, made them wild, and took off valuable pounds. None of these undesirable practices were allowed when working Richard cattle. It was slow and easy all the way, saving the horse, the cattle, and ourselves a lot of tension, wear, and tear. A slow pace conserved horse and rider for any real emergency according to dad.

Sometimes I felt things were way too slow and dull, but I didn't want to bring on Dad's chiding by rushing livestock. I often wanted people to see me on a galloping horse instead of walking my mount behind slow cattle.

Our riding may not have been exciting to the dude or non-rancher, but it was the genuine working rancher's way. Wildly chasing cattle, roping, and running them around were the methods of people who knew little about horses, cattle, or the business of earning a living from pounds of beef produced. We always called such behavior movie, drugstore, or city cowboy stuff epitomized by having your pants tucked inside your boots like Roy Rogers would do in some picture show.

My first riding horse was old Croppie. He was short-eared because his ears had frozen off in a mean Colorado blizzard when he was a colt. He was a prince and gentle as could be, never making a false move with any of us kids even when half a dozen lined up on him. We'd crawl under his belly and even between his back legs without getting stepped on or kicked. Dad had replaced the aging Croppie with a younger horse and made Croppie a kid's horse in his waning years. Croppie was a confidence builder for me since he never made a bad move. I seldom remember riding him alone or being in front holding the reins. I had older brothers.

As time passed I got to ride solo on some kind of horse. They ranged from quarter horses to plain nags. Jay soon was old enough to ride tall and white Teddy, the rough-gaited Arabian. Bob soon had his own horse, Spider, the son of Blackie our quarter-horse mare. Bob always seemed to get the best deal on horses, and I felt Dad considered him more of a rider than the rest of us. Larry usually rode Blackie or a cutting horse called Blue. Jimmy had Patches a small palomino with a white-patterned rear end. I had Dottie.

Dad took in Dottie after a Missouri timber worker couldn't or wouldn't pay the pasture bill. After he rode her just once, he said, " She isn't worth the pasture bill." Then he gave Dottie to me. I puffed up like a toad having my first horse. She was a true plug, but I loved her. It took almost an act of God to work her up to a slow gallop. She wouldn't rein worth a hoot and half the ranch was needed to turn her around, but she was a beautiful jet black and white. A real Indian horse, I thought.

Bob told me, "That plug isn't worth the bullet to kill her dead as a hammer. She's just a packhorse." I knew he was right, but she was striking in color and I liked her anyway.

We Richard sons over the years grew to compete for the best, fastest, and most worthy horses. All of us loved and defended our horses as extensions of ourselves. It was a loyalty we horsemen had, for an attack on a boy's horse was a personal attack, "...and the horse you rode in on too" sort of insult. Such attacks from those outside the family made us fist-fight them on the spot.

I used one of the old saddles Dad had accumulated. I dreamed of having a new saddle or riding Dad's with his "/ 8" and "2 -" brands and "CWR" initials stitched into the deep brown leather. That was as wild a dream as having my own riding boots.

But, along with my younger brothers, I made do, riding with high-topped work shoes for what seemed forever. Sure didn't make me feel much like a rider, especially when we were with other riders all decked out in high topped boots with big heels that caught a stirrup every time. I hated being bootless but Dad said, "It costs too much to get boots your feet outgrow in a year." So I waited as I did for the oxford shoes for school. I eventually got both shoes and boots. Mom eventually ordered me a plain black pair of boots from the Sears catalogue, boosting my pride.

When I rode with Dad, I had to do it all right and be on my toes. I felt safe and proud at his side trying my darnedest even if my mare was a plug. Riding with Willard Richard was a thrill and made me feel important, even just moving an old bull someplace.

Dad had acquired a young horse, Brown Shorty. His Shorty was a blocky gelding with quick moves and incredible speed. He was part quarter horse and had the stamina, strength, and quick cutting ability Dad wanted. None of us kids rode him while Dad developed Shorty into a fine cow horse. Dad said, "He is not a kid's horse and can hurt you." I watched with the eyes of a hawk how he used his horse.

Once I was with Dad working cattle for an Ole Dutchman neighbor, John Kuiper on the west side. Old John rode a big and striking palomino. An old wild cow left the bunch, got away from John, and headed out across the sagebrush with her tail up in the air, trailed by a low dust cloud. When John came back to the herd, Dad asked, "John, you want that cow back?"

"Yah, yah, but let ter go, Villard. We can't get ter." John wasn't much of a rider since it took nearly half an acre to turn his beautiful horse around. Dad took off after that cow like a shot and in a few minutes came high-tailing her back to the bunch, popping her with the end of his rope, teaching her a Willard Richard lesson.

"Villard, you did get ter!" exclaimed John with surprise.

"John, the son-of-a-gun doesn't live that can get away from me and this little brown horse."

John said, "Villard, you sure use a short rope."

"You bet, John, I have a short rope because I have a fast horse."

How I wanted to impress Dad with speed, but I couldn't ever get Dottie revved up to a gallop.

One dusk we were down at the horse pasture below the Two-Bar buildings with our riding animals clustered around us, fighting horseflies. We swatted their tormentors as we stroked and petted our equine friends. Bob boosted daring Larry up on Blue's back. As horses do in bad fly season when they had enough of the biting flies, they bolted. Blue raced off across the pasture at breakneck speed with Larry clinging to strands of black mane. Without a saddle, stirrups, or reins he rode as an Indian, naturally a part of the horse. Over soft ground of humps, across watery sloughs, and jumping the irrigation ditches all of our mounts ran wild and free with Larry as part of them. Finally they returned, and Larry slid easily to the ground. I knew there was another great rider in the family besides Dad.

One spring Dad and Jay were working yearlings at our La Rand pasture. Some of the neighbor's steers had mixed with our heifers. Jay was holding them in a fence corner while Dad cut out strays. One of the steers got beyond Jay and his tall horse Teddy. Dad took after it. In a burst of speed, Brown Shorty sped beyond the steer and encountered a group of badger holes hidden in the sagebrush. Even at a dead run, he missed some of them, but finally stepped in one and went down.

Jay saw the brown horse fall headfirst and roll over in a cloud of dust. When the horse regained his feet, Dad was hung up in the stirrup. Shorty bolted forward. The dragging dislodged Dad's foot as he fell into the sagebrush. Brown Shorty ran a few hundred feet and stopped. Jay dismounted and rushed to our father's side. Dad was white as a sheet, lying in the sagebrush and rocks.

"My arm's broken, Jay. We'll have to put a sling on it for me to get up."

Jay took off his shirt and ripped his undershirt into a makeshift sling. Gently he placed it over Dad's left arm and tied it behind the right side of the neck.

"How's that?"

"Fine! Now see if you can drive the car over here to get me to town." A little color was returning to Dad's face as Jay left him and ran the quarter mile to the car parked by the highway, maneuvering it back to the fallen rider in the grassy meadow.

"Catch and unsaddle those horses before we leave." Jay caught the two horses, unsaddled them, and put the tack in the car's trunk. He then helped Dad into the front seat of the car and headed for Dr. Morgan's office a dozen miles away in Walden. Jay had to stop many times when Dad got sick.

Eventually they arrived at the doctor's office. After a quick look at his arm, Dr. Morgan said, "I can't do much for this. I'm sending you straight to Denver. I'll get Dick Burt to fly you out."

Within a few hours Dad was in a Denver hospital undergoing surgery on his left arm. It was the first of several operations to restore use to an elbow and arm broken in seventeen places when the saddle's tree crushed it against the hard ground.

Dad's hospital roommate had been shot by a deer and was the first man to have that privilege in Colorado. Details had been in the newspapers how he'd leaned his rifle against a tree and moved to slit the downed deer's throat. It kicked and knocked the rifle over, discharging it. The bullet entered the palm of his hand and departed out the elbow shattering all his arm bones. He'd been through many arm operations and comforted Dad with sage advice on arm surgery.

Even after the operations, Dad was never able to fully straighten his left arm.

His stiff elbow limited roping but kept him from few other ranching duties. Strangely, Dad's own dad, Charlie Richard, had a ruined left elbow from an accident involving horses, being unable to extend it fully.

When asked about breaking his arm, all Dad would say was, "It hurt enough to set your hair." He was a man of few words concerning his injuries, never complaining.

Dad spent that year in left arm casts after the many operations. I could see his frustration as he watched from the house, car, or fence the cattle working operations done by us kids and his well meaning hired men. But never once did he show anger at our inefficient efforts.

Like a trooper, Mom ran the haycrew of a dozen haymen, drove a big team of workhorses on the plunger, raced to the house ahead of the haymen to prepare the meals as well as caring for five sons and a bunged up husband wearing a heavy cast. All was done cheerfully. Her only complaint that haying season was how the horses suffered so terribly from all the nasty biting insects.

Mom and Dad always tried to convey how dangerous all horses were, but it didn't always sink into my brain. When some ranch-hand or rancher was killed or dragged to death in our county, it increased our awareness. The folks wouldn't let us boys enter rodeos except to rope calves. They considered bronco riding events too risky. Just working cattle and riding on the ranch produced enough spills.

When Dad worked with green broke horses to make them into sound mounts, he never wanted to have one ever buck. He thought it was a failure if a new riding horse came unglued, got its head down, and bucked.

Over the years my brother, Jay, had two broken wrists and got blood vessels ruptured in a leg from falls and from being bucked off our horses. Dad always said that Jay was the best and most capable help on the ranch but wasn't the best of riders. Bob was the best rider. I accepted that without jealousy. After all, he was older and way bigger than me.

Dad often told us about his collection of horse mishaps before he was married. Once a horse reared over backwards, sending the saddle horn into his chest, breaking ribs. It hurt to breathe for weeks. Another horse fell with him into a deep washout, breaking both ankles. After he rode thirty miles alone back to town, his boots had to be cut off his swollen feet by the doctor. Horses had fallen with him, bucked him off, dragged him, rolled with him, kicked him, and bitten him. Yet, except for two broken ankles, two broken wrists, a broken leg, and a crushed elbow, his injuries had been rather mild, considering some of the mean horses he told of riding in his bronco-stomping days as a young man.

Dad also warned us about the dangers of horse manure, too. When he was a kid, a neighbor lady had hit her bare foot on the boot scraper outside Charlie Richard's front door. It brought blood. Everyone used the scraper to clean manure off boots prior to entering the big house in Brush, Colorado. Weeks later the woman came down sick and soon showed signs of lockjaw. She died a terrible death in convulsions so strong they broke the bones in her arms and legs before she succumbed. Lockjaw (tetanus) made a huge impression on my dad. He saw to it that we boys all had tetanus shots.

Perhaps because of the many spills he'd taken, Dad didn't show a lot of sympathy when we were hurt. Usually it was our own fault, and he sure didn't baby us. He expected us to carry on and be brave about our injuries.

Once I was unloaded in rocky sagebrush on my head and neck by a nutty white horse that was supposed to be green broke. There in the dust I thought I was dying when Dad rode up after catching my loose horse and insisted I get back in the saddle. I did. We pushed cattle all day twelve miles home teaching that horse a lesson, but it was pure misery with my stiff neck. I felt ashamed about being bucked off by a horse Dad claimed didn't buck very hard. Yet, it sure unloaded me.

Dad was a well-respected cattleman who could always be picked out of a group of horsemen for the way he hunkered down on a horse. It was that bronco rider's pose that distinguished him. He was far back in the saddle, had heels down and boot toes pointed outward. It was as if he didn't plan to give ground to any horse wanting to dislodge him.

His trail and riding codes I had to follow were staunch. Unless the trail or road was narrow, horsemen rode abreast so the talk could be side by side. Everyone kept up with the line unless someone had to ride ahead and open a gate. He was also one to let a horse rest, never wanting it "played out."

He preferred a slow lope of a horse as the best method of fast riding. Galloping full tilt was reserved for emergencies. He disliked trotting horses and when he did trot, he stood in the stirrups and held the saddle horn.

He showed me dignity and equality in the saddle. Everyone waited for the person who closed the gate before riding off. We rode side-by-side to give everyone an equal chance of seeing something and a chance to visit. If someone had to tighten a cinch, we stopped and waited, showing good manners. It was relaxed working horseback with Dad. He was never in a hurry and believed rushing and "ramming around," as he called it, didn't accomplish much.

Our horses were to travel, that is walk fast, and not bite at one another when they were being ridden. They couldn't be run uphill unless it was essential. "Too hard on 'em," Dad said.

A saddle horse was never run toward the house or barn when going home. To prevent having horses wanting to head for the house or barn all the time, we walked them. I hated that as I always wanted to race to the house after a hard days ride. How their ears perked up when they saw our buildings! Sometimes they wanted to run and pranced sideways, but we held them back and forced them to walk. "Hold 'em, they want their grain," he'd say. Overcoming the temptation to let them race for the buildings paid off because our horses were not "barn-sour." Every time a barn-sour horse runs after a critter in the direction of the barn, it heads straight for it, forgetting the job at hand.

When we worked cattle, I would help push a herd into a fence corner and hold the cattle. Dad would ride slowly into the bunch with Brown Shorty and cut out those he wanted. Our job on the outside was to turn back everything except those he wanted cut out. It was sort of a mind reading and observation test. He would sometimes say a word indicating the one he wanted out. But usually he expected us to know what he was doing by watching him.

My greatest riding took place when we moved our cows and calves each spring and fall. Trailing them took me out of school each year, and I was gleeful. We drove two bunches of cows and calves to the Norris Place the folks had acquired, twenty-one miles from home, as summer pasture. Then we had to move dry cows and yearling heifers to our La Rand pasture each summer. These three moves took a week. To my delight, return cattle drives home in the fall required more time out of school.

Several days of work were required prior to any major cattle move. This work involved sorting, pairing, and organizing the cattle. Dad called it "gathering." Once cattle were worked, separated, and in the right pasture, the entire Richard outfit went to work. I clearly recall one cattle drive with our hired man Kip.

After an early breakfast, we headed out to catch our horses. They milled about the corral with the milk cows as we each caught and bridled one. We led them to the big red barn. Some of us saddled our horses inside the dimly lit barn while others brought the tack outside and slipped on a blanket and saddle in the shadowy darkness. There was a final check of cinches, ropes, and coats before we mounted and left the Two-Bar's yard. Some of us led our horses the first hundred yards to the pasture gate. After a short pause to tighten the cinches again, everyone mounted, fanned out in a line, and headed cross-country toward the Illinois River. Ebony fish-ribbed skeleton clouds hung in the east, high over the Medicine Bow Range as the sky brightened. No one talked much early in the day.

Dad, we boys, and Kip rode slowly over the pasture with the sun rising behind us. Shadows of the horses and riders extended ahead on the frosty ground, making each rider and horse appear twenty-feet tall. Behind, the hoof prints resembled pathways of small, dark islands in a sea of white frost. Those first sun rays in late May gave a faint feeling of warmth across our backs.

Sparrows and wrens rose in front of the horses and winged beyond the line of riders. Horses gave short snorts while plodding along. Crows dressed in black and their cousins, the magpies, flew from the willows. Ducks scattered off the river with rapid wing beats and quacked repeatedly as they retreated downstream flying low over the willow trees, their voices echoing in the quiet morning air.

The crunching of gravel greeted our ears as the horses' feet left the soft meadow and struck the rocks on the gravel bars at the river's edge. As the noise level increased, more birds flew and a few cows started bawling. "V" shaped marks on the river's surface showed fish moving to deeper water, away from shallow riffles. A little ice clung to the sides of the stream, extending outward inches from grass and rock. Silver tips of ice attached to shore were crushed by our horses' hooves.

Our saddle horses extended their necks to muzzle the water and finally settled on a drinking spot. One horse pawed the water, sending icy projectiles onto adjacent riders. Then it was quiet, except for the noise of sucking water into their throats. Water silently flowed over the stream bottom and created "U" shaped cups around the legs of each horse. Riders turned in their saddles to survey the river and the scattered cattle beyond the clusters of willows. Each horse raised its head when it finished drinking and stood stone still. When the last horse had finished, Dad clicked his tongue, urging Shorty ahead. He splashed silver beads of water in the sun's rays above the Illinois River. Dad reined up when the last horse was on the soft pasture.

"Bob, will you ride down to the far end and be sure no calves are across the fence? I want to count 'em as we let 'em out the gate. Be sure and don't leave any sleeping calves, you guys." Dad then rode straight ahead toward a big bunch of red-and-white cows and calves.

We knew what to do. Larry took the far left as the rest of us moved out, pushing groups of cows and small red white-faced calves toward the west end of the pasture. We then began moving them across the long sagebrush flats.

Jay's mare snorted and jumped five feet sideways when three sage hens burst airborne close beneath her front feet. He managed to stay in the saddle, but Blackie pranced around showing early morning energy. As many sage grouse as the mare had seen, it was puzzling why the big birds scared her. Maybe she wanted something to spook at early in the morning. Horses are like that. They always scared me when they acted wild and crazy. I was never as fearless as Dad.

Jay and the rest of us slowly pushed cows and calves toward the west ridge fence corner. Red-and-white calves jumped up from their resting places and raced about with tails high in the air. Bawling and running increased as we pushed calves and cows off the pasture river bottom into the sagebrush. Their feet stirred the scent of sage airborne, refreshing my nostrils. That perfume whiff was always a pleasing surprise. We hung far back, not pressing calves. They hadn't been driven much and would run back if they had a chance. It was "slow and easy" until the calves settled down a bit and found their mothers.

We all knew we were in for a long day with new calves. They were all unbranded early calves and only little over a month old. They would tire fast, try to turn back, and lie down to sleep. So from the start we needed a watchful eye and loads of patience, which wasn't a kid trait. At times I wanted to whack them into some speed.

When the sea of cattle had been pushed into the big fence corner, Dad opened the gate. He sat atop Brown Shorty making up and down movements with his left hand. After counting the last cow, he rode around to the lead and headed the cows west across the seemingly endless expanse of sagebrush toward the towering white-capped mountains beyond.

We carefully pushed the last calves through the gate, shut it, and got the bunch organized. Dad, the hired man, and Bob rode on the flanks of the herd while the rest of us drove the bunch from behind. We called it "riding drag" or "eating dust." With Dottie, I couldn't do much else.

Without fences in sight, it was the flanker's responsibility to direct the point or head cows in the right direction. Also, they had to keep the herd somewhat narrow to avoid spreading the bunch out wide and slowing progress.

Those of us on drag pushed the cows and calves along, keeping them moving. Sometimes we had to move to the flanks and help push cows inward to narrow the herd width. If the cattle spread out too wide, the drag was unmanageable. Calves and cows would stop, turn back, and head for home. It was a constant job keeping them traveling and maintaining a narrow drag in the aromatic sagebrush.

I considered riding drag low-man-on-the-totem-pole work. It was slow and dusty riding from slow cow to slow calf and yelling to keep them going. Whereas on the flanks, it was riding beside cattle, standing, and keeping them lined out. It was a better job I thought, sort of a big shot job on cattle moving days. I hoped someday Dad would assign me to it.

There wasn't racing about or running our horses except when a calf quit the herd and headed home. Calves don't have too much sense and sometimes are impossible to turn back to the herd. They are swift and just keep running. Sometimes they had to be roped. When drag riders were chasing runaway calves, the flanks moved to drag, keeping the bunch going. If the entire herd stopped, calves would turn around and head for home. That happened one year, and everything headed back to the pasture gate requiring us to start all over again. Dad was unhappy and I remembered him calling a calf "a little bastard" as he finally got it back to the bunch. His words shocked me for he just never cussed around his sons.

By 11:30 we had moved six hundred animals four miles across the tall sagebrush. We rested the cows in a small hollow near the cream-colored dusty county road. Cows and calves quickly bedded down as we encircled them to keep an eye out for any trying to leave the bunch. By this time, both calves and cows were tired. Riders sat on their horses or dismounted and watched from a distance.

I found young jackrabbits wandering in the sagebrush and with the help of Larry chased two down. They fit in our cupped hands and were clear miniatures of the long-eared adults. "Cute as all get out," Larry said as we released them.

"Yeah, they never have a nest. Just hit the ground going, according to Harry's dad," I replied. Harry's dad was my friend's father who knew everything about wild animals.

Soon Mom arrived. We riders took our turns going to the truck to pick up roast beef sandwiches, oranges, and apples and then returning to our posts. After everyone was fed, and the calves properly rested, Dad started the bunch moving again by riding into them. Nobody yelled commands or signals as in movies. It doesn't take a lot of brains to move cattle since any semi-literate kid or stupid hired hand sitting a horse could do it with a little practice.

I, however, felt special and tall in the saddle moving our own cattle with my brothers and Dad since people passing by would notice what fine livestock the Richard outfit owned. I felt important on cattle drives that Dad called "moving cattle." There was a little showoff in me but none in Willard Richard the rider.

After lunch, the cattle moved better because they were being driven along the road west of Walden. About the only problem were cars wanting use of the dirt road, too. Those coming towards us could let the cattle walk past them. But cars moving in the same direction as the herd needed help from riders on drag to clear a pathway.

A car came racing over the hill behind us. The driver saw the cattle and suddenly slammed on brakes. The car slid up behind the cows and halted. Immediately, the driver started blowing his horn. Such behavior irritated us. Those of us on drag ignored the car since its driver was so impatient. Finally, the driver drove his car close behind the cows, hoping to make a pathway on his own. He bumped several. He kept moving until one of the cows gave a big kick and broke his glass headlight. The man stopped his car, got out, and inspected the damage.

"Come over here," the man yelled at Kip.

"What's the matter?" asked Kip.

"That damn cow kicked my headlight, and someone's going to have to pay," he yelled.

"You don't say."

"Yes, I do say."

"You'll have to take it up with someone else, I've cattle to move," replied Kip in his soft voice as he reined his horse, Red, off the dirt road.

The man returned to his car and approached the cattle again. "I want to see the boss," he shouted at Jimmy.

"I'm the boss."

"Like hell you are. You're just a little kid."

"What can I do for you?" asked the slender ten-year old from his little spotted horse.

"Somebody's got to pay for this headlight and get me through these cattle," he yelled out his window.

"Can't do'er," said Jimmy and rode off to push a slow cow.

The man honked his horn a few more times until Larry rode up.

"What the hell's the matter with you, anyway? If you don't stop honkin' that damn horn, I won't let you through these cows all afternoon. What's your big toot, anyway?"

"I've got places to go, and a cow kicked out my headlight."

"I don't think your business is any more important than anyone else's, and if you hadn't been such a jerk honkin' and drivin' into the cows, you'd still have a headlight. If you'd come up here like anyone else instead of all that honkin', I'd have helped you long ago," said the sassy twelve-year old straddling a blue gelding.

Larry rode beside the man's car for a hundred feet and nothing was said.

"Will you please help me through these cattle?"

"You're what we call ICKY! You know, Impatience Can Kill You."

Without another word, Larry booted Blue into the cows, spreading them apart for the car until the man finally cleared the bunch and sped away leaving us and a cloud of dust behind.

To the west, the blue sky draped downward to snowy white peaks. The sharp peaks extended across the horizon from south to north. Below the white snows extended blue carpets of dense evergreen forests blending into lower aspen groves giving way to the light green meadows below, showing our country's beauty.

Only a day and a half drive more and the cattle would be below the aspens in our summer pasture at the Norris Place. It would be so much easier moving them back home in the fall with calves six months old, much stronger, and easier to handle.

A cloud of dust to the east announced another approaching car. This time it had a sign across the top reading "U.S. Mail." The reddish-haired, leathery appearing lady behind the wheel was Mary Brands, or Queen Mary as everyone called her. Her family ranched west ten miles. She had a long mail route each day to west side ranches and was impatient. She honked her horn several times and waved her arm, motioning Larry.

"What do you want?"

"I want through these cows now! I'm carrying the U.S. Mail," she barked.

Her orders struck independent Larry wrong. Like all the Richards, he didn't like being told what to do.

"The hell with U.S. Mail. I'm not letting you through these cows," said Larry riding off. He rode over to me and said, "Don't you let her through, either. Just ignore 'er."

Mary followed the cows some distance. She honked her horn for awhile and finally gave up. I ignored her when she yelled my direction.

Dad sized up the situation and rode back from the point, cleared a pathway, and finally let Mary and the U.S. Mail speed away. He turned in his saddle and tipped his hat to Mary after he chased the last cow from her path. Dad never said a word to us on drag about holding up the U.S. Mail.

After a lot of dust in the afternoon heat, some of the smaller calves would have stopped to lie down if they could. Our horses would give the little guys a bump with their noses to keep them moving.

We riders made more noises as the cattle tired. Dad whistled. Jay slapped his rope against his leg and boot and made a "burr, burr" noise. "Get going, how how, gitup, yip yip yip, move on, ouh ouh, yah yah," were made by the drag people to keep the cattle going and the little calves awake.

Finally, about five o'clock, the North Platte River and its green meadow appeared ahead like the promised land. We forced the cattle down a small dirt road of two tracks leading through the sagebrush toward the first fence we had seen since leaving our ranch gate. Bob raced ahead and opened the gate. The old cows passed through and headed for the North Platte

River to drink. Refreshed, they turned back into the bunch looking for their calves. Once through the gate, the calves immediately lay down in the pasture. Cows bawled and in panic raced about searching for them.

Once they were all inside the pasture, we had to watch and wait for the cows and calves to pair up. If they didn't find each other, calves would crawl through the fence and head home. We'd have calves scattered ten miles back across the sagebrush. So we avoided the temptation of just leaving.

After what seemed a lifetime to me, there was no more bawling. They had all located their weary calves. Dad waved us toward the southwest. We left the pasture and rode to the Mallon Ranch with its huge red barn. We unsaddled our horses, left our tack in the barn, and turned our horses out into their corral. We were a tired, dirty, and saddle sore lot when we finished. My ankles and insides of my knees were rubbed sore because my stirrups were too long. So were Larry's and Jimmy's. All our butts ached, too. We headed for some great hot food and a good night's rest.

The second day, we saddled up early at the Mallon Ranch and gathered our cattle from the pasture. The drive was similar to the first day except there were more fences and pastures along the way. Bridges and ditches had to be crossed and that slowed the herd, but it would be an easier day.

Stiff and a bit sore, our calves were less prone to run back towards home. Also, the cows traveled better with fences on two sides. We had to keep someone in the lead, usually Dad, to close gates and keep other rancher's cattle and horses from mixing with ours. The move went well, and we horsed around a lot, goosing each other's steeds with an unsuspected kick in the flank or a slap on the rump to see who sat a tight saddle. Soon the monotony of the job settled in, and we settled down as drovers.

Bob always rode flank on his horse, Spider, the best kid's steed on the drive. Larry and I resented his bossing us around and spending so little time on drag. In one fenceless stretch, he told Larry to ride and keep the cattle from going north. Larry didn't like the dust and refused. Bob would impatiently push the cattle south and, in a huff, tell Larry again to keep them there. Larry still avoided going into the choking dust. After the third time of being ordered around, Larry told Bob, "The hell you beller. Go to hell."

Bob chased after Larry over the hill at a full gallop. It took two miles for Bob to run Larry down and rope him. When he finally caught Larry, Bob jerked him from Blue's back and worked him over.

They were gone a long time. When they returned, Larry had a big black eye, and he silently rode in the dust. I was unhappy with both because it had been harder riding their areas and keeping the cattle going when they had been out settling their differences.

Tempers grew shorter in the late afternoon. Kip, our hired man, wouldn't ride Red in the bad dust and hung back. Jimmy cut out one old cow and pushed her back to him, telling him to drive her since he wasn't doing anything. A grumpy, black-eyed Larry joined the act and told Kip, "You're fired for not riding in this dust and working like me!"

Then I shot off my mouth about his horse, "Great Red doesn't know a cow when he sees one, so why should he ride in the dust anyway."

Kip said nothing and stopped his tall red horse and removed his Bull Durham tobacco sack from his shirt pocket. He held one string of the white bag in his teeth, opened the bag and poured the brown tobacco into the cupped paper. He rolled his smoke with one hand as he rode back to the bunch. After a final tongue lick to the side of the paper, sealing it around the tobacco, he thrust the cigarette between his lips.

He stuck his tobacco sack in his sky blue denim shirt pocket, took a match, rose in his saddle, and scratched it across his Levi pants. His cupped hands sheltered his face as he lit up. We boys were amazed how he could roll a smoke with one hand while in the saddle, seeming to have totally ignored the nasty comments.

At the top of Kuiper Hill, I rode to the highest knob among scattered limber pines and looked down on Roaring Fork and Butler Creeks with verdant, vast meadow grass covering their basins. I imagined myself a hundred years back as a Cheyenne brave selecting a grazing bison to spear. The willows would have sheltered me as my horse neared the herd in the low gully to the north. We would have eased up the slope as I flattened myself against my horse to resemble a buffalo so as not to spook the nearsighted victims. Then a mighty dash from my great painted pony would put me upon the huge bison. My lance would strike home, bringing down the beast. I would return to my village in glory with a good food supply, saving them all from starvation. My boyhood dreamland had always been to be a free Indian. Where the idea originated, I never knew, but it was a part of me, something I carried all my life.

"Get the hell down here and start driving these damn cattle," yelled Bob from the lower slopes.

My return to drag was immediate. I had no desire to sport a black eye such as Larry was wearing. Worthless Dottie and I pushed the tired calves on up the mile-long hill to the west.

It was a relief to finally see the expanse of wide green meadows at the Norris Place. Dad loped ahead of the cattle and opened the last gate. He counted everything as we pushed the herd down the slope into the grassy meadow.

Some tired calves were afraid of the water and held up crossing a big irrigation ditch. Bob got off his horse and pushed them into the water, forcing them across. Kip got his rope down to catch and drag them. Bob lost his already frail temper and chewed out Kip for wanting to rope the calves and drag them across.

We were a grouchy bunch waiting an endless hour for the pairing up of cows and calves. We finally rode silently on to the Norris Ranch buildings a mile away.

When we were unsaddling, Kip told Dad he didn't think he could get along with the boys anymore and wanted to quit. Dad told him to come to town and draw his time the next morning. I felt a terrible sickening in my stomach. There was little talk during the ride back to the Two-Bar. We all liked Kip, and he'd been with us for several years, sort of part of the family.

Big mouths had done it again. I knew Dad would never reconsider once a man asked for his time. Being harsh had cost me a friend and all of us a good hired man. I knew the drive had to be repeated in a few weeks with the other half of the cows and late calves, but now without Kip.

It made the next drive harder, working shorthanded. Dad hadn't found anyone to replace Kip. On that drive, he rode drag a lot with Brown Shorty allowing us younger kids to sometimes be on the flanks and ahead of the herd. Way back then I never knew what my dad was thinking, but he always was. Today, I look back and appreciate how he didn't try to control our every move, letting us learn from our know-it-all and big-mouthed mistakes.

Dad's Brown Shorty was a steed no son saddled up and rode without permission. The chunky brown gelding wouldn't tolerate nonsense and proved his point by bucking. It was a fast trip to hard earth for boys who made foolish mistakes. He bucked if a rope got under or near his tail. Several Richards were unloaded for that sin. A hired man was also dumped hard for carrying a shovel and letting it touch Shorty's flank. Another man was bucked off for carrying a bucket of staples.

Everything was fine until they rattled; then the man met the good earth along with his noisy can. After having seen Shorty buck so hard unloading people, I was afraid of him while at the same time admiring the horse. That brown horse was like my dad, putting up with little nonsense while working.

Eventually, my turn came to ride Dad's wonder horse, and boy was I in tall cotton being so trusted. Brown Shorty was a bit lazy, but quick, smart, and sure footed; he seldom let an animal get away from him. It seemed as if he knew what direction a cow was going to turn before she did, and he was one jump ahead. It was Shorty doing the thinking and all the work completely naturally. It was such pleasure sitting in the saddle and feeling him work perfectly under me. Because he was a bit lazy, he didn't like chasing critters, so he didn't make mistakes to let any escape. He could turn on a dime and spin clear out from under me. Brown Shorty took off so fast and stopped so hard it took away my breath and made my insides hurt from the jarring. He kept me mentally alert and fearful of being unloaded.

That brown horse with a dark mane and tail had an inbuilt sense concerning his rider. If he was being ridden by someone who knew what he was doing, Shorty rarely bucked. But if the person wasn't a secure rider, he sensed it immediately.

During one calving season, a hired man, Merlin, had to ride Brown Shorty through the heifers each morning. Merlin wasn't much of a rider and consequently was unloaded by Brown Shorty in the snow. After that, Merlin would leave the barn, talking and saying nice things to Brown Shorty as he led him to the yard gate and mounted. No one ever talked nicer to a horse and still got bucked off on such a regular basis. Brown Shorty would send him into the air at least twice a week. Merlin couldn't figure out how Dad could get on Shorty anytime and never get bucked off.

One spring I watched Dad sorting cattle in the big corral with Jay. He was turning a steer when the front cinch of the double rig saddle broke. Brown Shorty immediately started bucking, and Dad went into the air. When Dad landed, he hit a grapefruit-size rock with his rump. One rein was still in his hand as the back cinch kept the saddle under Shorty's belly. When the horse finally tired himself out bucking around and around in a circle, Dad righted the saddle, got a new front cinch from the barn, and painfully finished sorting. For a few days Dad hobbled about, but his horse didn't get out of any work.

I didn't mess with Dad's horse, his gloves, his pocketknife, or his hat. Most everything else he had was fine to use, but those things I couldn't touch without his permission.

When Dad was a kid he was not allowed to use his father's hat, gloves, or horse either. However, he and his brothers once jacked up the family car and sold the tires to buy rabbits. Later they wrecked his car and were expelled from school, all without chiding words from Charlie Richard.

My dad was guided by a set of standards and wouldn't reconsider even when Kip said he'd stay if Dad wanted him to. I had begged him to let Kip stay confessing how we kids had been out of line. He listened but didn't change his mind. Sometimes I didn't understand my father, but I knew he was a gentle but firm person.

Willard Richard, at forty-five, was showing gray in his dark brown hair. His alert blue eyes were wide set in a face browned from daily outdoor work. His medium build was distributed over a five-foot-nine-inch frame. Not a big man, he was capable of doing almost anything he wanted.

His daily garb was a blue work shirt, Levi pants, and brown work shoes. Dad wore boots only when he rode horses. Otherwise, he hated walking in them since they hurt his feet that had been damaged in horse falls. His walk was brisk and peppy showing purpose and energy. The big western hat was avoided. He preferred the short-brimmed Stetsons many livestock men wore.

Willard Richard, a true rider and livestock man. Illustration by David Hartman

His manner was mild, not involving obnoxious behavior, cussing, or dirty joke telling. He was, however, quick to laugh, enjoyed talking, and loved visiting by the hour. Willard Richard would stand about on our town's streets, lean against cars, spit, and converse for hours with other ranchers and cattle people. They didn't congregate in saloons like ranchers did in the picture shows we saw up town.

My dad also didn't complain, gripe, or show immature behavior in front of us. He refrained from running down neighbors or dwelling on people's faults. He was a principled and fair man who set the kind of example difficult for boys to live up to.

The livestock-trading business and ranching were his loves. But I knew his first love was Mom. On her birthday and their anniversary, Dad usually remembered a gift. He would purchase candy or nightclothes and present them with a hug. They were never too affectionate in front of us. That wasn't a Victorian cattleman's way. I knew he loved her.

The week after Kip left, Dad shot a dry cow to be butchered. Three shallow holes were scraped in the rocky yard by the bunkhouse and each twelve-foot leg of a wooden tripod was placed in the depressions as we righted it up into place over the half-butchered cow. Bob, Larry, and I were helping with the butchering as Dad directed. A singletree was wired to the legs of the cow and a block and tackle hooked to the ring atop the tripod twelve feet off the ground. When all the insides were removed and the animal was nearly skinned, we pulled the six hundred pound carcass off the ground and removed the rest of the hide. It was time to cut the carcass in half with the meat saw.

Dad must have noticed something as he paused looking upward while sawing the slightly swinging carcass. He lunged forward, shoving Bob sprawling backwards. With his right arm, he then swept Larry and me safely out of the downward path of the falling tripod. It caught him across the shoulder and back. Dad lay there for some time, asking us not to touch him. Finally, we helped him up, and he indicated he'd better go to the house for a drink of water. Jay soon came home and helped us right the tripod and finish halving and quartering our beef.

Later, Dad came to see that all was up to snuff. He never said a word about protecting us, but I could tell he was hurting. He refused to see the doctor.

Later when I was sixteen, Dad acquired a buckskin with a black-and-white spotted rump. I was flabbergasted when he gave me the horse I later named "Buck." I was most pleased when Dad often rode him working cattle, making Buck a good cow horse. Buck was never a Brown Shorty, but I had finally arrived with my own decent horse and would no longer have to endure the teasing I'd taken because of Dottie.

Dad's saddle horse didn't pull back, run off, throw its head, or head for the barn. Dad had ways of breaking these acquired habits. His horse had to stop quick, turn sharp, and keep a tight rope on a downed critter. It had to turn into him when he put a foot in the stirrup, and stand or back-up on command. Overall, his horse had a job to do. He respected it. It soon knew what he expected.

When I rode horses with Dad, he was always the quiet steady leader. He could do it all. If anyone had trouble with an animal, Dad was there to take after the critter and get the job done. He never bragged, made fun of, or put others down because his horse and skills were better. He was a real rider.

On my own, once I got a little age on me, I'd saddle up and ride the Two-Bar as I pleased using different horses. Some kind of horse that I could use was always in the pasture or in with the milk cows.

I recall setting off on Blackie one day with Smokey at her heels. We rode among the workhorses in the Illinois green pasture. Ubiquitous blue iris clumps surrounded the herd under the clear blue sky on the soft verdant meadow. Slowly I worked into them, naming each of the sixty long-tailed beasts, trying to remember its team partner for haying. I knew each one and had petted and brushed them as they helped us put up hay. I really loved them as wild and free creatures until haying time tamed them into working horses.

I rode on north under the sandstone bluffs and stood on top of the saddle peering into caves high up that were unreachable on foot and looked for hawk nests. Then I rode right up the Illinois River channel for a quarter mile, spotting fish and wild things as the water often reached Blackie's shoulders while I ducked the overhanging willow branches. I worked my mare up the rock strewn west bluff and admired the ranch, viewing it all from high in the saddle. I could feel the puffing in and out of Blackie's sides from the strain of her steep climb. It was a wonderful green ranch with rivers holding wild things.

On the descent, I spotted a doe and fawn along the Michigan who melted into the trees after seeing my dog wander by. Smokey kept me in sight but wandered on his own seeking and probing his domain. Our dog was as independent as I was. We hugged the river bordering willows for a half-mile looking for the deer again. I spotted a big hawk leave a nest. The tree was branchless for ten feet, so I tied Blackie and stood on her back to reach branches for my climb. I found four warm eggs in the flat stick nest as the parent watched from a tall alder tree across the river. I was excited to know that later I would enjoy seeing the young birds grow in the nest and fly away.

Then I rode into one of my favorite small openings, ducking willows, and dismounted. There on the riverbank surrounded by trees and totally secluded, I sat and held Blackie's reins with Smokey resting at my side. We counted trout rise to the surface thirty times and saw seven diving ducks catch fish. I chewed on sweet ends of timothy stems and daydreamed as Blackie ate behind us.

Going home on the two-path dirt road, I opened up my beautiful mare to run as fast as she wanted. Wind blasted my face and tears came to my eyes as I flew free up the road with sagebrush and meadow flying by on each side. Smokey was far behind when I reined in Blackie. She pranced around and soon settled down as I walked her on up the ridge to the barn and unsaddled. Then I gave my trim black mare a bucket of oats and tenderly brushed her sleek black sides, mane, and tail. I felt as if I was a fairly decent rider, but nothing like my dad.

Chapter 3

PETTIN'

"She was the biggest skunk I'd ever seen."

My mind wandered, remembering as a kid that for only two bits I could see the Saturday picture show up town. One that stuck with me all my life was when I saw "The Yearling" in Walden's Park Theatre. The boy character, Fodderwing, was who I came to want to be. He had a huge pet bear that followed him around, allowing his deformed foot to seem unimportant and overlooked.

As little kid, I dreamed of having a big wild animal at my side, too. It would sleep beside me, protect me from enemies, and would cause people to pause and look. I would have settled for a gentle pet deer like my grandfather, Jay Monroe, had as a little boy in 1894 at the old blockhouse stage stop in the north end of the Park. A lobo wolf would have suited me, too, for it would have caused people to steer clear and give me respect. But, alas, wolves had been extinct in our area since 1929.

Although there were no bear or wolves on our ranch, smaller wild animals existed in large numbers. To have a wild animal as a pet was special and exciting to me, and if one escaped or perished, getting another one was usually easy.

Mom's and Dad's friends sometimes referred to our place as the "Richard Zoo" because of our many wild pets. Each spring my brothers and I found something wild to try and tame.

One time, Larry and I climbed a tree and found two young crows, which were grotesque, big-bellied, pinkish bald except for a few black pinfeathers. They were the kind of creatures only a mother could love. They tipped their necks upward and opened large pink-lined mouths, squawked, and begged for food. Home we went with them.

I adopted the crows, but of course I needed Mom's help in raising them. She was a willing partner with pets, and we took turns feeding them a mixture of bread and milk. We placed a teaspoon of bread soaked in milk in their open beaks whenever they squawked. And that was often, too. Our back porch soon sounded like a birdhouse. The crows lived in a big shoebox at first but quickly grew big enough to walk about. Dad said, "That porch and this house smell and sound like a bird house." Mom paid little attention to his complaints about our black friends.

Dad never made me get rid of the crows, however. They continued to grow as we added hamburger, earthworms, and insects to their diets. They soon developed slick, tar black feathers. Although I spent hours talking to Blackie and Croakey, they never learned to say anything. But, they were good companions, making "caw caw" sounds as they followed me around. I loved it when they each sat on my shoulders. Finally, much to Dad's relief, the crows were allowed out of the porch and into the ranch yard. Whenever the door was opened, they hoped to be fed, and they'd make a dive back to the house squawking like crazy, flapping their long black wings, and hopping up and down.

Mom and I debated whether to clip their wings since they were getting ready to fly by mid-summer. We finally decided not to. Begging for food they still flew in, landed on the yard fence, and gave their raucous calls. We continued feeding them into the fall.

Blackie and Croakey were beautiful, jet-black birds whose feathers glistened in the sunlight. They would rest on anyone's forearm and give low croaking sounds, while blinking their big black eyes. When looking for objects, they usually probed their beaks into creases in shirts, pockets, or coat cuffs. They loved to peck buttons. They'd steal matches and cigarettes, combs too, out of people's shirt pockets. If someone cared about the condition of their clothing, it was dangerous to allow them to sit on a shoulder. Little warning was given when they relieved themselves, and their droppings were not sparrow sized either.

Hopping about the yard, they brought in shiny objects, hid them, and searched about for things they had hidden earlier. The sunlight would bring out the glistening black and shades of blue in their feathers. They spent hours grooming and preening themselves. Because they knew we were their family, they stayed close and depended on us for hamburger and other food. Gradually, they discovered wild food sources and started ranging farther and farther from the Two-Bar house. They still slept on the yard fence or atop of the ranch house, however, and squawked at everyone's comings and goings.

One day in the fall, they disappeared. Heartsick I cried, feeling abandoned by my black friends. It was as if a part of me had flown away. How ungrateful--to leave me after all the time spent raising them. "It was to be expected," Mom said, "It's fall, and they probably flew somewhere else for the winter."

Amazingly, the next spring, two big crows landed on our yard fence and stayed close to the buildings a few days. Even though we couldn't get close enough to feed them by hand, they were unmistakably Blackie and Croakey, too tame to be ordinary wild crows.

For several springs, as if they had dropped by to say "hello", they returned and landed on the fences and house. As they became increasingly wary, they finally stopped coming. Never again were crows just big black birds to us.

After the crow-raising experience, which Mom said she wouldn't go through again, I decided to try a magpie. I brought Maggie, our magpie, home from the river nest. A naked pink with eyes closed, she was as helpless as could be. She could, however, open her beak, raise her head, and beg for food. Maggie slowly grew feathers and turned into a black-billed adult magpie. She grew extremely fast and hopped around our back porch, as had the crows. Since she was much smaller than a crow, we were worried that cats might get her. Maggie would have been easy prey, for cats naturally killed birds on the ranch. We kept her locked in the porch until, as an adult, she was able to fend for herself.

Our neighbor told us that a crow or magpie could be taught to talk if its tongue was split. That information didn't seem to make much sense. How could splitting a tongue make anything talk if the tongue was an organ for talking? Mom said, "That idea is poppycock."

We started talking to Maggie, as we would have to a parrot. We called her by name and spent hours saying, "come here," "go away," "dumb birds," and "Maggie." When someone sat down and talked to Maggie, she would turn her head sideways, roll her eyes, and make gurglings in her throat. Sometimes she would jump up and down, tip her beak straight up, and ruffle the feathers under her chin trying to talk. She made the strangest sounds.

Jimmy had a unique giggle. By the hour he and Maggie would play with matchsticks on the porch. She hid them in his clothing and under his shoes. She squawked when moving them while Jimmy giggled. Sometimes they played with Mom's clothespins. Maggie loved those wooden clothespins and carried them about. She placed them in first one pile and then in another.

When Maggie went outside to help Mom hang up the washing at the long wire clotheslines, she played with clothespins and challenged Mom for each one taken from the basket. When Mom returned from hanging out the wash, Maggie hopped along right behind her chattering. At that moment, Mom heard the first giggle from Maggie. It was a "Jimmy" giggle. As Jimmy continued playing with her, Maggie perfected the long giggles.

After that productive result, we talked more with Maggie. Soon, she was saying her own name and giggling to everyone while she rolled her eyes and hopped about on the window ledges of the porch. She became a clown with all the attention. Next, she learned to say, "Go away." Finally, after a lot of difficulty she mastered the whistle. Eventually she added "I love you" and "kiss me" to her vocabulary. The mass attention came as Maggie was in the final stage of becoming a full-grown bird. All this attention must have happened at just the right phase, for she learned extremely fast.

Using her strong wings, she was learning to fly. I decided not to allow her to fly away as the crows had. Since she could talk, I was determined that she wasn't going to leave us.

Taking Mom's scissors to her, I cut off half of Maggie's beautiful long black tail-feathers and snipped the ends of the black and white primary feathers on one of her wings. I didn't dream she would be scared, but she appeared to be half scared to death. It was the end of my close friendship with Maggie. She didn't want anything to do with me after I clipped her. I couldn't blame her, but it seemed unfair for her to hold it against me after all the nice things I'd done in helping raise her. Here she was, my magpie by claim of raising, and yet she fled me in fear. It broke my heart seeing her so friendly and talkative to everyone else, even total strangers, who didn't give a whoop about her. With a deep pain in my heart, I continued loving her from a distance, hoping she would eventually forgive me.

Maggie, now a flightless bird, had to hop rather than fly about the ranch yard. As a full-grown magpie, she had a powerful beak and an ornery disposition. She soon taught the cats the power of her peck, as she sneaked up behind them and pecked their tails. The cats howled and ran. Maggie queened over the cats, keeping them off her porch.

When someone called at the Two-Bar, Maggie was the first to greet that person in the yard. She hopped over and sat on the toe of one of their shoes. They would be impressed with our talking pet, as she poked her beak up under the end of the pant leg. Opening the beak she looked upward to see whether the visitor had on boots or low cut shoes. If they were riding boots, Maggie moved to the boot toe and pecked and pecked in frustration. However, if they were low-cut shoes, look out! She immediately pecked the owner's soft ankles as hard as she could. When the shoe wearer yelled and jumped, Maggie pranced on the ground, tipped her head back, giggled, and rolled her eyes.

Our Maggie who learned to talk, lightening all
our hearts. Illustration by David Hartman

Ole Bill Simpson, a rancher neighbor, walked by one day while Maggie was on the porch talking. He put his arm down, and Maggie hopped aboard and talked. He talked and she talked, each one getting more wound up all the time. The more he jabbered in Swedish, the more excited she became. She just had to peck something. Since Bill's right forearm was convenient, she let him have it. She took a small chunk of flesh out. Bill dropped her and cussed up a Swedish storm. Although he didn't mind the bleeding so much, he was exasperated when Maggie giggled and told him, "I love you" over and over.

Despite the few times she hurt people when she was extremely excited, Maggie was adorable and beautiful. She had a white breast that extended down to her knees. Black feathers covered the rest of her body except for some white on her wings. Her tail was many shades of blue and blue-black which changed colors in bright sunlight. Indeed, she was a strikingly handsome bird with a long black beak and clear brown eyes.

I felt proud when she reeled off a long chain of, "I love you, I love you, I love you, go away, go away," then giggled and said, "Maggie, Maggie."

When I told the kids at school about my talking magpie, they seemed unimpressed, doubtful. They even said I was spoofing. I couldn't understand why they wouldn't give me credit for having a unique pet. Mom wouldn't allow me to take Maggie to school, because Mom felt that something might happen to the bird. So I was stymied, and Maggie didn't even like me.

Maggie met her end in the dead of one winter. The folks had gone to Denver to attend the National Western Stock Show. They left a big mannish lady, Peg Clark, to care for us kids. She was a timber worker's wife and did the cooking for us kids and the hired man. She immediately disliked the hired man and said, "He looks like a sneak to me."

When I came home from school one cold January afternoon, Maggie wasn't on the back porch in the sun. Peg and I searched. We eventually followed overshoe tracks which led along the hired man's house. There we found Maggie stuffed in a big snow bank. She was cold and dead. Tears froze to my cheeks, and I became sick to my stomach, cursing who could have done such a black deed.

Peg Clark insisted that the evil hired man, Jim Parker, had killed our pet since Maggie was beside his house. I agreed with her. Refusing to have him at our table, Peg took his meals and shoved them inside his door at the cookhouse in total silence.

When Mom and Dad came home from the National Western Stock Show, I remember Mom's crying and saying, "I never want another darned pet around here." It always tore my heart out to hear Mom cry.

After he had heard Peg's story, Dad fired Jim Parker, who denied killing Maggie. We never learned why Jim had destroyed our precious pet. At his firing, Jim Parker stood in our kitchen as he protested his innocence. Dad silently gave him a check for his time. Mom wouldn't even be in the room near the man.

We all missed Maggie and her antics. I tried to get Mom to agree to let me raise another magpie the next spring. She refused. For her there couldn't be another Maggie. To this day, I clearly know how a pet can become a part of a person as Maggie was to Mom.

That next summer Jay brought home five tiny teal ducklings that our big blue dog had captured. Smokey had gently brought each one in his mouth to Jay without injuring any bird. Jay and Bob dug a hole in the ground against the hen house and buried a large washtub level with the ground. They screened in a six-foot area that included the swimming pond. A shelter box with hay inside served as a sanctuary. The tiny ducks were also given bread soaked with milk and grain in a shallow pan. The little ducks fed themselves, unlike the helpless crows and baby magpies. How those five little guys went after the food with their small flat bills! They moved their bills back and forth in the milk as they searched for pieces of bread, wiggling their little behinds and shaking their tail feathers around the feeding pan.

Holding them was a tender experience. They sat quietly and explored the creases in my hands and between fingers with their small bills. Sometimes they nibbled rapidly, tickling, but were always trusting and gentle.

For a few months we enjoyed our rapidly growing ducks. Having developed long wing feathers, they had lost their baby duck cuteness. Blue patches on their wings and white crescents near the eyes clearly marked them as blue-winged teal. Nothing had been cuter and more precious than our flock of baby ducks. Now nearly grown, they were ready for their freedom.

Shortly before we were to release them at the river, Mom found the cage empty. A hole had been dug under the screen barrier, and all five were gone. Duck feathers were scattered near the corner of the chicken house. We knew from the size of the hole that something small had made off with our little flock. Each time I had to face the loss of a pet I felt sad, but I gradually realized animals do die.

I couldn't apply death to family members, however. Sometimes I even feared that the folks wouldn't come home when they were away on overnight trips. Their being away worried me a lot as I always asked in my prayers in night's darkness for their safe return.

A week after the ducks vanished, Mom heard a racket out in her chicken house. Rushing out, she saw a weasel chasing her hens in the roosting area. Clumps of white on the henhouse floor indicated that several hens had already been killed. Quickly, she locked the main door and blocked the small hole that led to the outside. She rushed back to the house, grabbed her .22 rifle, and returned with her determined stride to the hen house. She shoved the cartridge into the gun's chamber, slammed the bolt shut, raised the butt of the gun to shoulder level, and smashed out the glass panel. She jerked the rifle to her shoulder and shot the weasel dead with the first shot.

Later, we asked her why she hasn't asked anyone for help. "I simply didn't have time. I just had to get that weasel who'd killed my hens and probably our little ducks, too!"

Mom used guns but was mildly opposed to hunting, except for meat. She encouraged me to learn to shoot well and to hunt, since shooting was a family tradition. I found myself eventually feeling as Mom did. Animals were to be loved more than killed. Little did I know then that my eventual career would involve teaching about animals.

Skunks, which abounded on the ranch, were Smokey's addiction. Many times each year our blue dog wandered home after a night's rampaging, smelling to high heaven. Mom wouldn't have him in the house until the stench had vanished. Smokey acted sheepish and dejected. "Hung dog" as Dad called him. But when the very next skunk came along, Smokey attacked it promptly. Often wounded, the black and white carnivores crawled under the house or outbuildings and left an odor that would sting the eyes for days.

One summer, there was a full week when I couldn't be in our kitchen long because of Smokey's addiction. I remember having to eat and run. Then, Dad had to tear up part of the porch to get the dead skunk when it started to decay. Poor Smokey was really in the folk's doghouse.

When Smokey barked in the willows and pastures, I hurried because I knew our big pal was probably playing and battling his archenemy before closing in for the stinky kill. I had an extremely difficult time getting the big blue dog away from a skunk once Smokey engaged. I had to yell at him in as mean a voice as I could muster before he'd slink away like a whipped hound.

Our hired men told me that a skunk couldn't release its stink if its feet were off the ground. That information seemed incredible. Dad said, "He lied as fast as a horse can trot." Smokey soon located a skunk, and I had to see if it was true or not myself. I undertook the task of catching it without its giving off the repugnant odor. Usually the encountered skunk with tail held high will hiss, stamps its front feet, and face the enemy. When the range is about six-feet, the skunk will do a sudden whirl and spray the attacker with a horrid yellow fluid of stench.

My technique was to hold Smokey back and have fearless Larry keep the skunk's attention in front. I then sneaked up behind and swiftly grabbed the upright tail and lifted the skunk off the ground. The skunk was unable to squirt and was now mine. Heading for the house, we made sure that its feet didn't touch anything. We handed it back and forth as we walked.

When Mom saw us in the kitchen holding a big skunk by the tail, she had a fit. She informed us in no uncertain terms to get outside with that "darned skunk" before she crowned us. One time we had two skunks in her kitchen before she noticed and chased us outside.

Only once did a skunk stink us up. Larry was sprayed as he approached the skunk from behind. He smelled so repugnant that it hurt our eyes to be close. Mom put his clothes on the outside clothesline where they hung for a full week until the odor was gone.

One day when I was down on the Illinois River exploring, I heard Smokey give his "I've-got-something-cornered" barks. He was in a thick clump of tall tangled willows where he was facing a large female skunk when I reached him. Reluctantly giving ground, she was still facing him. I sat down on a big limb as he backed the black-and-white stinker with her bushy tail held high right to me. One quick grab and I had the biggest skunk I'd ever seen off the ground.

Now, how was I to get her out of the willows and not allow a paw on a branch? How was I to prevent becoming a stinking mess? Since the willow thicket was such a tangle, getting her into the open was impossible. I decided to shorten her body length by grabbing her behind the neck. Then I would be able to weave her in and around the branches to reach open meadow.

When I attempted to execute my plan, she twisted her head around in her loose neck skin and bit my thumb. Pain shot through my hand. I slowly dropped her to the ground, yet she didn't let go. There she stood for what seemed forever with my blood running out of her mouth. Eye to eye, we were both wondering what to do. Finally she released me. I dove away from her and avoided the spray as I fought my way from the entangling limbs. Once clear, I examined where the teeth holes had punctured my thumbnail and caused the blood to ooze. Quickly, after I had wrapped my hand in my handkerchief, I dogtrotted the mile home with my big blue dog at my side.

Mom soaked my thumb in Epsom salts, her cure for almost any wound. Soon healed, I was much the wiser about Smokey's enemies. We never gave rabies a thought.

Later Jimmy and Larry captured a small skunk and took it to the vet to be deodorized. The operation was a success, and the skunk became a house pet. Rather shy, she hid much of the time despite handling and attention. After many baths, Flower still retained her musty odor. I learned that all skunks naturally stink a bit.

When we had visitors, Flower sometimes walked across the living room and scared the socks off them. Much like a cat, she took her milk well. Flower, however, never reached our expectations as the perfect house pet. Perhaps because she was older than thought when captured, she never became tame enough.

Smokey totally ignored Flower. Why he didn't tear her to pieces as he did all the others skunks crossing his path was beyond us! Flower never became a cat-like pet. She somehow escaped from the house, and we never saw her again.

I said, "Mom, Smokey must have killed her."

"Nonsense," she replied. "He would never do that to a pet that he's supposed to leave alone."

We sought more pets. Woodchucks, also known as marmots, were another of our experiments. Bob and Jay brought them from an abandoned cabin in a mountain pasture on Newcomb Creek where Dad summered some steers. I immediately fell in love with our "whistle pigs".

These fist-sized young marmots were playful and easy to handle. Eating everything from seeds to grapes, they held food in their tiny paws and gnawed away with four yellow buckteeth. They sat up on their hind legs as they ate grapes and nuts, their foods of choice. We let them run about on the kitchen table when Dad wasn't home. While Dad wouldn't tolerate wild animals on his eating surface, Mom would.

These young clowns rolled on the floor and curled up into furry balls. Sharp whistles kept them in contact with each other, when they were carried apart. They had black noses, gray faces, and three toned brown hair with short tails tipped with black. I thought them the cutest hairy babies on earth.

Because Mom decided five woodchucks were too many, she made Jay take three back. I went the twenty miles with Jay in the little jeep to the abandoned cabin where he released the three woodchucks, but there we were also exposed to a terrible animal situation.

After releasing the whistle-pigs we walked around in the trees and in the neighbor's pasture, exploring in thick aspens, willows, and wildflowers. We discovered a set of vacant old buildings snuggled in the aspens beside a shallow stream that was filled with tiny, white finned brook trout. In the corral were half a dozen strange appearing horses, which had no manes or tails. Bony thin, they had a deathly look about them. At first we didn't know what to make of the situation, but Jay figured it out. He reasoned that the person who was pasturing the horses had seldom checked on them and hadn't wired the pole gate open, as Dad always required. The poor things had probably been in the corral fighting bugs and flies, when they rubbed the gate closed and trapped themselves inside. There was water running under the poles on the far end of the corral, but there was nothing for them to eat. They were so starved that they had eaten each other's manes and tails. They had also eaten all of the horse manure on the corral ground, which was picked bone clean.

After Jay opened the gate, we watched the poor things slowly stagger out. They lusted for green grass and ate it as if wildly crazed. Watching them hobble and wobble about was a pitiful sight. Jay said, "Stupid people shouldn't have horses unless they check on 'em."

Back home, Woodie and Wooda, the two remaining woodchucks, provided great fun until they started backing up against walls, showing their long yellow teeth, and challenging me to pick them up. By putting cloth over them, I could handle them for a while. As they became more and more wild, I could no longer pick them up without being bitten.

Someone, probably Mom, released them, and they soon populated the Point of Rocks formations where the rivers met with generations of beautiful marmots. Distinct woodchuck whistles always greeted us in passing as they scurried into their sandstone caves.

After the woodchucks, Jay became more occupied with working on cars, talking to girls, and being with older school buddies. He left the pet stuff to his little brothers.

Together Larry, Jimmy, and I captured gophers, chipmunks, and assorted birds for pets. Often we were able to capture them because they were injured. Later, they usually escaped, healed up, and were released or died. Sometimes another animal got them, showing us the intertwining of life and death.

While we were raising wild pets, we also hunted wild animals and raised our domestic animals for someone's eventual food. The whole routine with animals seemed natural to me as a ranch kid.

Having lots of animals around overshadowed some of the other material things other kids up town talked about. Such things didn't seem important at the time. Our big family's existence on the Two-Bar was Spartanly simple. Each of us had to share a double bed with a brother in an unheated bedroom. We had a drawer or two in an old dresser which held a couple of pair of Levi pants, some black socks, white underwear, and a few plaid shirts. We wore our clothes all week, changing them and the bedding on Saturdays when we took the weekly bath. We washed our hair with Lifeboy, Lava, Babo, or Ivory soap. One pair of shoes was for everyday, and a good pair was for school, town, or special occasions. Each fall we had a new school coat ordered from Sears and Roebuck catalog. We wore our old coats around the ranch, until they became too tight, wore out, or were passed down to a younger brother. We had hats, mittens, and overshoes, which got handed down too.

Not to be lost, reordered, or replaced, wearing apparel was to be taken care of. That was Dad's biggest issue, "Take care of things, and don't replace them needlessly. Money doesn't grow on trees on this ranch."

When I had the gall to complain about having to wear mittens for a second year, Dad reminded me of hard Depression times when people lived on nearly nothing. He strongly recommended that I look around at poorer kids in our community. "It isn't what you have that matters but what you are inside that really counts," Mom added.

To earn a small allowance, we boys did regular chores that the folks assigned by age. Doing chores kept things going on the ranch and around the house. Our receiving an allowance kept us on equal footing with most kids at school. However, we were way ahead of them with our great pet experiences.

In the home ranch house, we all got the same colds and diseases at nearly the same time since everyone drank from the same water dipper from the metal bucket. We used the same washrags and towels too. We never had table napkins, tissues, or paper towels because they were too expensive. After a run to the two-holed outhouse in the middle of the night to do one's business, one wiped with old slick pages of last year's discarded catalogues. Thunder mugs or chamber pots were used only when we were far too ill to reach the outhouse under our own power.

Dad called us each morning with, "Up, up, up," echoing through the bedrooms. Rising with my brothers, I gathered with them on the far end of the front porch where nobody could see us in our long handled underwear. We urinated as far as we could down the sloping gravel hill behind the house to relieve ourselves. We often had a contest to determine who could piss the greatest distance north each morning. It saved us all long trips to the outhouse on the far west side of the house and wasn't different from how we relieved ourselves around the corrals and meadows.

Each spring Mother Nature exploded new life on the Two-Bar as domestic livestock provided abundant offspring. The new and beautiful young replaced those sold or lost over the past seasons.

Mother was as deeply interested in our profit-making animals as she was in wild ones. The beautiful tame creatures shared the ranch with us. Important to us, we enjoyed them.

We named some of them; we gave them homes. Mom who was tenderhearted, insisted that all animals be treated humanely. Because she never wanted anything to suffer, she insisted that those beyond hope be dispatched at once. She said, "I gained respect for animals by watching my father, Jay, take good care of his. I won't put up with any meanness with animals."

Dad was more matter-of-fact and seldom showed open affection for animals and pets. I knew he dearly loved his horses, but he never talked about them in loving terms. Instead, he showed his feelings and respect by the way he treated them. Dad who never abused or intentionally mistreated any animal wouldn't tolerate such practices.

He said to me many times in my growing up, "You have to be smarter than an animal to teach it anything. Fighting with or hurting one never accomplished much. They are just dumb animals and don't understand; be patient and never lose your temper." Willard Richard, who was tolerant of our many pets, and somewhat indifferent to them, always saw they were cared for properly.

Although Mom could hold and hug both wild and tame creatures, she never hugged me. I didn't really expect Dad to hug. Ranchmen didn't do that in North Park, at least not in front of other men.

An assortment of beautiful domestic animals also graced the Two-Bar, getting a lot of love from us. Horses, sheep, milk cows, cats, hogs, dogs, and range cattle were ever present. These animals came and went.

Mother Nature allowed most of our cows and heifers to have their calves by themselves. Playing mid-wife to all of them would have been impossible for us. Always we lost calves and some cows during birthing. We grieved and mourned our losses and were proud when we saved an animal. There were times during storms when chilled, long-legged, newborn calves wobbled about in Mom's kitchen. Mom kept each one fed and warmed, until it could be reunited with a waiting cow.

Our sheep, with their thick wool, gave fewer problems during lambing. Ewes needed less help and had more multiple births than our cattle. Sometimes a problem occurred when there were lambs with no mothers. When a ewe died or had more lambs than she could nurse, lambs were left without a mother. We called them "bum lambs" because as orphans they tried to bum milk from other ewes.

I helped Mom feed these motherless lambs on the bottle. Several times a day Mom heated cow's milk and filled glass bottles to which she attached long, black rubber nipples. The bums played about the yard and ranch buildings. Whenever the back door of the house opened, they came with tails wagging. As bum lambs grew larger into summer, they started eating green grass and required fewer feedings of milk. Begging and living up to their name, Bums still hung around the yard much of the time.

To the dismay of Dad, we kids usually taught a couple to butt. Bum lambs would butt each other, the dog, and whoever fed them. As they grew in size and gained confidence, they would butt anyone. If they butted a person once and got away with it, look out. They would be peeking around the corner of the house, sneaking up behind, and knocking that person flat whenever they had a butting opportunity.

Larry and I enjoyed bringing friends home from town and setting them up. One lamb, Tiny, would act friendly around our playmates, who, when they turned their backs, went down. We watched an astonished friend prepare to get up with Tiny standing just a few feet away neck bowed and ready to butt again and again. If I screamed at Tiny, he would retreat. I had fun chasing Tiny off and "saving" my friends.

Once, Tiny sneaked up behind Dad and knocked him flat. Dad, who promptly took a stick to the bum lamb, taught him whom to leave alone.

One summer a workhorse stepped on a bum lamb in the corral. Because the lamb's shoulder was broken, Dad was sure he wouldn't survive. I adopted the lamb and named him Peekin' Squeezer, because he squeezed through tight places and peeked around corners in a shy manner.

He lived and grew, but poor Peekin' Squeezer was a three-legged cripple, a condition I was unwilling to accept. Of course, my brothers teased me about him. They asked why I didn't adopt a healthy lamb instead of wasting my time on a crippled, ugly one. Peekin' Squeezer lagged far behind the other bum lambs. He hobbled along after them on three legs. When he lay down, he had a real problem getting up. It took several tries for him to make it up onto his feet. I liked my Peekin' Squeezer even if he was little, pathetic, and hobbled along. He was always last, but I hoped that he might someday use his leg. Because of my small size, I was also often chosen last at school, too. I just could not give up on him. Trying to get his leg to work, I moved and rubbed it, and I prayed for a miracle.

When fall arrived, it was time to put the bums with the other sheep in the pasture. I just couldn't let Peekin' Squeezer go. I was afraid that he would probably become lodged someplace and die, being unable to rise like the others. Dad let me keep him with our bucks (rams), the male sheep we kept separate from the ewes and lambs except during breeding season. Peekin' Squeezer trailed the bucks around the ranch buildings, lagging far behind.

One Sunday after church, the Town Marshall, Charlie Snow, called and told Mom that our bucks were again on Main Street in Walden. She quickly took Bob, Larry, and me to town. Sure enough, there were all eleven big bucks and Peekin' Squeezer bedded down on the sidewalk in front of Mr. Mankin's drug store. They were peaceful as could be, chewing their cuds. Embarrassed, Mom drove off quickly. She left us afoot to drive the big bucks and my pet back to the Two-Bar.

One day that fall when I came home from school, I couldn't find Peekin' Squeezer anywhere. Frantically, I searched the ranch buildings. When it became dark, I still hadn't found him. No one had seen him. I went to bed heartbroken. The next morning I futilely searched again.

When I came home from school the next day, I noticed the hired man as he flanked loose hay over the fence to fill our big feedrack. A six-foot high slab fence backed the feed rack. Our bucks often enjoyed bedding down there in the afternoon fall sun. Now the feed rack was nearly full of hay. It dawned on me that Peekin' Squeezer could be under the hay that had been unloaded the day before. When they had started pitching the hay over the high fence, the men couldn't see what was on the other side. The bucks could have all jumped up to leave, but Peekin' Squeezer would have had difficulty getting up. My brothers helped me move the huge hay pile. Sure enough Peekin' Squeezer was there. He was just fine because he was close to the fence that protected him from the total weight of the hay pile.

Peekin' Squeezer was special. Since he had a harder time in life, I found him more lovable. I don't think my brothers ever really understood. Mom did. Yet, after we discovered him alive under the hay pile, they stopped teasing me about my lame lamb.

Later that next fall, when we sold some sheep, I gnashed my teeth and agreed to let Peekin' Squeezer go, too. No matter how much I tried to help him and wanted him to get along as a normal sheep, he was still limited. I had a heavy heart as I helped load him in the truck with some other sheep, which were to be sold in Denver. I went behind the loading chute where Dad couldn't see me and I cried because I'd given up on my pet.

The next spring, a crooked-necked lamb with a nose bent nearly to the ground couldn't raise its head high enough to suckle its mother. Dad said that someone should knock it in the head. Instead, I carried it away and fed it warm milk, holding it on its back. At night, I kept it in a big cream can bedded on soft hay. Within a few weeks its neck straightened out and it could eat standing. I had at long last saved a lamb. Although Mom said, "Paul, all we need around here is another darned bum lamb," I knew that she was pleased.

She wasn't so pleased, however, when I rescued a nest of pink deer mice after Smokey had chomped their mother. I fed the orphans milk with a tiny doll bottle. At night I took them to bed in a matchbox full of cotton and kept them warm beside my body. Mom, who had a fit one morning when she found them in my bed tried to convince me that rodents didn't belong there. I changed her mind and never rolled over on them. I raised them a couple of weeks until they were haired out and big enough to release in a hay pile.

"Is there something wrong with me, Mom? I care more about pets than my brothers do."

"I know you do. It's because you're special in those ways."

Later I told Bob what she'd said while I was doing dishes for her.

"I don't think you're anything special," he said. His remarks made me wonder, since being special still left me small, blond, and farsighted. I swore to drink more milk to get bigger. I felt like a runt who was never destined to grow. I yearned with all my heart to be as big as Jay and Bob. I wanted to show people my pets and have people accept me for the animals I tended.

Being surrounded by so many pet animals as a kid had a big influence on the kind of adult life I later sought. Pets seemed to be a part of me. My working years, because of such an animal-rich childhood, were always filled with studies and caring for pets and wild things.

My father had always seen most animals mainly for their utilitarian use. Dad had raised rabbits as a kid, encouraging us in that effort. Our hutches were full of black and white does. They stomped their big hind feet if we neared their adorable babies. Adult rabbits also kicked and scratched like crazy when I tried to hold them. Dad had a fit if I picked them up by their ears, as most people did. He'd say, "How would you like to be picked up by your ears?"

When spring green grass appeared, we released our rabbits around the ranch yard's hay piles and out buildings. The rabbits made holes under porches and in hay piles to scamper into when Smokey and I tried to catch them. Foxes, coyotes, and hawks reduced their numbers, as did barn cats. By fall, we trapped and hutched the survivors. The remaining few had enjoyed freedom, but their numbers had been thinned. Mom would never kill one to cook and eat as Dad often suggested. Dad's talk of delicious rabbit meat fell on deaf ears in her kitchen.

We people on ranches could sell, hunt, kill, and eat the same kinds of animals that we loved and raised, but we Richards did not eat any of our personal pets on the Two-Bar Ranch.

Chapter 4

SPRINGIN'

"It's May! Let's go get magpies."

Sitting there in the warm midday North Park sun, my view of our two rivers prompted my mind to focus on the best time of the year when I was growing up. Spring in all its glory.

Long ago as a teenager, I had often watched a giant broad-winged hawk fly over our buildings as a feisty little bird gave chase. With bated breath I observed the tiny blackbird after the sharp-shinned hawk. The huge hawk rolled upside down and snapped its killer talons after the tiny attacker, who nimbly avoided their sharp grasp. Big and small went spinning and rolling across the blue sky in combat. Why would a hawk flee from a minute bird or a tiny bird take on a hawk?

I had many more questions about the dozens of kinds of wild birds on our place, trying to understand why they did what they did. Each spring as I was growing up, the return of these flyers brought songs to the Two-Bar's silent landscape as feathered ones sought their old spots along river and meadow to nest and feed.

In April, very early spring before full green-up, sage grouse congregated in large groups. At dawn and dusk each day, hundreds of the chicken-sized birds assembled in the sagebrush. In bare flat openings between expanses of snow-filled sage, the big gray birds stood about for an hour or so on the brown grass. From late March to early May, some of this bird activity took place on the ridge just outside our ranch gate. As a kid I didn't really understand that the sage grouse were displaying, strutting, booming, and breeding to produce a new crop of birds. Nobody told me. I just knew that when they stopped their activity the first week in May, there was green grass. It seemed like forever since I'd smelled the green grass, the surest sign of spring.

Our river ice also broke up in April when the greening occurred. Ice jams blocked the rivers sending melt water across the tan meadows where its surface froze each night. When the ice jams broke, the water rushed downstream in a small flood and left abandoned layers of ice on the meadow. After the rivers settled down within their banks, they were peaceful for a month.

I watched the spring earth open up and pour out life. Plants shot up. Gophers emerged from the thousands of holes along the ditch banks and ridges across the ranch to eat the new greenery. Badgers, in their efforts to dig out gophers, piled up chocolate mounds of dirt all across the Two-Bar.

These Richardson's ground squirrels, sometimes called gophers, scampered across our dirt road, stood erect, and whistled when we walked home each afternoon from school. And of course my brothers and I chucked rocks at them.

"It's May! Let's go get magpies," shouted Larry as he threw his books on the kitchen table.

"I've waited for this all winter," replied Jimmy.

"Let's hit the river," I said in total agreement.

"Maybe we can make some good money, if Dad pays better than last year," said Larry.

The North Park Stock Grower's Association, of which Dad was president, had again proclaimed in The Jackson County Star:

"Kids can earn reward money for bird pests. Magpies and Crows peck the eyes out of newborn calves and damage their new soft hooves. Also, they peck open sores of all livestock. One cent per egg, five cents per hatchling, and a dime for adults will be paid to control these pests. Reward money can be collected from any association member."

Dad sweetened the pot by doubling up on what the association paid. Because the money was prime motivation, magpie hunting took my spring weekends. However, I had not seen any birds do the dastardly deeds the cattlemen listed in our one local newspaper.

Adult magpies are hard to approach because of their lookout system that has one bird watching all the time while the others eat. Often they were my warning sentinels along the rivers. When a magpie spooked, squawked, and flushed skyward, I knew something was coming. No wonder the cattlemen went after the young and the eggs. We boys would not get many of the sharp-eyed adults.

Our two rivers were bordered by willows that housed an abundance of nesting magpies and crows. We knew that magpies and crows laid clutches of eggs in late April and early May. If something happened to those eggs, the birds would immediately lay another large clutch. So, we decided to raid their nests in May when they first laid their eggs. Then we'd allow the birds time to lay a second batch of eggs for later profits. We didn't let Dad know about our plan which would allow us to make double money plus Dad's doubling the reward on top of that.

During the Two-Bar spring lambing and calving time, we headed for the nests along the rivers. Ours would be a systematic search of all the willows on the ranch. Armed with our trusty bows and arrows, we made a statement, "Look out birds; money is to be made." We carried a woven reed creel and several gallon coffee cans.

When we reached a big bunch of willows, we spread out and climbed trees. Magpies nested eight to twelve feet off the ground. The rounded, tall nests had an open door and a stick roof over the top. From six to eight eggs rested on soft grasses lining the nests. We carefully handed the eggs to someone on the ground who gently placed them in our creel or the cans. The olive-green-speckled magpie eggs accumulated rapidly as we worked beside the rippling rivers.

Crows' eggs, a turquoise blue, were larger than magpie eggs but not as abundant. They were found in smaller willow stick nests, without tops, and always higher up the trees. Crows laid about four eggs in each clutch, making them poor money-makers for us.

I thought that our ranch crows hated owls because the owls ate the crow eggs and young. I'd often see dozens of crows mob an owl in a big alder tree along our creeks. I couldn't tell whether they actually hurt the owl, but the noise was thundering.

Because adult crows and magpies were shy, they departed when we climbed their nesting trees. Sometimes we shot arrows at them, but we seldom hit one. Neither crows nor magpies stayed around to defend their eggs or to dive bomb us.

Although we were great willow climbers, able to shinny up almost any tree on the Illinois or Michigan Rivers, we had our share of falls. Larry was once left hanging upside-down with his foot caught in a fork between two limbs before we rescued him.

As we worked our way from willow to willow and to lighten our load, we paused at the riverbank and punched small holes in each end of the eggs with our knives. Then we placed each egg to our lips and blew out the contents in order to cut down the risk of a soggy mess if we broke eggs.

We hopped single file, high hump to high hump, across the lumpy meadow low wet places where cattle feet had unevened the sod during years of grazing soft pasture ground. These humps were natural grassy stepping-stones across the shallow sloughs of cold water. While magpie hunting we saw other creatures. Smokey helped find shy mammals and wild things hiding along the willows.

Under the greening trees we'd pause and cut the small willow branches, tap the bark with our knife handles to loosen them, and slip the bark off the branch. Then by cutting a 'V' notch and a flat reed hole near one end and replacing the bark, we had created fine Indian flutes to play as we hunted for nests. Crude music flowed from us from among the dense willows.

At day's end we counted our eggs on the back porch in front of Dad, and he'd pay us cash for the Stock Growers Association and also his portion. Then he told us to take the eggs outside and to crush them. One time, instead of crushing them, we resold them back to him. It worked fine until he realized that he had paid exactly the same price the day before. After that, he took the shells outside and smashed them himself. Feeling guilty, I vowed never to hornswoggle him again.

On one magpie hunt Harry Rosenfield and I cornered a pair of animals in a clump of willows. The weasel-like creatures poked their light brown heads out of the twisted branches and hissed. They were strikingly beautiful and new to us. The pair finally ran off up the Illinois River. Their bodies were two-toned yellow brown, like a Siamese cat. They ran like otters, all humped up as they leaped along.

We finally learned from Harry's dad, Old Harold Rosenfield, the savvy outdoorsman, that they were pine marten. What they were doing in our river bottom meadow, seventeen miles from green timber, we never knew.

I didn't know another kid at school who'd ever seen a live marten. Harry, my age and my best friend, and I were eager to tell about our discovery.

"I think you guys are just making up this stuff, and my mom says you can't handle little birds and eggs as you and Harry say," snapped Ted after hearing our bird and pine marten stories.

"We do handle them!" answered Harry indignantly. Shy Harry, who seldom argued with or debated others, usually left the verbal jousting to me.

"Yeah, but she says birds won't hatch them eggs and will abandon all the young you touch to die. They can tell if you guys were there," responded Ted.

I chipped in, "Well, we do handle some bird's eggs, and the parents still hatch and raise the whole lot too," I said.

"You two are just full of it, always telling tales of wild things," jeered Bud.

"Just bring some of these animals and show us. Then we can see if it's just lies," said Ted.

"We don't take animals out of the wild," replied Harry.

"See, I told you its all lies to make themselves big deals," said Bud as he and Ted walked away for class.

On my way home after school, I thought, "The heck with them." Having seen two marten made me feel important anyway.

"Don't worry about them, Harry, they're stupid."

"Or jealous," Harry said. My good friend had a sister, Jane, one year younger, and a younger brother, Warren, whom we called "Wart." Larry, Jimmy, and I spent loads of time at their timber worker place close outside the ranch gate on the edge of town.

Near the end of May, magpie hunting stopped. We could no longer ford the rivers, and we had raided most of the nests for the early egg hatch.

The snow at higher elevations now started melting, swelling our rivers to over-capacity. Water, sometimes a quarter-mile across, filled the flood plains of the Two-Bar. It was a temptation for us.

Harry and I dragged old railroad ties to the water's edge, laid them side-by-side, put inch boards on top, and spiked them all together. Ten or so ties made a nice raft. To pole the raft into the current, we used long willow branches. We wanted to float downstream the length of the Two-Bar.

We set out poling the raft into the main current. It was difficult to keep the bow forward in the swift, brown water, so we were swept along. Our raft spun around and around much of the time, despite our efforts to control it. Sometimes we couldn't even touch bottom with our poles. We were totally at the mercy of the current. Willows along the banks were half under the water and debris collected in their tangled clumps. Sticks and old hay from upstream meadows made the willows nearly solid and blocked the water's passage through their branches.

I glanced at my shipmate as fear increased in my heart. Harry, always collected and calm, seemed unfazed. So I labored with him to keep the raft in the current. It was a fast trip as our raft sped along. Smokey who was standing on the ties with us, tongue half-extended, apparently enjoyed the spinning ride. Our biggest problem was to avoid hanging up in willows, since the river was ignoring its natural main channel and sweeping us down the valley and through the trees.

We struck the edge of one snag willow. The far side of our raft went under for a moment, dumping Smokey into the icy water, forcing him to swim back to the raft. We collided with several more willows at glancing angles. We were both now very uneasy since we couldn't control our raft, and the current was stronger than we had anticipated. The water was much too cold for us to swim ashore. Up ahead the sight of thicker willows struck fear in my whole body. Unable to get out of the rushing current, we were powerless to pole to a safe shore. I felt numb craving to get ashore any way possible.

As we approached a long chain of willows that rose about half way out of the brown water, we hoped that we could hit one of the few openings between the trees. Helplessly we hit a big willow. The raft buckled beneath us and tipped under water to stand on edge, flat against the stout willow. Instantly we grabbed onto the willow branches and stood on the ends of the wooden railroad ties that stuck above the boiling water. Smokey was swept downstream in the current. He swam valiantly toward shore, but he was making little progress. The last we saw of him, he was swept down the valley. We knew he could take better care of himself than we could ourselves. From our perch atop the willow, we watched the deep water rushing by on each side. Harry squinted at me and said, "This is real bad."

"How do we get out of this?" Harry just shook his head from side to side, looking blankly.

With a branch, Harry tested the rushing water's depth. It was over our heads and icy cold. The closest willow was a dozen feet away. We couldn't stay where we were. I was scared to death that if the willow with the raft against it broke loose, we'd be swept downstream and drown. To give a lifeline weight, we took off our belts, shirts, and undershirts, tied them together, and attached them to a stout branch we cut from the willow top. We took turns flinging our makeshift line and stick at the next willow until the stick caught between two strong branches. We jerked hard to make sure it would hold. For a while we just watched the fast water rush between the next tree and us, looking at each other without saying a word. We had been in tight places before but none this scary.

Finally, Harry grabbed the end of the last shirt and jumped as far as he could. When he hit the ice-cold water, the current carried him immediately downstream. He pulled himself hand over hand up the lifeline, grabbed branches, and climbed out, cold and shaking. After he had tied a stick to the end of the line to give weight, he threw it back to me. Trembling with fear, I went into the frigid water, which took my breath away. We followed the same procedure in crossing two more willows until we could wade ashore in chest-deep frigid water as the spring wind kicked up from the west. Although shaking cold, no two kids were ever more grateful to be on dry land.

Smokey happily rejoined us and three soaked, cold, and much wiser rafters set out on a long walk south to the Illinois River highway bridge, which was the only place where we could cross the wide river to loop back north and reach the ranch buildings. Gusty spring winds bit our wet bodies and froze our pant legs stiff against our flesh. We hurried along happy to be alive.

Since Bob considered himself a better sailor than his little brother, he and Gus Harris decided to navigate the river a few days later. Having boasted that any boat was better than a raft, they wanted to show what they could do in Bob's twelve-footer. In making his boat over the winter in the barn, Bob had used pine boards that he sealed with tar.

Feeling confident when they first set out, they soon lost control in the swift water, too, and hit a willow. The boat went under, carrying Bob below the surface and entangling him in the lower branches. Bob almost drowned before Gus got Bob's head above the water's surface. Frantic in his effort, Gus finally was able to extract Bob's body from between the boat and willow. When the two great sailors finally returned home, they looked like a couple of drowned rats, defeated by spring runoff.

Bob was unhappy to have met the same disaster as his little four-eyed brother. However, his wrath was nothing compared to Mom's, who banned us both from navigating the high waters of spring runoff across the ranch. After our long winter of cold and snowy isolation, running river water was hard to leave alone.

During normal water times each summer, my brothers and I kept a good railroad-tie rafts beached at good spots along both rivers, by sloughs, and at duck ponds behind the huge red barn. We used these many rafts to hunt, to fish, or to reach islands or opposite shores. Smokey rode with us and quickly abandoned ship anytime trouble arose.

Once the rivers had gotten back within their banks about mid-June and new clutches of eggs had hatched, magpie hunting resumed. Freedom from school allowed us to hunt any day. Because snowmelt mud blocked the logging roads in the mountains where he and his dad cut and hauled mine props, logs used to shore up ceilings in mines, Harry was able to join us. This time we gathered no eggs, waiting for all the eggs to hatch. We got five cents per hatchling from the stock growers, plus the same amount from Dad. And it took only five birds to buy a ticket to see the picture show uptown in Walden.

Along the rivers we again climbed the now fully leafed trees and tossed young birds down from the nests. We put a stick across each bird's neck and pulled quickly on the body to remove the head, bringing swift death. Non-feathered heads were worth five cents, but the feathered heads of nearly mature birds we could sell for a dime--big money for us.

Smokey barked and ran around chasing crows and magpies from limb to limb. They were out of the nests, but they couldn't yet fly away. We couldn't catch them all, as we scrambled and climbed after them. Adults dive-bombed us, while their young moved to the highest thin branches out of our reach. There was a lot of excitement with barking, yelling, and squawking in the dense trees.

Since we had to bring in only the heads, neither the stock growers nor Dad could determine whether a black-feathered head belonged to an adult or to an immature non-flying bird. So, we sold loads of immature bird heads for adult bird prices.

With the discovery of a square wire-and-wood magpie trap on the Illinois River in thick willows near the neighboring Post's ranch buildings, we became even more greedy. The open bottomed wire trap had been placed over a dead horse. Magpies and crows could hop down into it to eat carrion. Once inside they couldn't fly out of the trap. We entered the trap cage and caught the adult magpies, which used their black bills to peck and pinch. Their pinch felt as if someone had pinched us with a pair of pliers. The pain brought tears to our eyes, yet it didn't keep us from secretly raiding someone else's trap and taking all the adult magpies we found worth a dime each.

One year, we gathered enough magpie and crow eggs and heads to win the first-prize cowboy boot bonus offered by the North Park Stock Growers. I was elated to have my name, as the winner, in the local newspaper even though Larry, Jimmy, and Harry had worked as hard as I had. I sported the shiny new boots around school and soon passed them on to Larry when my feet grew too large.

Although Mom didn't say much about the bird-hunting effort that kept me busy at the rivers, she wasn't totally pleased. However, I was sure we were doing the right thing by destroying birds as Dad wanted, helping cattlemen protect their livelihood. Our efforts didn't seem to put a dent in the crow and magpie populations, as they laid eggs in the same numbers year after year.

Reflecting back on it today it has a totally different feel than in my rash youth when money was hard to find for any ranch kid. Was the money really worth all the birds we took? Not now, in my adult view, since I am well beyond being a greedy kid.

Magpie voices often led me to the dead. Since magpies were part-time scavengers, they'd find and eat almost any dead critter. When I saw a flock of adult magpies fly up, I went directly to the site, knowing something interesting awaited. Many times the animal was recently dead, swollen big, and bloated tight as a drum. I'd launch my sharp-pointed arrows into the big belly and listen to the hissing of rot gases exiting. Holding my nose and turning my head, I waited for the stench to subside, then, sometimes gagging, I dug my arrows out. To shoot arrows into a body, once alive, was realistically different from my usual targets of stumps, posts, and trees. When I attacked the dead, I often pretended to be an Indian hunting buffalo or attacking fat fishermen.

We boys revisited these death scenes again and again, as we tried to ambush the animals that came to feed upon the decaying flesh. Eventually, the bones would show. We'd use the scapulas to bat rocks on the river gravel bars, and we carried the toothy jaws as whitened pistols in our pockets and belts to use in pretend gunfights in the willows. Sometimes, imagining them as big game, we used skulls for target practice with our arrows.

At times after we had drunk clear river water while lying on our bellies, we rose to find a dead and bloated critter around the next river bend upstream. Knowing we had drunk that water, I always said, "It would gag a maggot." But none of us died from drinking below the dead on the ranch.

I learned more about death too one spring when I saw a beautiful cow with her calf half-born gasp her last breath, realizing that only a few young of most animals ever grow up. I wondered at times whether we boys would all make it. One of our brothers, born--years before me, had died of pneumonia at age one. He would have been between Jay and Bob in age. Mom and Dad never talked in detail about his death. Mom became instantly sad whenever his death was mentioned. I noticed human death was not a topic people visited very often. However, in my river wanderings, I often witnessed death as animals died there all the time.

When an animal became sick on our Two-Bar, Dad doctored them. Those that died were dragged by horse team or vehicle down onto the big ridge by the swimming hole and abandoned to nature. Dad wanted their stench away from his buildings. If sick animals went to the river to quench their fever and died in the water or if they died in the willows or pastures, they decayed where they fell or they washed downstream in spring high water.

I often played on the graveyard ridge and sneaked up over the rise in the tall sagebrush to watch the scavengers fight over the dead dragged there from our corrals. There was a lot of life competing for these dead. I often told my brothers that when I died, I wanted them to drag me down on the ridge and let me rot where I'd do something like a coyote or magpie some good.

Every wonderful spring, young life kept shooting up around me, keeping my mind off the dead. When I saw wobbly young gophers wandering about, I remembered that life has a cycle each season. Clumps of foot-high sky-blue iris and pinkish evening primrose blossomed in bunches along the foot of the ridges amid the new grassy areas riddled with gopher holes.

Once a mother with four young in single file led her little skunks across my path. I held Smokey. I never killed the young, except crows and magpies, and then only for profit.

Having watched a red-tailed hawk carry several young gophers to her nest, we climbed up to it when she was away. Her young were a snowy white with brilliant yellow beaks and snappy black eyes. Half-eaten rodents ringed the edge of the stick nest. Each week we climbed to see how much they had grown. Their growth was rapid, and soon they were fully feathered and standing in the nest hissing at us. We proudly showed them to a young hired man who poked at them with his hat and said, "Let's kill 'em. They're chicken killers."

Jimmy and I protested that the hawks were ours since we had found them. Although he finally left them alone, he insisted that we were crazy. Soon they were perching on the branches outside the nest. On our next visit they were gone. I felt cheated, as I had expected them to linger longer so we could get to know them better.

One spring day, Harry and I were sneaking along in the willows like a couple of Huron braves, when we saw five turkeys on the railroad right-of-way. We ducked in the willows and raced to the house to see whether Mom would let us use the 410 shotgun to blast them for a great meal. She informed us that there were no wild turkeys in North Park. We returned and upon taking a closer look discovered that they had bare necks with red heads, vultures. We had never seen them on the ranch before. We laughed at the thought of how they might have tasted had we killed one, cut off its head, and had Mom cook it.

By the two rivers in the spring, we picked the fragrant leaves of the square-stemmed green mint plants, placed them in a tin can of clear river water, and made ourselves mint tea over a willow branch fire. Mint tea had a strong tart taste and a great smell. Sitting around on the grassy riverbank surrounded by thick willows, we drank our tea, listened to the water murmur along, and watched birds fly up and down the creek. Chirping yellow warblers, jabbering magpies, peeping sparrows, and a host of other birds landed in the willows. While kingfishers made loud cackling sounds that we could hear a quarter mile down river, great blue herons glided by in silence as their gray blue wings, nearly six feet across, brushed near the tops of the willows which we sat under.

Across from us, one of the long-legged herons glided to a rest on the rocky riverbed just above a riffle. Once it caught sight of the four of us in the tall grass, it frantically flapped away upstream, pooping a white stream in the water.

"Now that's what I call a real shit bird," said Larry.

"It must be real tough taking off because they crap every single time," said Harry.

"Look at all those huge mountains. What if they were bird poop? Its like they have us corralled," said Larry.

"I'm glad they are rock and trees not crap and where big game lives," said Harry. Our focus shifted to the mountain ranges surrounding us.

"It's like a big wall keeping everything out of the Park," added Jimmy.

Growing Up Wild

"Wouldn't it be nice to keep all the people out and have this for ourselves?" Larry asked.

"We could make it ours for all the animals and just us," I said, dreaming of running great herds of buffalo and antelope.

"All other people would have to get our permission to come in to hunt and fish. We wouldn't let a cow or sheep in to ruin it for the wild things," said Harry.

"We could be kings of North Park," said Larry, "I'd like that, living like Utes."

Larry Richard, who loved horses and action. An independent boy in every sense of the word. Illustration by David Hartman

"We'd have to strike gold to buy all of it," said Harry.

"If we had it and lived wild then they would come in and take it like they did from the Utes," I said.

"Even if we owned all of The Park and had bought it with our own gold?" asked Jimmy.

"Well, the Utes owned it too, and weren't using it like white people liked and look what happened to them."

"Let's find a mother lode of gold and buy it anyway and just see. Since we aren't Utes, and are white, maybe they would just treat us like big game or bird ranchers and leave us alone," said Harry.

"Yeah, but where is all the gold, under all this water and dirt?" snapped Larry.

I said, "You just have to find it like we find birds and fish."

Birds were always around us, enriching our lives on the ranch. Around the acre of wooden corrals, if I remained totally still beside the pole fences in the late spring, young flying bluebirds and swallows would land beside me. Slow hand movements under the pole and a quick grab netted a live bird barehanded. I usually said to others that the birds were adults since they were fully feathered and colored. However, I alone knew they were the unwise young. Still, to catch a bird required patience and the catch caused me to feel special and big, though I was still ninety-six pounds and four-eyed, and still often lost my glasses along the rivers.

During my spring birding time, there were serious efforts going on under Dad's supervision to raise our hay crop and to keep the ranching operations going. The first signs of greening up suggested the need for spring work. Pussy willows made an appearance along the plum-red willow twigs that were slowly turning yellow-green. These puffy gray-white pussy willows showed themselves at the tips of branches in tiny bunches. Soon new leaves made a slow appearance. At the same time new growth of grass showed itself along the meadows and on the hillsides. The green seemed to say there was a new crop of hay to be grown. For Dad, the rancher, it was time to think of spring work.

How free I had felt each late spring when I stowed away the high-buckled black overshoes that had weighted down my feet for six weary months. I knew emancipation when I didn't have to give a rip about footgear.

Our cows, looking for freedom from dry hay, foraged from place to place for a few bites of the delicious green. Their newborn calves were small. To have had irrigation water on the meadows would not have been wise because the small newborn calves might have fallen into it and drowned. Before the ditches were opened, cows and calves were moved off the meadows to pastures and were driven to summer range at the Norris Place.

After our new calves reached pasture with their mothers, the mark of Richard ownership had to be placed upon them in early June. On two weekends we boys and neighbors joined in the branding operations at our Norris Ranch. Branding was an exciting event in the big wooden corrals along the twisting, tiny Norris Creek below towering Pitchpine Mountain.

The big red and white-faced Hereford calves kicked me, ran over me, and knocked me about. They bawled under the hot branding iron while we five boys suffered from the heat, from wind-blown dirt in our eyes, and from the hard work. We held the calves down while the men did the easy work. Bob and I often wrestled calves together, functioning as a team doing a good job and not competing against each other. All of our new calves had a big Richard / 8 or 2 - burned onto their left hips. When Bob and I released the last calf, I felt proud to see our new brand on the animals and to have been part of the branding operation.

Dad always broke out the whisky bottle after we finished branding. I, too young to drink, watched each man pass the bottle around, take a big swig, make a sour face, and say, "That's sure good."

With the meadows free of cattle, the dragging operation quickly took place. A fourteen-foot log with three old dump-rake wheels attached was pulled over the soft meadows. In breaking up and scattering the winter's accumulation of cattle manure and uneaten hay, this contraption helped fertilize our land. Then to help get the manure into the ground, river water was spread over the meadows by a series of ditches to nurture a new hay crop.

The meadows soon became a bright green. Water-bird time on the Two-Bar had arrived. Ducks flocked to the meadow water from the south and moved to the ditches, sloughs, and rivers for spring nesting. Other water birds like terns, snow geese, loons, curlews, and phalaropes stopped by for only a few days, then winged on north.

Grebes, avocets, killdeers, white-billed coots, and a dozen kinds of sandpipers stayed at the duck ponds behind our big red barn and allowed us to see their young grow. We rafted out to their nests and handled their young amid the reeds, cattails, and tall sedges, listening to the pleasant calls of yellow-headed and red-winged blackbirds. Bitterns made mournful pumping calls in the cattails as we watched the wonderful duck pond with its tall muskrat houses and swarms of birds. Watching the action along the water's surface just at dusk was better than a picture show up town. The duck ponds were Harry's, Larry's, Jimmy's and my special spot. I kept the sacred place a secret from the town kids and school classmates because I didn't want them to discover our bird treasure.

About mid-June, irrigation of the meadows brought an airborne mosquito invasion. The insects lighted on all parts of my body, biting through light trousers, shirts, and socks, puncturing all exposed skin as the females sought blood meals. They flew into my throat and nose and sometimes my ears. To escape the wrath of these mosquito devils, I had to seek high ground as our horses did, or leave the low irrigated areas, or pray for stout winds. Or, I had to just learn to live with them—not letting their bites bother me. That was Dad's answer since he never seemed to let their blood sucking bother him as much as it did us boys and our workhorses.

On still late spring days, the biting bugs nearly drove our herd of work horses crazy, forcing them off the wet pastures up onto the highest place behind the high-board fence where I was now sitting in soft dirt. My spot was where the horses had always huddled together, whipped their tails, tossed their manes, and stomped their hooves for protection. In those late spring days, winds had provided true relief, keeping the insects from being airborne. Spring, despite the slow increase of the hordes of mosquitoes, was still the best time of the year on the Two-Bar because of the new life that returned to the land.

Chapter 5

MOVIN'

"Where's your dad? I'm gonna kill 'em!"

Much earlier, my parents had once vacated this beautiful North Park. I too remembered leaving and losing another home place when I was a small boy, yet it had not seemed as difficult as contemplating the upcoming sale of my Two-Bar Ranch.

Sitting by the fence and remembering our ranching past and what had influenced my life, I had to journey back in time to when my newly wed parents had fled North Park, riding out the Great Depression hard times on the great plains. Our lives would have been so different had we stayed at those lower elevations. Dad and Mom had moved to eastern Colorado near the old cattle trailhead and railroad town of River Bend during the horrible 1930s. My early years had been on ranches on those plains, too.

The year before 1929, they had started out as newlywed cattle people in Colorado's high mountains. Dad had been tending 3,700 head of cattle in North Park for a few years with his father, Charlie. He had earned a decent share in the large herd, enough, in fact, to buy a good ranch when the cattle were to be sold.

Dad didn't want to be an actual rancher and had promised Mom he was going to own a ranch, but not live on one. Having been raised on a ranch, Mom swore she would never marry any rancher. And Dad's promise had finally convinced her to marry him. He wanted a ranch as a place to keep the livestock he purchased before he sold or traded them. His dream was to be a speculator in livestock following in his father's and grandfather's footsteps.

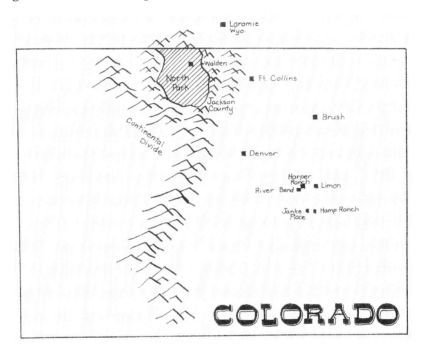

Colorado map of where the Richard family once lived.
Illustration by David Hartman

Mom and Dad had relocated from North Park to eastern Colorado at River Bend and made a down payment on the Harper Ranch. This put them closer to Charlie Richard and the cattle trading center in Brush. Dad planned to pay off the Harper Ranch the next month with proceeds from his share of the 3,700 North Park cattle. A week after they purchased the eastern Colorado ranch, the Depression of 1929 knocked the price of cattle to rock bottom. My parents lost most everything they had accumulated, and they were stuck on a barren ranch with only milk cows and saddle horses.

My grandparents on both sides were also financially crippled by the Depression. One grandfather lost his ranch and his health while the other battled to keep from losing a vast agricultural business. Our grandparents were in no position to help my parents much. It was from riches to rags during the Great Depression of the 1930's for both the Richard and Monroe sides of my family.

It rained very little during their six-year stay on the Harper place. They usually had some spring grass from scant winter snow accumulations, but there were several years without any good rains.

In the early 1930's, dust was terrific. Black clouds, miles high, would roll in. Mom then hurried to cover dishes on the table with towels. When she removed the towels, dust was soon in everything and a part of each meal. Windows and doors were covered with wet towels and cloths to try and keep the dust out. It was of little use--eventually dust penetrated every opening. Once the dust cloud was so thick and black that Mom's chickens, thinking it was night, went to roost during the middle of the day. Dozens of the black blizzards came and went each month across their grassland ranch in the depths of the dark 1930s.

There was no spare money. Livestock wasn't worth much of anything. Few people could pay the interest on their ranch loans let alone any of the principal. Such was the case with the Richard family. President Hoover said, "Things will be better if you only wait." It wasn't true. Usually the bank went along with people like my parents, extending credit just to have someone living on the ranches rather than having buildings stand deserted. Few who owed a bank could really expect a working ranch to pay any principal in the early 1930s. The Richards hung on by their fingernails, having land, some grass, a garden, and a roof over their heads to keep them going which was more than most people had.

Jay was born in 1930. Mom had had no experience with children since she had been an only child herself and was raised in severe isolation. She often said Jay scared her to death because she didn't know the first thing about babies. She raised him by following a government booklet advocating a rigid clock schedule.

My folks made it, in part, because some friends of Charlie Richard pastured steers on the Harper Ranch some of those dry summers. That provided income of fifteen dollars a month. Also, Charlie Richard had his bank send them twenty dollars some months.

Antelope were the mainstay of the Richard diet due to Dad's accurate shooting. Later, when the antelope gave out, bacon squares, fatback, and the milk from a few cows, plus Mom's garden, and some chickens kept body and soul together. Dad bought a separator so cream could be separated from the milk and sold in Limon. The $2.50 for a full cream can was wonderful. Mom made her own butter and cottage cheese and did everything the hard way. Dad cut up old discarded ties from the railroad for fuel. He took every opportunity to earn some money just to acquire an animal or two for the nearly vacant Harper Ranch.

Time crawled along during those dusty days. A second son, Dale, was born in 1932. Mom now had enough experience not to raise him exactly by some book and the alarm clock. But the dust was terrible much of the time. At one year of age, Dale came down with pneumonia in both lungs. They rushed him to town, and the only local doctor, who later turned out to be a drug addict, sent them home saying Dale would get better. Mom felt Dale was far too sick to go home, but the doctor insisted, and they didn't know what else to do. There was no hospital. Mom had never been around a terribly sick child.

Mom and Dad watched helplessly, doing all they knew how as the tiny blond boy gasped and fought for each breath. Dale died near morning in the dusty little shack on the Harper Place amid the sounds of turkey gobbles. It was a horrible blow to lose a tiny son. Mom was bitter, thinking it was due to her inexperience and poor doctoring. All of her life, she hated that doctor and refused ever to speak to him.

A year later, Bob was born as the third son. He came at a difficult time, long before she was past her loss of Dale. It was the lowest and most desperate time in her life. Mom and Dad hadn't been off the dusty ranch socially in ages. They hadn't even seen a dime picture show in four years. It had been years since Mom's last new dress, but the family was still eating.

At last, they accumulated more cattle than children. They were a motley looking bunch, all colors, all sizes, and all shapes, but Mom and Dad had done without everything to accumulate them and were proud of their small herd.

Dad talked the banker into a loan from the Limon Bank, increasing the herd to a hundred head. Charlie Richard then brought 500 steer calves from Texas to pasture on the Harper Place saying, "The only way these things can lose money is to lie down and die!" Some of them were eating cotton cake as a new feed, appearing to adjust well to the Harper Ranch. Those calves plus their own herd gave the Richards hope of getting back into the cattle business. Hope hadn't been visible beyond the black dusty skies for years.

In November of 1931, a month after they had received the Texas calves, a big blizzard struck without warning, bringing bitter cold driven by howling winds. It went on for three days--a total whiteout ground blizzard not allowing anyone to see more than a few feet ahead.

In the early and worst part of the blinding storm, Dad wanted to ride out, find the cattle, and move them nearer the buildings for some protection. He knew it was the kind of storm in which cattle drifted into fence corners, humped up, and froze standing. Mom urged him not to go, but he said, "Good grief, I have to do something. They're all we've got."

Willard, Edith and Richard boys barely existing on the Harper Ranch during Great Depression hard times.

He fought his way to the barn in the wind whipped snow and saddled short-eared Croppie. When Dad opened the door, his trusty horse refused to go outside into the howling blizzard. Willard Richard tried every thing he knew to force the horse out, but it was to no avail. Croppie braced his hooves and balked. Mom always later said, "We would have lost Willard if that good horse hadn't refused to leave the barn. He would never have found the way back to the buildings in that freezing blizzard." And later my dad agreed saying, "Croppie had more sense than I did."

Fierce winds drove snow through the many cracks and into the old barn for several days. Croppie, the workhorse team, and milk cows tromped it beneath their feet. As it piled up, they moved upward. Their backs were at the top of the barn in the high rafters when the wind finally ceased. Dad had to shovel a stair-stepped ramp to get them down.

When the blizzard subsided, Dad rode out on Croppie and nervously looked for cattle. Mom was baking bread and her heart just sank when Dad, half frozen, walked back in the tiny house and told her the blizzard had killed 106 head. She fell into a kitchen chair and sobbed.

A couple dozen head had drifted onto the railroad right-of-way and had been killed by the Denver-bound train. Hungry people from Limon trudged the miles out to get meat from the dead animals. There they stood in the whiteness, skinning the dead animals in thigh-deep snow. Hides might even bring a quarter each. Dad was on the other end of the ranch skinning away on the eighty dead for hide money, too.

Family disaster struck again when a train hit Charlie Richard's car in La Salle, Colorado and killed him in 1934. This stunned Dad and Mom for he had been a guiding light. Now, Charlie was gone and everything was in the hands of his partner and a bunch of lawyers in Brush, Colorado, sixty miles north of River Bend.

There was little Dad could do with so few cattle left, but he kept busy with a new plan to get into the sheep business. He hauled old ties by wagon and mule from the railroad track that spring and used them in building a shed for sheep protection. He planned to talk the bankers into a loan to buy sheep. He knew they wouldn't listen unless he had sheds for storm shelter.

Hungry men by the hundreds rode the Union Pacific Railroad and walked the tracks past our Harper Ranch buildings asking for work or a free meal. Most wanted money, but many worked for room and board. Dad had food but no money to pay a wage. Destitute men were happy to have a few square meals before moving along. Mom fed several men before they could work since they were so weak and starved.

It had been tough for Bob to be born following a lost brother, a lost cattle herd, and a lost grandfather in a time of lost hope and in a nation lost in deep economic depression. Two years later, I was born into this dusty, dark, and dank world adding a new sibling and another mouth to feed.

But Mom was optimistic; with a new blond child, maybe things would get better. The bank still couldn't lend money even with the big railroad tie sheep shed completed. Dad then worked a deal and took over some sheep owned by his two brothers who didn't think they could make any money with them. Dad assumed the loan from Dora Richard, his mother, in Brush to take over and buy the 500 ewes. That started a sheep business, since Dad had plenty of room to run the five hundred head on the vast Harper Ranch.

Our neighbors, a family of Jehovah's Witnesses named Browder, told Dad that Armageddon, the end of the world, was coming, so there was no need to buy kids' shoes or get coal for the coming winter or buy any sheep. And, in those days on the isolated prairie, if people didn't stock up on coal in the fall, they didn't get it delivered on the bad winter roads. Dad got both coal and shoes for his boys. The neighbors didn't, and Mr. Browder and his family spent the coldest part of the winter in bed. Without heat, there was no other way to keep warm in their shack-like house. Dad always said, "Those people have got religion real bad."

We were now in the sheep business in a big way, having a huge railroad-tie sheep shed that looked like a medieval fortress to protect them from snowstorms. We had a sheepherder, sheep dogs, and sheep wagons that resembled small prairie schooners.

Quickly the two crops from the sheep, wool and lambs, started getting the Richards back on their feet. Since it was wartime, wool was bringing high prices. After two years, we had eight hundred sheep and had paid off what Dad owed on them. He bought more.

Dad decided it was time for a change in locations. He paid the bank the back interest he owed on the Harper Ranch and told the banker he wanted to move. The banker offered to sell the ranch back to him for less than the original loan. Dad refused. He'd been there seven years and couldn't pay anything on the mortgage, just interest. He was washing his hands of the outfit.

He soon leased grazing land north of Limon. It was 1937, I was only one, Bob was three, Jay was six. We lived in another shack that was once a granary. Dad built a lean-to kitchen on it from old lumber. It was a stark poverty-flats kind of a place. Mom had to carry water nearly half a mile up a hill to the house. That spring she was cooking for a half dozen Mexican helpers during lambing and shearing. The hardest part was taking care of us kids and washing the clothes. She had to "break" the hard water with lye and skim the crud off the surface before the water was usable.

She always told me how she detested that place. The old house was full of bedbugs, and she fought them at night, hunting them down with a flashlight. When the bed sheets were turned back, away they would scurry in droves. If she didn't try to control them, we kids would have bites every morning. During the Depression, everyone we knew had bedbugs and smelled of them—a musty odor. Most any visitor who threw down a coat spread the bugs to a new location. The old granary house had plenty of biting little bugs, but Mom's efforts cut numbers down.

Our neighbor, Earl Solzs, came by and visited with Dad. The poverty-stricken man was from a dirty outfit that rarely bathed.

He said, "You know Willard, it's really been hot lately. And, yesterday after dinner I went in to take a nap. The pillow on our bed was just covered with those bedbugs. I got mad and threw that damn thing across the bedroom against the wall. Then I got a new one out of the closet. Damned if it didn't have just as many!"

"We have the things, too, Earl. Edith keeps after 'em, but ours don't sound that bad."

"I think the bugs and damn dust storms are going to take the place. Maybe if our bedding wasn't so darned dirty, we'd be better off. Guess I'll have to get the old lady to wash better, but the water is hard an soap too expensive."

"They don't bother me much, but they raise welts on Edith and the kids. One bite and she's out of bed after 'em. I just sleep through it all."

My folks kept trying. They stayed less than a year at that miserable place north of Limon, then leased the Hamp Ranch and moved again.

The Hamp ranch, a dozen miles south of Limon, had been settled by a wealthy family of English people in the mid-1860s. They had killed and eaten a young horse a year, seeming strange to their neighbors. A huge house was hidden down in a protected draw filled with cottonwood trees. It was livable despite some doors being riddled with holes from knives thrown by the people who had lived there just before us. It had a nice spring with cold water piped into the house. Mom was thrilled. It was like heaven compared to the barren dry waterless place north of Limon.

Sadly, it had a mass of bedbugs. The folks used cyanide to fumigate, and when they opened the house after the two-day treatment, there were no bedbugs or mice anymore. However, the fumes had escaped up the chimney and killed birds roosting at night in the trees above.

Growing Up Wild

Larry was born there in May of 1938. That was the year we feared grasshoppers were going to take the country and all our grass. I remember seeing the giant yellow-green creatures crossing the roads in groups. Huge masses of bulging-eyed mouse-sized locusts marched on the Hamp Ranch eating everything in their path. Soon gulls and hawks appeared by the tens of thousands and controlled the grasshoppers within a week. The birds disappeared as abruptly as they had appeared once the hoppers were gone. The neighbors contended God had sent them, but Dad contended they were just hungry birds.

As an adult, I read how a similar situation had happened to early settlers in Utah as hoppers by the millions descended on their fields, but arriving birds saved their crops as they has saved our pasture grasses. It was considered a miracle in their religion, but not to my matter-of-fact Dad.

Jay, who seemed big to me, was now going to school and had lost a tooth. Mom had him put it under his pillow for the tooth fairy. He was amazed to find a nickel the next morning, a miracle to him. A few days later, Mom raised Jay's pillow and a large horse jaw with numerous big teeth stared up at her.

Things continued improving rapidly in the sheep business at the Hamp Ranch. Soon Dad had acquired over three thousand head and could also pay the lease and get money ahead. After three good years, he wanted our own place.

In 1940, he and Mom purchased the Jankee Place only three miles from the Hamp Ranch. Jimmy was born into the world in 1941 as we entered the Great War after Pearl Harbor. We kids purchased war stamps, and I remember Dad buying a five-hundred-dollar war bond when Jimmy Doolittle bombed Tokyo early in the war. We were all told to hate Japs and Hitler. We couldn't really hate Germans because Dad had a German background.

Over the next years, our sheep increased to nearly 5,000 head. Dad began to buy cattle, too. He worked constantly and improved the rundown place, making it an adequate sheep and cattle ranch. It also had some dry land farming ground that he worked with a John Deere tractor he purchased. Yet, the Jankee Place had little protection for livestock from the frequent grassland killer-storms. Dad, remembering the 1931 storm, was afraid a big storm would one day wipe out all the sheep and cattle he was accumulating. He felt a dark cloud was hanging over us, ready to knock us back into hard times.

However, the Jankee Place was a handy location, having a school close by. I wore blue bib overalls and high-topped brown work shoes to the first and second grades in the one-room Hopewell School with its thirteen pupils. Jay, the oldest kid in school, and Bob, six years younger, were my brother classmates and kingpins in my life. They were there to protect me on our daily horseback rides and walks across the grasslands to school. Larry was not ready for the first grade yet.

I was the pathetic blond kid who wore glasses, which were always being lost or broken, who had to share a desk with a girl, for which I was relentlessly teased, and who was such a little twerp that a boy named "Haystack" attacked me and forced me to fight him, which I did, dropping to my knees and socking him in the belly until he stopped pounding on my head, breaking my glasses. My brothers said I won the fight despite the battering I took. I wasn't sure, but my status improved. I was not always being chosen last to play ante-over at the Hopewell School or kick-the-can.

I remember three times getting out of Hopewell School to see something special. The first time Dad and Mom collected all the kids and the teacher, red-faced and gray-haired Mrs. Vermillion, in our old pickup. We bounced across our grassy pasture until we saw an airplane resting on its belly. Long plowed cuts in the green prairie sod led to the huge plane where the pilot sat writing in a little black book. We kids crawled over the P-38 Lightning fighter and its twisted off engines.

I felt special having an experimental plane downed on our place. I imagined myself as a daring pilot when my turn came to sit in the cockpit. My thick glasses, alas, would never allow me to be a real pilot. But once the military police arrived in their jeeps with guns to guard the secret aircraft, they wouldn't let people within a hundred yards of the aluminum flying machine. The next day, they hauled it away on long green trucks right out our gate across from the house. Dad wanted to do his part in the war effort and refused any damage payment for the pasture saying, "It will heal."

Larry asked one of the officers to give him the little jeep he drove. But the officer only responded with a laugh.

Later that spring Dad picked us up again for a trip to a windmill in a nearby pasture. At its base were half a dozen dead animals. Lightning had hit the metal windmill tower and was conducted to the base where steers were seeking shelter, killing them all. After that we were even more scared of lightning on the flat plains. We boys had been told that it strikes the highest point and that meant us if we were walking in the rain. We were never to get under a tree in a storm. But we boys all knew if our suspenders on our bib-overalls were twisted, lightning would never get us. A sheepherder had said it. So I always wore mine twisted at least once.

We got out of school again when a prairie fire was burning across pastures and they needed the older boys to help fight it. The men had barrels of water and piles of gunnysacks in the back of several rusty pickups. They would wet the sacks in the water and beat at the racing wall of fire, then race to the pickups to get soaked gunnysacks and exchange their steaming black ones. We smaller kids stayed in the pickups with the women drivers who kept the vehicles ahead of the firewall. I watched the frantic firefight amid the blue smoke and saw Jay helping soak the gunny sacks for the men. They finally contained the flames at an old road.

Dad's sheep raising was not as exciting as airplane crashes and prairie fires. My quiet Dad kept at it, understanding both the cattle and sheep business. Although Dad kept a small herd of cattle on the prairie, most of his efforts were keeping the sheep operations going and our sheepherders in line.

Good herders were hard to come by as the Great Depression was ending. Many of the better ones were from old Mexico and spoke little or no English. I went with Dad to meet the bus from Denver in Limon to pick up a new herder from the employment agency. With his trusty Spanish dictionary in hand, my dad would try to communicate. Most herders were eager workers wanting to please the boss when they understood what he wanted.

A good herder was dedicated to his sheep and watched them more than he herded. Dogs were directed by whistles to do the work. A sure sign of an inexperienced herder was one rushing around and waving his arms trying to drive sheep, so Dad believed. Top herders had the know-how, doing little things to handle the animals and his dogs.

Our herders worked in bad rattlesnake country. One young herder hated snakes and killed all he saw one summer and collected their rattles. By summer's end, he had a quart jar completely full of rattles. Some were huge with up to ten sections. I wanted some of them but didn't know how to ask in Spanish and neither did my father.

A rattlesnake once bit a neighbor's sheepherder as he crawled under a barbed wire fence bordering our Jankee Place. He was struck in the side of the neck and was found, not far away, dead. The folks said the man probably was scared to death from the bite and probably didn't die of the poison. We had dogs, horses, cattle, and even sheep bitten by the snakes each year. They would swell up but never died.

Snakes were a big part of my grassland life. I remember coming home from school and seeing Mom's turkeys circled around a big rattlesnake in the yard. Jay took a long tree branch to it. Within a few minutes they had another cornered for Jay to kill. That evening Mom gave us a ride in the pickup to drive in the milk cows and as Jay stepped off the running board he almost stepped on another prairie rattler. Six more were within the small area around the pickup. She drove us to another spot and let us off, urging us to watch for snakes as we drove the cows to the barn a half-mile away. I wasn't afraid with my big brother Jay there beside me.

A few days later we found a huge mass of snakes in an old caved-in well. Bob and I watched wide-eyed as they oozed about one another in a creepy mass. It scared the wits out of Bob and me, giving us what Mom called the "willies," whatever that was. Dad set the tumbleweeds afire above them, but the heat couldn't reach them. I had nightmares about falling into that pit with hundreds of rattlesnakes crawling all over me.

Mom shot two snakes one day close to Larry and Jimmy as they played in their sand box near the back porch. She blasted them good and proper. However, she didn't hate all snakes blindly and even allowed a six-foot bull snake to live in our basement because it would kill and eat rattlesnakes and mice even though it never killed the big dirty black rats living under the house.

Once Dad brought home six little ducks that we kept in a little pen beside the house. We let them swim in our big black stock tank between the house and the barn. One morning the ducks had vanished. I found a hole beside the house's foundation and reached inside, retrieving a dead duck, then another, and another. Finally, the rat bit me clean through my finger. I cried like crazy, and Mom doctored me with Epsom salts. Jay and Bob dug up half the sandy yard trying to get the rat, but never did.

Each exciting spring a shearing crew came to our big barn. It was a busy couple of weeks when valuable wool was removed and sacked. I loved playing on the mountain of sausage-shaped eight-and ten-foot long woolsacks filling our barn.

We kids had the job of hauling drinking water to the five-man shearing crew. Jay had a paying job tying each woolen fleece with twine after a shearer had removed it from a sheep.

A long burlap sack was suspended below a wooden tower and hung downward. Jay tossed the fleece up on the tower and we dumped it into the sack. I helped tromp each fleece tightly and could get out of the long sack only when it was nearly full. I stayed down in the bottom enjoying swinging to and fro. I picked the spider-like red sheep ticks off myself and the sides of the woolsack while I stomped wool along with my other brothers.

Once sheared, our sheep were naked, skinny, and strikingly white. I felt embarrassed for them being as white as I was. Our chickens flocked to the sheared sheep and fed on the ticks that now had little wool in which to hide.

My dad gave the crew one sheep for every five hundred they sheared. The cook cut its throat and chunked it up into small squares and added it to the small barrel of boiling mutton stew he kept going. The men ate when they were hungry, and shearing continued all day for a week. They had mutton stew and tortillas. They ate hot chili peppers like we ate popcorn. Dad ate with the crew. Jay tried their hot chili peppers and was in agony for a long time, drinking water, which didn't seem to help. He said, "Never again."

After shearing one year, I recall Mom spotting a lone figure stumbling across the flat prairie east of the Jankee Place. As we watched, the man fell to the ground twice, only to right himself and stagger on. He would move to the left then sway to the right, obviously disoriented and trying to reach the dirt road. A twinge of fear went through us as Mom strained to identify him. From over a quarter mile, she couldn't determine who the dark figure was. She knew something was dreadfully wrong.

"Jay, get in the pickup and go see what in the world's the matter with that guy. Be careful!"

"I won't even stop unless I know him," replied Jay the eight grader running out the kitchen door eager to drive for any reason.

Anxiously we watched the dull green pickup clear the long row of stately cottonwood trees and bounce along the washboard rutted road toward the solitary figure on the barren flat prairie. Mom said, "I wish to heaven Willard was home to handle this kind of thing."

Jay, had a shock as he drove up beside the tall staggering man. He saw scarlet red blood blanketing the side of the dark skinned face and running down the neck inside his shirt. Joe, one of our Mexican sheepherders, staggered up to the pickup and placed his two bloody hands on the half rolled down window and peered at Jay with wild, drunken eyes.

"Where's your Dad?" Joe said, bracing himself against the pickup. "I'm gonna kill 'em. Look what he did to me."

Jay figured Joe was referring to Allen, our Osage Indian herder, and said, "Get in." The two herders had never gotten along well at their adjacent sheep camps and were always arguing and fighting. With Joe inside, the pickup jerked forward several times and died.

"God, kid! When are you goin' to learn to drive? Can't you see I'm bleedin' to death?" muttered Joe, gazing at the floor boards in the old pickup and clutching his cut hands together in his lap.

Pumping the foot feed and trying to get the pickup started, Jay noticed how Joe's teeth showed through the big slash in his left cheek. The bloody opening ran from near the ear to the corner of his wide mouth. It sagged at the center, exposing dirty brown teeth from years of chewing tobacco. He was drooling and bleeding as he slumped forward and placed his hands on the dashboard. Blood dripped in dark red spots onto the floorboards. Finally, the pickup started moving. Jay led Joe into the house and Mom sat him on a stool inside the dining room. She frantically tried to contact Dad. She repeatedly cranked the old black wall telephone, but there was no answer at the neighbor's ranch where Dad was looking for some strays. Joe kept falling off the white stool in the corner. Each time he got back on, bloody spots and red handprints were left on the floor, wallpaper, and chair.

I stood horrified by all the man's blood and how scary the Mexican herder was as he swore, whined, and bossed Mom around.

"Do something! Mrs. Richard, do you think I'm goin' to live?" muttered Joe.

"Of course you are," Mom replied, "Just keep your shirt on. It's just going to take us a little bit to get you to the doctor."

Mom knew we couldn't all fit into the cab of the pickup, and she wouldn't take Joe to town alone. No telling what he might do since he was so drunk. On the stool, Joe continued to sway, cuss, and clutch his cut hands in a towel Mom had given him, and to mutter to himself how he'd kill Allen, that damned Osage.

I stood with my brothers wide-eyed and watched the wounded man's performance. Joe continued raving and wiping the blood from his face with the now crimson towel.

Mom and Jay decided to get Joe to town. Jay, Joe, and Mom were in the front and the other four of us were sitting in the back pulling out of the yard when Dad and a neighbor drove up.

Mom leaped out of the pickup and rushed to Dad telling him Joe was all cut up. Dad walked over and asked Joe, "Who cut you like this?"

"Allen--that dirty Osage."

"Did he get cut, too?"

"No, I didn't have a knife," replied Joe, peering at Dad and holding the bloody towel over his left cheek.

"We'll get you to town right away, Joe," said Dad.

Dad asked the neighbor to drive Mom and Joe to town in our car, told Jay to take care of the other four of us, then jumped in the pickup and headed for sheep camp where he found Allen, with two big black eyes and a badly swollen face. Allen acted sober as a judge out herding his sheep, calm as could be, but Dad saw Allen was beaten up badly.

"What happened to you?"

"Nothing, I guess, Boss."

"By the looks of you, something happened, Allen."

"Well, I guess Joe and me had a fight. He was a lot bigger than me, Boss. So he beat up on me."

"Did you cut him?"

"No, Boss," said Allen, "I had no knife."

"Are you sure?"

"Yes Boss, I had no knife. I swear, no knife."

"How did Joe get cut then?"

"I don't know. He had the knife, Boss!"

"You don't look cut up to me."

"Look where he cut, Boss," muttered Allen, turning around and showing where a knife had cut through his heavy sheepskin coat, shirt, and underwear. Allen had a deep bloody gash over a foot long across his back.

"Come on, Allen, let's get you to town to be sewed up."

On the way, they stopped briefly at Joe's sheep camp, picked up his bedroll and personal belongings. Allen knew Joe was being fired and he still had a job. Often, herders were jealous, fought, and argued over grass, campsites, or good sheep dogs, but when they started using knives on each other, Dad rolled up one's bedroll thus ending disputes.

Things were usually more peaceful when Allen and the other herders were widely separated at sheep camps. Dad now had six herders with a thousand head of sheep each. It took a lot of pickup trips to tend and supply their camps each week. I rode with Dad in the back of the pickup to different sheep camps seeing all the herders, sheep, dogs, and tiny sheep wagons on tall wheels.

One herder I visited with Dad had the skins of snakes, rabbits, ground hogs, lambs, and ewes on his sheep camp fence along with coyotes skins and a dog skin. Dad laughed telling us at the table that night, "I tried for two weeks to get him to skin the dead ewes so we could sell the pelts. Finally, I got my knife out and started skinning one and said, 'Vamoose the pelt.' Now he's really got the message and skins every dead thing he finds. And now I can't stop 'em."

Skinning of animals didn't bother me a lot, however the actual killing and butchering was a different matter. When I was seven, I was with Dad when he caught a ewe and tied two legs together, took out his pocket knife, and slit her throat, allowing dark red blood to cover the grass. Another time I was startled when he and a hired man strung three turkeys up by the feet on a corral gate and used an ice pick to poke them in the brains through the roofs of their beaks. The idea was a brain kill loosened the big feathers making them easier to pluck. He also stuck a giant hog with a big butcher knife, letting it bleed to death. After it was dead, Dad scalded it in a huge barrel of boiling water to remove the hair so cracklings could be made of the inner hide. I had a hard time eating any of them thinking of how the poor pig had squealed as it died. But the turkey killings had seemed the most terrible to me, giving me nightmares. I didn't want Dad to know how I felt about using our own animals as food.

That year, I lost or broke my glasses three times, forcing trips to Dr. Gayle in Denver to fit new ones. I could tell that Dad wasn't happy about the extra trips and expenses. Mom didn't say anything, but taped the new glasses to my nose with adhesive tape. I felt like a freak since nobody else in the family wore glasses taped to their skull.

Dad usually carried a rifle in his pickup in case we saw coyotes when we tended sheep camps. Coyotes killed lambs in the spring and some ewes at other times. Woe to the coyote that showed up at the wrong time in the wrong place. Dad was a good shot and few escaped. I remember pickup-coyote chases when the rifle wasn't along or Dad was out of ammo. If there were no fences near and the terrain fairly level, Dad would take off full tilt. Up, down, across draws and gullies, he always pushed the coyote with his pickup at about thirty miles per hour. This would wear one out in a few miles.

Bumps were easy for Dad to contend with since he had a steering wheel to hold onto. I bounced sometimes clear to the metal ceiling as the pickup raced where pickups were never meant to go. It was a grassland speedway. Swerving, turning, dipping, bouncing, and sometimes a bit out of control we raced. Sometimes the coyote escaped by finding a fence or rough place the pickup couldn't cross. Usually, however, the pickup ran over the exhausted coyote as it ran slower and slower. I felt sorry for the coyotes thinking we might take them somewhere else instead of killing them, but I didn't dare say anything. To me they looked like small dogs I could tame.

My dad concluded that dead coyotes meant more live lambs and sheep. All coyotes were considered "bad" and "fair game" when a family's livelihood came mostly from sheep. Dad said, "Only one coyote in a hundred kills sheep, but we can't tell which ones do and don't."

We lived a long dozen miles from town over bad dirt roads. Jay was now about ready to enter high school, so the folks finally decided to move when they got a chance at a new place. Dad and Mom sold our Jankee Place to a preacher who said, "I am fascinated by the rolling hills." Since it was mostly flat,

Dad thought the man was nuts but sold anyway. He also sold all the sheep except 300 head.

Mom and Dad were returning with five boys back to North Park and safer mountain ranching. Our new home was to be near Walden, in North Park, on the old Two-Bar Ranch that belonged to Mom's grandmother in California. We were going to be leasing the place, then maybe purchase it. The ranch was on the edge of town and getting to school would be no problem for Jay and the rest of us. We boys could walk as we had to Hopewell. Dad was excited about having cattle again on a mountain ranch, but Mom wasn't too happy about it.

There was much talk and anxiety about moving. We flatland boys wondered what the future would be. I recall Bob's crying in bed late one night after overhearing the folks talking. Bob was upset and cried to Mom, "I want our radio and Croppie to go with us." She reassured him that they were taking everything, including Croppie and the radio, to North Park. I was greatly relieved, too, but leaving frightened me.

It was now 1943 and, through a lot of hard work and some luck, the folks had gotten back on their felt. But they had five boys to educate. In early May, we loaded everything we owned and headed for Walden. I remember riding in our Ford car with Mom and the other kids as we left our prairie home.

I left our grasslands during late May, the most beautiful time of the year. It was a verdant green plain, dotted with white, yellow, red, and blue blossoms of thousands of spring flowers decorating the landscape as far as my eyes could see.

We had had our share of trouble and grief during the Dust Bowl and Great Depression days. My folks were proud to have never been on the dole. How my parents survived is a tribute to their "doing what had to be done with help from some relatives."

We boys, however, had such unique fun to remember. We ate dozens of huge grasshopper legs in the pasture after Dad had said the Chinese liked them. Jay once made Bob eat a gray cutworm and me a big red angleworm in order to play in the barn with him. Jay even made Bob eat pigeon eggs by breaking them open, one at a time, into his up-turned mouth. I nearly gagged watching it and was thankful I didn't have to do that to be with him to hunt salamanders in the pond north of the buildings.

We sadly bid the prairie farewell when we entered the irrigated farming areas of Greeley and drove on west to Fort Collins. I was a bit bigger and heading into the third grade, but still didn't see well. A new place, a new school, and new kids worried me, but Mom said it would be fine.

Mom drove the car along as mountains with foothills grew to our left. I could see splendid snow-capped peaks, expanses of green forest, and rocky outcrops more clearly as we gained elevation with each mile heading from Fort Collins and Laramie toward North Park. None of us kids had ever been in the mountains.

Dad and his friends were bringing tractors, cattle, and the household things. All were strung out someplace between Limon and Walden.

Mom dreaded returning to North Park for several reasons. The winters were too long. More importantly, she felt bad about not having her parents on their ranches. They had worked so long and hard carving them out of the sagebrush. Her Dad had rheumatic fever and had developed a bad heart when he was a young man and had later literally worked himself to death in developing his own ranches. The fact that he had lost them in the Depression really hurt Mom. She said, "It won't be any happy going-home-again for me." Some wives would surely have raised a stink if they had to move where they didn't want to go. Our mom didn't. She always said, "When a man has to make the living, where he goes, I'll follow."

On the trip, Mom showed us Laramie, Wyoming, where she was born and had spent her life until she was my age. We boys were excited crossing the Laramie plains as the Ford crept up Woods Creek Pass, soon entering the forest with its miles and miles of lodgepole pines. It was beautiful tree-covered rolling country with beaver ponds and an occasional meadow bordered by aspen trees.

Mom pointed out a small sign saying "Fox Park" at a dirt side road leading into thick green timber. As a kid in 1920 she had returned to North Park with her mother on the train from Laramie for Christmas vacation from her boarding school. The snow was deep and the winter had been awful. The Union Pacific train had their largest snowplow mounted on the engine. It became stuck and the snow continued to fall. The train was unable to make it on to North Park or back to Laramie.

So Mom and her mother spent a week snowbound on the train at Fox Park, Wyoming. Its railroad buildings were buried under ten feet of snow and she told of climbing down tunnels to the warm railroad cookhouse to eat. She slept with her clothes on in the caboose of the train with other passengers. In those winters, the train was the only safe way in or out of North Park.

Our cattle and sheep were coming to Walden on the same steep railroad line. Jay, Dad, and our hired man, Ben, had driven them seventeen miles to River Bend and the railhead from the Jankee Place the day before. It had rained the entire day, and Jay told how old Ben had chewed tobacco, spit, and cussed all the way in the rain. Finally, they reached the train and loaded our cattle in three cattle cars and the sheep in double-decked sheep cars. They put a saddle horse in each car with the cattle. In a few days, they would arrive on the slow Laramie-Hahn's Peak Railroad. How I envied Jay's being able to drive cattle on horseback.

Traveling along as slowly as the old train, Dad was far behind. He drove his bright yellow-and-green John Deere tractor pulling a hayrack loaded with possessions and equipment for the new ranch.

The evergreen smell in the thin mountain air greeted my nose, refreshing me. I had never smelled pines before. I had been, as Mom put it, "around and about," meaning, "around home and about out of shoes." During the Depression, I never went anyplace far away like the mountains. We were hard up and didn't waste gas on silly pleasure trips.

Dad had said it would be nice living in the cool high mountains where it never reached 90 degrees in summer. Summer would be cooler at the new ranch, what little summer there was. Mom quoted our great-grandmother, Lindy Monroe, who had always said, "There are nine months winter and three months late-in-the-fall in North Park."

Finally, we broke into the open basin of North Park. It stretched forty miles long and thirty miles wide. Mountains and trees surrounded the valley. I could feel the fresh air and see the beautiful mountains about me. Mom answered questions as fast as she could while I pressed my chin into the back of the front seat and peered out the windshield.

The Park's floor was slightly rolling. In the west, a butte and a hogback rising sharply against the surrounding mountains were the only obstructions in the rounded park. It was great summer cattle country, according to Dad. Yet much of the valley was sagebrush and greasewood. In the sagebrush, I could see grazing herds of red cattle and white sheep.

Only 2,300 humans resided in Jackson County in 1943. A total of seven Richards, including five boys, were being added to that population. Mom turned the car westward and there were the grand ranch buildings near the edge of the small town. I was now home on the Two-Bar (2-) Ranch.

There had been no pristine running river water and few mosquitoes when we lived back on the dry plains of eastern Colorado where all we boys were born. Mom said that we would have to get used to biting insects and lots of running water on the new ranch.

All my growing up years I enjoyed listening to my folk's tales about when they lived on the grasslands those fourteen years trapped in the Great Depression during hard Dust Bowl days. However, I also always remembered the green plains myself and never got over leaving their wide expanses where our sheep roamed.

Even today as an adult, I have a deep love of the peaceful prairie. Losing the Jankee Ranch by selling it and moving was not a big worry to me since we were going to another better ranch. It was not like enduring the upcoming loss of a total way of life that I soon had to face.

Chapter 6

RIVERIN'

"Lord knows what it died of!"

Stopping my daydreaming and picking myself up off the dusty ground by the high-board fence, I trudged across the manure filled corrals and down the ridge a half mile, admiring the wild things flushing ahead of me along the waters of the ditches in the grassy pasture. Near the end of the ridge, I climbed to its top where I could see the two river valleys, the ranch buildings, and the high mountains directly beyond Walden. Again my mind raced back to the past, remembering what went on along the ranch waters when I was a kid.

Our North Park ranch's two rivers held treasures of rainbow trout, brook trout, and German brown trout along with suckers and creek chubs. After these swimmers left the Michigan and Illinois rivers, they moved into our larger ditches during high water irrigation time each spring, not being able to distinguish a ditch from a small river channel. Such fish misjudgments were a boon to my boyhood, giving me some of the best days any kid could have in growing up.

I first saw these sleek water creatures after a small ditch below the ranch buildings had been shut off, causing the water level to drop instantly. Dad and our hired men walked the rocky-bottomed ditch ahead of us sons finding trout in the small pools of the remaining standing water. "They'll soon die and rot if we don't collect 'em," Dad said.

Soon, I chased two light green, swift fish up and down the ditch's shallow water until in panic they beached themselves. Springing on them, I lifted one skyward in each hand. Although I wanted to rush my prizes to the house to show Mom, my brothers objected.

Never had I seen any animals so strikingly beautiful and perfect. I stood with shock, pride, and amazement as I gazed at my first fish. The rainbow trout had perfect green and black marks on their backs with snow white on their lower halves. And down the sides there were brilliant blood red stripes that seemed to have been painted in a straight line. The trout's red gill covers moved in and out showing fiber like red arches, but I had no idea what they did. They were slick, wet, and smooth feeling not scaly at all. What nice looking animals these were, and I had caught them.

"I want more," I said.

Then Jay, Bob, and I raced up and down the ditch together. We covered a half-mile, catching trout after trout in a delightful frenzy. Within two hours, we had two galvanized washtubs, one full of big trout from thirteen to twenty inches and another of a foot and smaller. We helped Mom clean them for freezing for our haying crew in August. Mother, who liked the smaller ones for our family, said, "They're the better eating."

As I helped Mother clean the trout, my mind raced. What a way to fish! At my age I hadn't had any luck catching trout in our big streams since I lacked the equipment to pole fish. Fish confined to ditches sparked my imagination since they were out of the deep river holes where they always lurked in hidden blackness. I could get at them in small ditches.

Later that same afternoon, Dad spotted a green state pickup weaving between mud holes as it came down our lane from Walden. I was sure we were all going to be arrested. We hurriedly covered the washtubs with boards. A game warden stepped from the vehicle and visited with Dad on the porch regarding beaver dams in the Michigan. He never noticed the nearby tubs. I breathed more easily when he drove back up the road.

"Dad said, "It's the law to allow the ditch trout to die and rot, but if we use them for food, it's illegal." I just knew that Dad was right and that the game wardens were wrong.

Sometimes I went along just to watch the irrigating in the hay meadows. Dad and the hired men often saw fast trout in the shallow water. When they ran across a nice big trout, they'd try to spear it with pitchforks as it streaked up a ditch. Suckers, a trash fish, were also in our ditches in large numbers. Dad and the men could spear them more easily and pitch them out onto the banks.

Ditch water nurtured frogs by the tens of thousands. They croaked in chorus across our hay meadows all day and into the cool of the nights. Through my open bedroom window in the summer, I always fell asleep while listening to their singing on the Two-Bar, comforted to be serenaded every night during irrigation time.

In places, the frog-infested meadow sod became so waterlogged and soft that it would shake five feet outward from a person walking on it. No horse or vehicle could cross such a soggy meadow. The waters of spring dominated and claimed the meadows and limited activities there.

Soon light green hay stood above the meadow flowers and moved with grace in each gust of wind. By this time, the crop was over half raised, and the ditches were full of fat trout, feeding on the insect hordes of North Park. It was mid July and time to shut off the big irrigation ditches across the Michigan River.

"Dad," Larry said, "Can Paul and me go down and shut off the head gate?"

"Well, I suppose, if you guys can stop the water."

"We can."

"You'll need a bunch of gunny sacks to fill with sand and some wire to tie 'em. Tell Paul to be sure the trash and willows are cleared in the head gate before you guys lower the gates down in the slots."

"Can Paul use your gumboots?"

"He can. Be sure to go over to the river and tear some of the dam out before shutting that head gate. That water has to have some place to go. It just can't back up behind the dam in the river once you drop the head gate," said Dad. "I don't want that head gate or dam washed out if it backs up!"

"Is it O.K. if we take Jimmy along?"

"Sure, if you both watch him."

Quickly Larry, Jimmy, and I headed for the shop where we located gunnysacks and baling wire. I wanted in the worst way to shut off the big ditch. Being in charge was a big deal, as was who got to go first, and who got to tell of an adventure. This time I had put Larry up to asking Dad, as I hadn't wanted to face him myself, fearing he might say "no." My father was the kind of man who didn't always say "yes".

"Jimmy, you get the shovel. Larry, get the big seine and the landing net," I ordered as I got Dad's gumboots from behind the shop door. I was thrilled to now be big enough to be able to wear the gumboots, even though they were still too big. There are big fish in that ditch, I thought, as I fastened the boot loops to my belt and checked my hunting knife, knowing I might need it to clean the trout.

What an opportunity to shut off the big ditch and do it my way! We'd just close it down fast, instead of lowering the gate slowly as Dad always did. That way all those trout wouldn't get back into the river, and we could get some.

Smokey was standing in the shade of the bunkhouse watching, knowing something was about to happen. He was always ready to go. It was a hot July day without a cloud in the sky as our dog joined us.

"Hurry up, you guys. You're as slow as the seven year itch," I barked. Heading for the buck-and-pole fence, I carried the seine and gunny sacks under one arm, then waited on the top pole for my two little brothers. As we crossed the fence and started down the hill, mosquitoes began swarming around our heads.

At the railroad tracks we paused. Without speaking, we each pulled out a large white handkerchief and removed a cap. We helped each other adjust one end of the handkerchief under the earflaps of the cap, until it hung evenly from temple to temple around our heads. With earflaps down and the handkerchief hanging below, we looked like kids in the French Foreign Legion. Finally, we turned our shirt collar up, and buttoned them over the handkerchief. All of us were wearing winter caps and long-sleeved shirts. Mom had taught us to use these technique our grandfather, Jay Monroe, employed to keep mosquitoes from biting anything other than face and hands.

"It's skeeter land ahead," Larry muttered happily.

We headed down the railroad tracks. Hundreds of mosquitoes rose from vegetation in the standing water around us and swarmed about us in dark clouds. Jimmy carried the big spade that was almost as tall as he. We hurried along. We didn't pause as Smokey chased whistling gophers that raced for their burrows along the two tracks.

Once at the wide clear river, we stood at the dam for a moment and watched the clear water spill over the green algae-covered logs and fall into a deep foamy pool. Log pilings stood starkly erect above the dam. A beaver-like dam of poles, logs, sod, driftwood, rocks, and old hay formed the barrier that raised the river's water level and forced it to the open-mouthed box head gate to the north. Other water flowed over, under, and through the crude dam. Trout, rising upstream of the dam, took insects and left behind small rings on the Michigan's surface.

After dropping our gunnysacks, we moved onto the narrow dam and began tearing out two big holes. I worked in one spot while Jimmy and Larry tore a hole in the dam nearer shore. As we removed more materials, the water roared loudly over the dam.

"That's enough," yelled Larry, "let's go!"

"Whoa! No, it isn't! Remember what Dad said," I shouted above the roar of the water. It griped me that Larry was always in such a big hurry.

In a few minutes we moved off of the dam. Water flowed freely through the two big holes, lowering the river level above the dam. Smokey led the way along the river, as we walked single file through the waist-tall hay. We entered the willows and soon came out at the river's rocky edge. Across the river we could see the iron wheel atop the big head gate that lowered the plank gate, which would stop the ditchwater.

"Hop on, Larry," I said, as I stepped down off of the bank and onto the jillion small, slick rocks on the river bottom. We always piggybacked. No need in everyone getting wet. Besides, I had Dad's boots.

Placing his arms around my neck, Larry climbed on my back. I grabbed each of his legs and started staggering against the current toward the other shore. Twice, I nearly lost my balance but regained it. When I reached the other bank, I dropped Larry on his butt and the shovel in the grass.

"Isn't that big kid pretty heavy to be toting?" came a voice from the willows.

"No, I like my brother dry."

I whispered to Larry, "While I go get Jimmy, you see if that guy has permission. If not, run him off."

As I waded back into the river to carry Jimmy and the sacks across, Larry walked through the tall grass toward the man.

"Any luck?"

"Got a few," replied the fisherman.

"Big ones?"

"No."

"Can I see 'em?"

"Can't you see I'm busy fishing, kid? Besides, you and those brats are scaring the fish, wading in the river and stomping around," said the man, as he reached for a match to relight his pipe.

"Who said you could fish?"

"None of your business," replied the man.

Larry saw us approaching through the tall grass. "My Dad owns this ranch, and you haven't been to the house to get permission," shouted Larry.

"How do I know if your dad does?"

I answered with a blast of words, "Well, he does, and you had better pack up your gear and get the hell out of here, mister. Don't you have enough sense to ask permission?"

"Now listen, sonny, your dad doesn't own this river, and I don't have to take any talk from snot-nosed kids."

"Well, we own the land you're standin' on, mister, and we pay taxes on the land under the creek, too. So, unless you can tread water, buddy, you're trespassin'."

"Shall I go get Dad?" asked Jimmy bravely.

"It's pigs like you who don't ask permission to fish that spoil it for nice people," yelled Larry.

"I should just stomp the holy-hell out of you all and kick your butts," said the man, who was getting red-faced as the mosquitoes continued swarming about him.

"Try and catch us, fatso," snapped Larry.

As we started backing away, I said so that the fisherman could hear, "Larry, you keep an eye on him. Jimmy and I will go over to the bridge and let the air out of his tires and then get Dad. Dad'll get the sheriff and show this big bird a thing or two." Although the man must have heard me, he said nothing.

We whispered to each other on a rocky knoll about a hundred feet away.

"Larry, you rock him. Jimmy and I'll go over to the head gate. He'll think we went for his car and Dad."

"I can outrun that pig anyway."

"Don't hit him in the head. We'll meet you at the head gate," said Jimmy.

"Good plan," I replied.

As we walked away, there came a big splash in the water, which was followed by a cracking against the willow branches. A sharp blow hit the fisherman's knee and almost knocked him down.

"Get the hell out of here, you fat puke," came Larry's voice from the tall grass. "I'll rock you to sleep, you fat fish hog," he shouted as he unleashed another volley.

We soon looked back. The man was walking away with a string of trout in one hand and fishing pole in the other.

"Next time you sneak onto our place, I'll have my big brothers kill you. You're a dirty flatlander, no-good, invading trespasser," hollered Larry. He then used all the dirty language learned from the hired men and threw rocks at the fisherman until he was far out of range across the river.

After poking with my shovel to clear sticks and rocks from where the plank gate would fall down in the two groves, I waded down in the head gate mouth. The head gate was a six by ten-foot wooden box, open at the top. The gate had to fall flush with the bottom to stop most of the water.

Jimmy was perched on the gravel bank atop the head gate when Larry jogged up.

"Got him once in the leg, Paul."

"Did he chase you?" I asked, leaning on my shovel in the thigh deep water.

"No. When you guys left, I hid in the grass and loaded up with some ammo. I missed him the first shots; the rock landed in the water. He thought it was a big fish. He was a perfect target when he turned to look in the water, but I got excited and blasted the willows. Finally when he was turned around, I got him in the knee and I dropped in the grass. He never saw me. He just took off to his car. I bombarded him. May have hit him again when he crossed the river."

"Well, the ole goat deserved it," said Jimmy.

"Next time we find one like this, let's tie him up and torture him like Indians would," said Larry.

Even as an adult today, I still feel somewhat violated by what these men did by sneaking onto our place and taking our fish. They probably got exactly what they deserved from us. For all they had to do was ask permission, and we would have given it.

Soon we had the wooden gate cranked down in the head gate to stop the water. To close the gate had taken half an hour. We heard splashing in the shallow channel which led to the big pool in the ditch below the head gate. When we looked around, Smokey was standing over a splashing fish as it fought upstream. He probed his nose under the water and blew bubbles as he sought the slick prey. Finally, he clamped his teeth on the sucker's back fin, hauled the fish out, and dropped it into the pea-sized gravel beside us. It was the first time we'd seen him bring a fish ashore.

"What a pooch! We'd better get goin' before he out-fishes us," Jimmy said.

"Are there many more, Paul?" asked Larry, as his gaze fell on the large half muddy pool.

"You bet! Big ones here this year. We shouldn't waste time. Down below, the water will dry up. These up here will come upstream to the head holes where we can get them later. Why don't we leave our seine here, come back tomorrow, and bring Harold along if his dad doesn't have him workin' in the woods."

"Yeah, once the water down there has dropped, they can't cross that culvert at the railroad track, either. We can get millions," said Larry, who had experienced ditch fishing before.

Jimmy was already hiding our seine in the willows beside the head gate. Carrying the shovel, Larry walked one bank.

With the gunnysack over his shoulder, Jimmy walked on the other bank, and I waded the ditch.

"Look," yelled Jimmy, "there's a real big one ahead."

Larry was first with Jimmy right behind him. I struggled in the ditch with water above my knees. A "V" shaped wake was moving along the shallow channel. Half a green back with a two-inch dorsal fin protruded above the water and showed the fish's good size.

"Whoomp," Larry's shovel hit the water behind the swift trout.

"He's a huge one," yelled Jimmy, as he scrambled into the water.

"Get him, Larry," I shouted and prepared to stop the giant fish from entering the deeper water with my landing net. Swiftly, the trout turned and headed back past Jimmy downstream.

Twitching and quivering, the brook trout lay on its side after Larry hit home with the big spade. Jimmy grabbed the big fish. "I got him!"

"I was the one who killed him, damn it, Jimmy!

"He must be at least twenty inches long. What a beauty!" said Jimmy, ignoring Larry.

Larry squatted in the tall grass and looked at the fish. "I have the biggest one so far."

"Jimmy, look at your shoes. Boy, are you going to get it when you get home," I said. My little brother, who was standing ankle deep in mud, was holding the big trout with red spots on its sides and pearl white margins along its fins.

"Isn't it big?" asked Jimmy, as he held the fish out at arm's length.

"He's really a dandy brook. I thought he would get away in the deep water," I said, as I took the fish from Jimmy for a closer inspection.

"Not a mark on him," said Larry. "We don't get many big brooks here, either."

"Let's put him in Jimmy's sack and go. I noticed lots of 'em in that hole back there. Most of them suckers, I think. They really thumped my boots as I waded."

"I'll bet we find some monsters at the rock dam," said Larry, barging through the tall grass down the grassy ditch bank.

Smokey bounced along in front near a tangled pile of old gray fence posts at the old flume. With his ears straight up, Smokey jumped, and rose stiff-legged above the tall hay. Again and again, he repeated his jack-in-the-box performance. He located his prey, but it ran under the pile of posts. His barks brought Jimmy to his side. Smokey raced from end to end as Jimmy quickly tore away the parallel posts. A gopher whistled underneath as Smokey, sniffed, whined, and made snorting noises. When the last post was removed, the gopher attempted to race into the waist high thick hay. But Smokey pounced, and soon the rodent was lifeless.

When Jimmy and Smokey caught up with us, we were at the rock dam. I was feeling far back under the dirt banks, while Larry, who was on the exposed rocks, was reaching between them for wily trout.

"Oh, there are some damn big fish in this hole," I said, as I righted myself. The front of my shirt was dripping water. Having reached in to my shoulders under the bank, I had felt slick sides and bumped huge trout. They were too far back to grab.

"Smokey killed a gopher," said Jimmy.

"Atta boy, Smokey."

"I think tomorrow we can get these with a seine," said Larry, moving from the rocks up onto the bank.

"I just felt a huge one under this bank!" yelled Jimmy." It must be long as my leg."

"That's not so darn long," replied Larry.

"Let's go on down to the deep bend," I ordered, and we moved out.

"Hear that?" shouted Larry.

Listening, the three of us froze. We heard the familiar sound putt-putt...putt...putt as the railroad section car approached. The rumbling sound changed as it crossed the tin-covered bridge to the south.

"Get down! Hold Smokey," I yelled and crouched against the side of the ditch.

Larry and Jimmy fell into the tall hay on each ditch bank. Larry who was holding one arm around Smokey, pulled the big blue dog into a prone position. From the tall grass we watched the small motorcar move slowly along the railroad tracks eighty yards away. Dark complexioned men gazed across the meadows of our tall hay. Occasionally, we could hear Spanish and Indian curse words above the noise of the putt-putt car.

"Are they gone?" inquired Larry.

"Hold your horses! Just stay down! They're almost to the other bridge now. Okay! You guys keep your eyes open. We don't want to get caught, catchin' trout by pole is the only legal way."

"Do you think they saw us?" asked Larry.

"Doubt it."

"Remember when you were fishing before season opened down where the rivers meet, and those two game wardens with the big black dog chased you?" asked Larry.

"Didn't you have two sage chickens, too?" asked Jimmy.

"Yeah, I had the sage hens, but the big problem was you guys were on the rocks with Harry, yelling half the morning how the game wardens were coming because I was fishing before season opened. Then, when they really did show up, I wouldn't look, and they nearly got me."

"They were just running their beaver traps," said Larry

"We really cussed them out from the rocks, too," giggled Jimmy.

"When I finally saw 'em and reeled in, they were right after me. Remember I headed for the thick willows across the slough and they couldn't find me? I was really scared and raced home. I took all of the fish out of Mom's freezer and hid them in the bunkhouse. That's as close as I ever came to getting caught by the law. I thought they would come to the house, search the place, and arrest me."

"Yeah, but we wouldn't tell 'em who you were or where you went. Harry kept tellin' them 'you were nobody'," Larry said with a laugh.

"They only got one beaver, too," said Jimmy.

"I hate game wardens. We should kill 'em all, maybe build a fire on their chests when we have them staked out as the Shawnees did to whites," said Larry.

As we approached the big bend, the fish raced for the banks in the thigh deep water. The big bend of North Park No. 5 Ditch was about ten feet wide and ran five feet of water during irrigation time.

"Can I wade in? My feet are wet anyway and the water will clean off my shoes," Jimmy pleaded, as he smacked a large horse fly on my shoulder.

"Sure." I said, "Larry, you hold the net at the end of that big bank after we stir up the water so they can't see. I'll poke into the net for you. Don't move it 'til you feel a lot of 'em," I kicked and stirred mud up from the bottom of the hole. Fish continually struck my gumboots from all angles.

Mosquitoes hovered above his head as Larry lay on the bank and waited with the landing net in one hand. Smokey stretched out beside him and lowered his nose to rest on his paws. Larry stroked the big brown-eyed dog while Jimmy and I muddied the water. I moved to the overhanging bank and reached under it.

In a low voice, I said, " Holy cow! There are just hundreds of fish under here as far back as I can reach. Jimmy, give me that big stick. I'll poke 'em your way, Larry."

"Wow, look at those!" yelled Jimmy, as Larry swung the big net up on the bank beside Smokey.

Jimmy and I reached under the deep bank and started pulling out trout with our hands. We tossed them up to Larry for him to thrust into the wet gunnysack.

"I got seven in the net that first time. Let's do that again, Paul".

"How many do we have now?" I asked, as I tossed another small yellow-sided German brown trout onto the matted grass beside Larry and Smokey. It flopped madly.

"We must have about fifteen," replied Larry.

"Well, here's another one," said Jimmy, who smiled as he raised a foot long rainbow trout from the water. Jimmy's arm was dripping and he was wet all over except for one dry spot on his back.

"Look at that fish's tail. It's been chewed," Larry pointed out.

"Boy!" Jimmy exclaimed.

We stood huddled about the limp trout with the lower half of its tail missing. Bloody red edges, bordered by white loose scales, marked the bite of some predator.

"There must be a real big old trout like Grandpa in this hole. Those big browns are cannibals," replied Larry.

"Let's shake a leg and move down below in the real low water," I said. The ditch is smaller and they're easier to get and we want to get 'em before the crows and herons." I headed down the ditch, trailed by my two brothers.

Cackling at the edge of a slough, killdeers faked injury to lure us away from their long-legged young. We had other things on our minds as we walked ankle-deep in irrigation water amid the thousands of singing frogs who fell silent when we got close. Because mosquitoes blanketed our bodies, we continually slapped our faces and hands, killing hundreds.

Late afternoon shadows were upon us when we heard the ringing of the dinner bell atop our log cookhouse. Picking up a heavy sack of fish, we hastened up the railroad track to the big ranch house on the hill. As we hurried along the tracks, black clouds of also-hungry mosquitoes followed us, attacking. Frogs by the millions serenaded from the soggy meadow sloughs, as nighthawks cried eerie wails, twisting high overhead catching flying insects.

Being able to put fish on the family table, especially since the folks loved eating trout, made me feel ten feet tall. I felt big having shut off the ditch. I was so puffed up with pride that I could have busted the buttons right off my shirt. But Dad said nothing special, as he never was one to easily hand out praise.

The next few weeks, when Harry's dad didn't need him to load mine-prop logs from the mountains, we had better fishing days playing in the water and catching trout in the big holes below the head gate. When fishing with Harry, we made sure to give a bunch to his family.

It was sad to think about how many fish perished every summer in the hundreds of ditches across our North Park. The Game and Fish Commission didn't have manpower enough to work the ditches to save them. At least we put them to good use as food for the family and the hay-crew. Sometimes, when Mom didn't want any more fish, we would catch the trout anyway, place them in a bucket of water, and dump them in the nearby river.

Hand-fishing had been a tradition on the Monroe family side. Early on, Mom told us how as a kid she, her dad, and her grandmother, Lindy, had caught trout in the head holes when they shut off their ditch water. When I first tried hand-fishing, I found it was easier said than done, as trout zipped away from my every grasp.

If the technique had been passed down three Monroe generations, why couldn't I learn it? I spent long spring days chasing fish up and down our ditch below the house. When I cornered a fish under a bank, I'd flop down on my belly, thrust my arms into the cold water, and try to grab it. I practiced first on suckers, since they usually exceeded trout in numbers. Round and slow-witted, they could be more easily caught by hand. Finally, I learned to catch suckers since their coarse scales and lack of zeal made them easy to grasp.

Trout are shaped like a football in cross section. They have fine scales, and are quite slippery. I spent hours failing, until I finally came up with the right technique. I learned that I had to approach trout more slowly and very gently. Just a soft touch here and there with my finger tips. They probably thought that it was just another fish bumping them. Any strong contact at first sent them zooming away. From touching, I had to estimate the size of the fish and to mentally calculate the location of its gills. I had to place my hand under the dark bank, around the gill area slowly and very gently. I found the right location just behind the gills, used a sudden iron tight squeeze, held on tightly as the fish struggled, and finally wrested it out of the water.

When I was only twelve, I caught a twenty-one inch German brown under a ditch bank behind the ranch house. At least six inches from belly to back, he was a hock-jawed male beauty. Although the folks were pleasingly impressed when I showed my catch, their visiting friends, the Chedseys and Snells, heaped on praise and embarrassed me. I felt like a king, however, when I was able to do something my older brothers and the town kids couldn't.

After I mastered trout, I taught Larry and Jimmy. I was so proud when they learned to be hand-fishers, and I was dismayed that Bob wouldn't let me teach him.

We didn't need all those hooks, line, leaders, sinkers, sticky worms, minnows, and fishing poles. It was all in our hands with the magic touch. In growing up, we never heard of other kids in our county who caught trout with bare hands.

As we grew up together, I craved to eat fish and live off the land, wild and free. With my little brothers, I wandered and feasted in the wild where our beautiful rock-bottomed streams meandered. Bordering willows cut off the view of our ranch buildings, parents, and civilization. Whatever took place down at the river's waters was a secret kid-world.

Although most ranch kids had one pristine river to talk about, I had two. There was magic in their waters. Rippling flows allowed a fresh start every moment, as the past moved out of sight and mind down stream among the dense willows, forever forgotten.

Richard range cattle on the Illinois River amid willows and wild iris clumps.

Harry Rosenfield usually went along with my riverin' ideas because we were friends. Larry and Jimmy often followed my plans, since I was older and had Harry along. I tried to be a good leader, as I wanted to keep everyone happy.

Once when out scouting like an Indian, Jimmy's sharp eyes spotted a white object deep under a willow on the river bottom rocks. We used long willow branches to probe and move a huge dead twenty-five inch rainbow trout. After we had worked it ashore, Larry suggested that we smoke and eat the giant since it was nearly as large as Grandpa and clearly the biggest trout we'd ever seen.

We cleaned it. It didn't seem to stink when we gave it the "sniff test." So we hung the big trout in the hot smoke to cook over our willow campfire. Later we cut it into sections and ate the white rainbow meat. We washed it down with tangy riverbank mint tea we'd boiled in an old Hills Brother's coffee can. It was tasteless and a bit raw--we didn't know what smoked trout was supposed to be like--but we couldn't lose face by not eating it.

"Good eating," we all said.

When Mom learned of our trout feast, she got mad as hops and made it clear we weren't to eat any more dead fish we found. "Lord knows what it died of," she snapped. "Don't you kids have a lick of sense? It could have killed you all!"

Our myriad of river adventures would not have happened had not Mom been the sole granddaughter of the Monroes. She was as strong as the spring river currents in keeping us sound and going onward.

Mother, a dynamic storyteller, was a lady of true grit. She had those strong traits that the pioneers possessed. I suppose she followed a tradition, since she was a descendent of the first settlers of wild North Park. With dark brown hair and fair complexion this mostly Norwegian woman with a bit of Scottish thrown in, didn't appear to be anywhere near her age.

That she could be the mother of five sons didn't seem possible. Only five feet four, she was still mighty in her determination. She also had an instinct of helpfulness about her. She had pride in her family and pride in being a Richard. Above all, she wanted to do things right. Edith Richard was dauntingly honest and extremely strong willed.

Mom, however, was not affectionate. I never recall her having hugged me. I was amazed when I saw other mothers hug sons my age. I often wondered why Mom never did.

However, raising her five sons and educating them and helping the family were her life. She wanted us to "amount to something." Raising us on a ranch where we often were out of sight was an adventure that tested even her keen eyes and strong fiber.

She had beautiful dark brown eyes that flashed when she told stories. She had the hands of a hardworking woman and seemed to be constantly busy cooking, cleaning, and washing clothes. Most of my conversations with her occurred on the move while she worked about the ranch house. It was a treat to talk when she sometimes sat down and churned cream to make butter or stopped to peel potatoes. Her nature was mild and her patience great. Because she'd seen alcohol do so much damage to other people's lives, she was against drinking liquor. She admired hard work. She loved flowers and animals, as well as her five boys.

Mother gave scanty details about her own mother, Evelyn Monroe, on the Rawlings side of her family. She talked mostly of her father, Jay Monroe, whom she greatly admired. I suspected that she wasn't too proud of her mother, although she did relate how Evelyn graduated with honors from the University of Denver in 1905. Good in music, she had taught school in North Park before she married our grandfather, Jay Monroe.

Mom's grandfather Rawlings had abandoned his family. Mrs. Rawlings, her grandmother, was an accomplished musician who supported the family of seven children by giving music lessons in Durango, Colorado. The woman, however, "couldn't boil water" as a cook. The care of all the children fell to Evelyn, the oldest daughter.

Mom said, "Taking care of all those younger brothers and sisters soured my mother on kids. Then I was born about nine months after she married my dad, and she never wanted me." That's about all we ever heard about the Rawlings side of the family. We never saw Evelyn, our grandmother.

My parents never saw a lot of what we kids did either. They tolerated our feasting in the wilds along the rivers since they couldn't supervise us all of the time. If they had tried to watch our every move, neither would have had time for much else.

Once, after Dad and Mom returned from a Denver banking trip, they told us about how good frog legs tasted. We quickly went down to our boy camp at The Point of Rocks where our two rivers met. There in a reed-lined slough we caught green and yellow spotted leopard frogs. We built a fire, dropped the frogs into an old dented frying pan, and boiled them. We ate their hind legs and their front legs and tried a few other unspeakable parts. They were tasteless. So, we concluded that North Park frog legs were too small and weren't worth the effort.

At our other river camps which we named McGillicutty and Lafayette, we'd snuggle in the dense trees, build fires, and place meat on green willow branches over the licking orange flames or glowing ruby coals. Eating ducks, sage grouse, and fish, we tore at their meat with sticks, with our bare hands, and with our teeth as cave people in the picture shows did. We even tried big red-sided suckers but found them full of tiny bones. Once we tried muskrat legs that tasted like tough beef.

Mostly, we ate canned goods from Mom's basement pantry or jam sandwich lunches from the ranch house. Hot dogs, when roasted over an open fire, were a real treat. As we were almost always in a hurry or on the move, we many times ate hotdogs raw and later suffered intense bellyaches but never understanding why.

We avoided mushrooms, since we knew that one mistake in identifying them could lead to our being plowed under. Wild onions were in good supply in the pastures, and we dug them with our hunting knives and devoured them on the spot. We huffed our stout onion-breaths in one another's faces. As part of our hunting and gathering diets, we loved picking and eating red late-summer gooseberries growing among willow clumps.

"You guys be careful not to step off in some hole and drown in that river," Dad warned. "It's real high this year." It was much like his saying, "Don't shoot your eye out with those BB guns." We gave as little heed to his warning as we did to Mom when she often stated, "I hate those darned rivers. Be careful. They're so dangerous."

We watched for whatever lurked in the blackness of those deep water holes, especially following the heavy spring runoff as it changed the river channels and deepened existing holes in the thirty-foot wide Michigan and Illinois.

Sometimes we employed weapons against the two rivers' treasure of fish. When we'd spot a fish in the river's current, we let our arrows go zipping into the water. If an arrow hit home, the shaft would dart back and forth. We joyously pulled the arrow with a fish on it out of the stream like South American Indians. Often, when fish came to rest against a bank in the river, we all fired in unison. Good synchronization would pin the fish to the stream bank below the water's surface and put fish covered with corn meal sputtering in lard in Mom's frying pan.

We made seines of old grain sacks and stitched them together. At each side, we attached upright sticks as handles. With one of us holding each stick, we'd move the seine through deep pools. The fish would be caught in front of the seine and swept forward as water passed through the fabric. We loved seining because we never knew what would be in the seine as we slowly pulled it through the water and up on shore. We scrambled wildly in glee to capture the fish before they flopped or rolled back into the water.

Most summers, around the 4th of July, we'd used firecrackers on our aquatic prey. We'd tie five-inchers and M-80s to a small piece of iron, light the fuses, and throw them into deep holes. When the explosion occurred, water would swell and splash high into the air, and the fish would come belly-up, stunned. There seemed to be an inexhaustible supply of fish in our ditches and rivers. In fact, there were more fish than we had money for firecrackers to stun them.

Often we flopped on our bellies and drank from the river water we fished. Sometimes we used cupped hands to take up the pure fluid. Fist-sized rocks just below the surface held a unique world on their algae-coated slick surfaces. Green, black, and brown six-legged insects, some in square cases, along with snail egg globs clung to the algae-covered green surfaces. We figured out that trout ate the insects, and we then ate the trout, all of us dependent on the clean snow-melt river water.

Occasionally, Bob got his fly rod and told Mom we were going fishing. Soon, Bob was back with a nice mess of fish to brag about, and I was soaking wet. Bob told of what fabulous luck he had had and how I'd fallen in the river.

We actually had gone down to the culvert that carried ditch water under the railroad tracks. Trout in the ditch spooked and swam into the thirty-foot culvert to hide. Bob had a big landing net. As the older brother, he'd order me through the steel culvert. I would proceed in the cold water with my nose pressed to the top of the twenty-eight inch culvert, in order to get some air. Lying on his belly at the other end, Bob held his net over the mouth of the culvert. As I forced the fish out of the culvert, Bob got them. I later sent Larry and Jimmy through the same culvert while I too netted good-sized trout.

Every long winter I planned fishing trips and dreamed of the big rainbow trout in the deep river holes and under the willowed grassy banks. Spring days found Larry, Jimmy, Harry and me heading again toward the river on expeditions. Smokey accompanied us at our heels. We carried our array of fishing stuff and bows and arrows. We played so hard that we often lost track of time.

When we were gone too long, Mom went to the cookhouse and rang the big dinner bell. Since none of us owned a watch, we observed the time as well as the weather from the North Park sky. When we heard that distant sharp bell clang across the Two-Bar's river bottoms, we knew it was time to scoot home, regardless of what we were doing.

Mom required me to be back from the rivers in time to eat at mealtimes. If I wasn't there at noon or six o'clock, I was in trouble, or I got the leftovers. Mom used to tell me, "Listen up. I don't run a short order cookhouse. Be on time for meals, or take what's left."

Wet to the hips from wading and wet to the shoulders from hand-fishing for gorgeous mountain trout, I often has to scurry for the house to eat. Dark clouds of mosquitoes usually trailed me as I slogged along feeling water slush in my soaked shoes.

Unbeknownst to me in my youth, adventuring in the waters along our rivers had a profound influence on my thinking and later life's work. A love of wild aquatic things was slowly growing within me, developing a curiosity and a true love of nature that would later become my career.

Chapter 7

PROTECTIN'

"You have to help with this outfit and protect this ranch…"

At the top of the flat ridge and before I could "park my carcass" as a hired man often said, I looked across the willowed valley of my kidhood, seeing an open bend in the Illinois River where something awful had once happened to our sheep, something we had not been able to protect against. Even our best rifles could not be everywhere to defend our livestock, and there were threats on many levels to every ranch, ranging from relatives, to legal and financial issues, to predators, to rifles, and even to our own foolishness. I finally sat down on the seat of a long abandoned dump rake without wheels, surveying the lush land we boys all had had to take care of despite our rash and sometimes thoughtless behavior.

As a kid I craved to get my hands on a .22 rifle to blast around the Two-Bar, to get a chance at those animals beyond the range of my trusty arrows. When would Dad say I was old enough to use a gun? Jay and Bob could use guns anytime they asked permission, but I still had to wait in silence. Sometimes I thought Dad considered me younger than I was because of my shrimp size.

Guns were in the ranch house but ammunition was scarce and expensive, and my folks weren't about to supply it for kids. Also, I didn't dare touch the big rifles that Dad used to protect our livestock. Yet I had longed for years to fire some rounds from the old lever-action 32-20 or from Dad's sleek scoped .257 Roberts to see how much the guns kicked. I wanted to blast large and dangerous animals to protect us and to bring home wild meat for the dinner table.

Before graduating to real guns, I used the BB gun. All one fall I had begged for a BB gun and finally got a Daisy at Christmas. Mom warned, "Don't shoot yourself in the eye." I assured her that my glasses would protect my eyes and that I would not be shooting at myself.

To test my marksmanship, I shot at everything that moved--from barn cats to my brothers. Chickens were my favorite targets around the buildings. The inexpensive copper BB's bounced off the feathers of running and clucking targets. In the corral, I sneakily shot the range bulls in the testicles. To my amazement, getting shot there didn't seem to bother them. But I knew that Dad would have blistered my hide if he had seen me in the act or had found out about my choice of targets.

Soon Harry and my little brothers had BB guns, too. We shattered every empty jar and bottle on the ranch in our shooting lust. Often we had BB gun fights. The rule was, "No shooting anyone above the waist." If everyone adhered to the rule, no one would get hurt, just stung a little, or so we thought.

A few weeks later in the tall dark willows where green herons nested east of the railroad bridge, we had a BB gun fight with the Wilson and Rosenfields which soon developed into a fierce battle. To our horror, during one of our charges, Jimmy accidentally shot Harry Rosenfield in the eye. The BB stuck right there in his eyeball.

Terrified, we rushed Harry up to the ranch house and Mom drove us to Doctor Morgan who removed the copper BB. Harry lost part of his sight. Dad paid the medical bills, but he never scolded any of us for he saw our remorse. It broke our hearts having our Harry no longer perfect. The lure of BB gun fights was never again the same.

However, I couldn't contain my lust for real guns. I had to start out by tagging along with an older brother who had a 22 rifle, and begging, "Can I shoot-- please, just once?" If he were generous, I'd maybe get to fire off a round or two. For the pleasure of shooting his rifle, I'd usually have to do one of his chores for him.

When I was finally old enough to use a gun by myself, I saved my money to buy ammunition. I bought 22 shorts, longs, and on rare occasions expensive long-rifle shells. Although I dreamed my folks would one day buy me my own 22 rifle with a seven-shot clip, they never did. Dad wanted me to use Mom's old heavy target rifle that she had won in a turkey shoot way back in the 1920s. This old gun was highly inaccurate and had the barrel shot out. There was also a single-shot 22 rifle in the house. Dad said that it saved shells and would make me a better shot. Dad preached, "One shot, meat. Two shots maybe meat. Many shots, no meat."

One winter at an indoor target range in Walden, Dad worked to teach his sons the fine art of shooting. Although I tried my best, I was never more than an average marksman. Dad, however, was wonderful. I'd watch him shoot six shots into the bull's eye from a rest with his .257 Roberts. When we reached the target, we could touch all six holes with a quarter.

Dad set up an axe blade in front of two-gallon cans of water, one can on each side and a foot behind the blade. He, John Riggen, and Doc Morgan would, in a prone shooting position, try to split bullets on the blade and shatter the cans into two twisted masses. Seeing such wonderful shooting, I was green with envy. But Dad said, "I'm only average compared to Jay Monroe, your grandfather. He used to drive nails with his 22 high-power."

Since our ranch was adjacent to town, local dogs plagued us. In packs they would chase our cattle, our sheep, our calves, our chickens, and run horses and bulls. Dad put a warning notice in the *Jackson County Star*: "Any dog trespassing on The Richard Ranch will be shot." Dad told people, "If you want your dog, keep it at home."

When I was in the seventh grade, we boys owned a band of sheep that our folks, who thought that we should have an early start in the livestock business, had purchased. My share of the price came from my haying wages and trapping money. I was miffed at having to pay because some of my brothers never paid their shares. But they still claimed the sheep as theirs and got money from the sale of male lambs each fall. I told Mom how their share of the sale money should go to pay what they owed. Mom said the matter was between Dad and her, that it was none of my business, and that I should be above spitefulness.

Edith Richard, 1926, who was determined, ethical, and always willing to listen. Illustration by David Hartman

Growing Up Wild

We kept our flock in the corrals and pastured them on the Illinois River west of the ranch buildings. Because the pasture was downhill behind our high-board fenced corrals and out of easy eyesight, we could not watch them closely, but the flock did well the first couple of years, increasing in numbers and profits.

One spring morning, when our little lambs were old enough to travel, I helped turn them out of the corrals and into the large Illinois pasture. The black-and-white lambs played and frolicked about their mothers. Running in bunches and sometimes in a long line, lambs would do the stiff-legged bounce. Ewes paid little attention for they were only interested in the new green pasture grass. White sheep with black faces playing and grazing on a verdant pasture beside a blue stream in front of a mountain backdrop was a strikingly beautiful scene.

Late that afternoon I walked with my brothers to drive the band of ewes and lambs back to the corral for the night. In the bend of the Illinois River, we found thirty-five of our little lambs slashed and ripped apart. Tracks in the mud along the bank told how dogs had run the lambs back and forth, killing them. Several ewes had their ears, eyes, and legs badly torn by dogteeth. They had to be destroyed. One ewe dragged her guts along behind her. I helped hold her down and my brother, Jay, cut her throat to put her out of her misery. My having to do that nearly made me throw up.

Those dogs had killed just to be killing. They didn't eat any of the lambs they had slaughtered. Though I never saw the dogs, evidence of their savagery left marks deep in my heart that I've carried all my life, knowing how pets can become savage in a pack.

Dad said, "Town people will never see this kind of killing or believe their pets capable of it. They'd blame it on coyotes. But the tracks in the mud are dog. I know the difference."

To better protect our sheep, we built a five-acre woven-wire, supposedly dog-tight pasture fence to keep them safely inside at night. During the day, we continued to let them out to graze, and we put them back in each evening. Since we had only a couple of hundred in the flock, we didn't hire a herder to look after them—too expensive.

Early one morning, the telephone rang. In a booming voice, Stanley Bulis reported that he had just shot at a pack of dogs on his place. He offered to help catch them in crossfire, as they were heading toward our sheep pasture.

Dad sent me running to get his extra rifle on the saddle in the barn and the hired man. Dad, the hired man, Bob, and I spread out and took positions at holes in the high board fence on the hill that overlooked the sheep pasture. Larry and Jimmy were slightly north and west on the ridge near the railroad cut. To the south a pack of ten dogs was moving along the far side of the Illinois River. In the far distance, Stanley's pickup was slowly approaching on the southwest to cut off the dogs' escape.

Boldly, the dogs approached our south line fence at the riverbed. Having dug and squeezed their way under the woven wire, they steadily moved toward the sheep, which were bunched against the gray board windbreak in our sheep pasture. Frightened and trembling, two hundred sheep watched the canine attackers as they approached. The few old rams stood at the exposed perimeter of the sheep flock and waited. Although the bucks and ewes with lambs stomped their front feet on the ground at the approaching pack of dogs, without horns they were no match for their opposition.

The pack stalked the sheep like a bunch of wolves. Just at the moment when the sheep appeared to have no chance at all, an ear-splitting blast rang out in the early morning stillness. Seeing that the long-haired brown dog was down, Dad cranked another shell into his .257 Roberts. Now we could all fire.

The pack halted for a split second, then ran south and north. The dogs were too late to escape southwest, for Stanley was shooting and blocking the escape route across the Illinois River. After Dad's first shot, the booming and crackling of rifles became intense. A red dog died instantly before it hit the ground. Another dog dragged itself along. A third, severely wounded in a front leg and bleeding from its shattered shoulder, was slowly limping away from the rifle fire. Additional shots ended their misery. Other dogs, unscathed, ran south in their confusion. I was firing so fast that I wasn't sure I'd hit a thing.

Two of the ten dogs escaped. After I had seen one dog crossing the railroad tracks to the south, Jimmy and I followed it and found the dog unaware. I shot it through the head as it faced us on the icy duck pond. Around the prone dog's head, there grew a great pool of crimson red. Since I had never before killed a dog, someone's pet, it made me feel sick in the pit of my stomach. Then I remembered our dead lambs. Knowing that I had probably killed one of the killers made me feel a little better.

To see the carnage of dead dogs was awful, and to see the dozen sheep ripped up at Stanley's place was equally pitiful. Had Stanley not warned us when he did, we would probably have lost large numbers of our sheep. Better to have killed the dogs than to have lost more of our valuable sheep to them.

Our successful ambush was a rare occurrence, for dog packs usually escaped and left the sheep owners with a large number of dead and injured and a loss of income. And Mom would have more bum lambs to feed.

A month later two Huskies were in our sheep one morning, and Dad chased them to town, and into Vern's place. Dad knocked.

"Good morning, Willard. Come in," said a smiling Vern, swinging his kitchen door wide. Vern was a sandy-haired big man who welded, repaired, and built equipment for us and other ranchers. He was rough and tough.

"Vern, I'm afraid your two dogs have been in our sheep this morning."

"Willard, that just can't be! I just let them out of here about half an hour ago."

"I followed them back here just now!"

"Let's have a look," snapped Vern, who headed for the back porch and called his two Husky dogs.

In silence, Dad watched Vern discover blood on the faces and noses of both dogs. Sheep wool was stuck in their teeth. The big friendly dogs wagged their tails as Vern inspected them.

"Go on in and have Jane give you a cup of coffee, Willard. I have to take care of these dogs."

Inside their house, while he was visiting with Jane over coffee, Dad was surprised to hear two shots behind the house. Startled, Jane said, "Oh, no, he really loved those dogs, Willard."

Soon Vern entered the house. Tears welled up in the huge man's eyes as he sat down at the table. Jane placed a cup of coffee in front of him.

"They won't be killing anybody's sheep from now on, Willard. I won't have dogs doing that."

To protect our livestock, I was quick to shoot at dogs. I had no problem blasting as they raced along at a distance. However, when one wagging its tail came close and walked toward me, I would chicken out and lower my rifle.

We weren't alone in dog warfare, fighting the packs of poor animals simply dumped by people when they left town involved our neighbors, too. All the ranchers around the Walden city limits were plagued with stray dog problems each fall.

One fall Dad spotted a pack of dogs crossing our place and sent Jay to intercept them. I tagged along. Jay hunkered down in the wooden head gate on the ridge and got a resting bead on the lead dog with his 32-20. He had already killed four before the pack of a dozen stopped milling around and decided to run off. He downed five others on the dead run. "Nine dogs with only eleven shots! Almost Jay Monroe shooting," Dad said with pride in his oldest son.

During summers, we trucked our sheep to the Norris Place where we didn't have to deal with stray dogs. Coyotes, however, were the menace there at the mountain's edge. Most years they took only a few lambs, but one summer they killed over fifty lambs. Dad had had it. Confronted with the loss of so many sheep both at home and at the Norris Place, Mom and Dad decided to sell the remaining sheep rather than help us continue trying to build a herd. We just couldn't protect them.

The proceeds from the sheep were divided equally among the five of us. Once again, I felt cheated because some of my brothers still had not paid their shares when we bought the sheep. Although I let Mom and Dad know what I thought to be fair, they didn't increase my share. But the worst part of it all was to not have our beautiful ewes and cute lambs on the ranch. I had dearly loved them.

Dad, in a sort of compensation, soon purchased five Black Angus cows, one cow for each of us to help get a cattle herd started. For me, the cows didn't replace the sheep since I liked sheep better and rarely saw my one black cow in Dad's big herd of five hundred red and white ones.

When dogs were chasing our bulls one day, Mom assumed the role of protector, too. She recognized one dog and called the owner about her dog's behavior. When the woman told her to "prove" it was her dog, Mom said, "Next time, I'll just have the men shoot the damn thing and call you to come get the carcass." Then she slammed down the phone. The dog was not on our place again.

I also remember how angry Mom became when Dad wanted to rent our La Rand heifer pasture to the neighbor. "I won't let him rent it, even if he was the last man on this earth, considering what he did to my Dad," she raged, with hate flashing in her eyes. Dad had hit a nerve and dropped the idea as Mom continued to protect us from the evils of the past.

It wasn't smart to get Edith Richard fired up and angry. For months, electricity had been live to a power pole on the ranch, but the Rural Electric Association manager up town had not kept his promise to make the necessary connection for power to the Two-Bar. After having called the REA many times and waiting four months, Mom went to the hardware store in Walden and purchased light bulbs for her newly wired house. Then she burst into the REA manager's office, cornered him, and said, "Are you going to get electricity hooked up at the ranch for my family or do I break every one of these bulbs over your head?" We had power hooked up the next day, and Mom sent him a thank you note.

Mom came from a long line of protectors and once told me that she would have died as a child if it hadn't been for her grandmother, Lindy, who had made arrangements with Mrs. Thobro, a friend, to look after her when she was a baby. Mom and her mother, Evelyn were living in Laramie. Mom's dad, who was sick and wasting away, was in Arkansas for most of that first year. Mrs. Throbro came daily to check on the Baby Edith and finding her blue, cold, unfed, and dirty, would whisk her home across the street and get her warmed, cleaned, and fed. Evelyn, who didn't want her baby anyway, didn't care who had her. That first year, Mrs. Thobro and her daughter, Louise, kept a close eye on Mom until Jay Monroe, the father, returned. His presence in the home assured Mom's physical survival.

I always had Mom's support except when I did something wrong. Then in private she would express her disappointment in my behavior by saying, "I expect more of you than you're showing, Paul Willard Richard."

After having leased the Two-Bar for a few years, we were hoping to buy the ranch ourselves. A threat to lose our place came unexpectedly when, Lindy Monroe, now in her eighties and living in California, decided to make a new will. Though she was no longer mentally competent to handle her own business affairs, she made provisions in this new will for her only living son, Brush Monroe, to get the ranch and for Mom, her only grandchild, to inherit three houses in Long Beach, California. We felt totally naked, unprotected, and confused by the change.

Our days on the Two-Bar seemed to be numbered, for surely we would have to move from there shortly after Lindy's eventual death. Worried sick, I prayed at night under my heavy blankets for God to help us keep the home place.

Mom's Uncle Brush, who the family said was as crooked-as-a-dog's-hind-leg, had pressured elderly Lindy into changing her will so that he could get the ranch. Suddenly, however, Brush had to flee to Canada for using an illegal device he had copied from Eastman Corporation to direct bits in oil well drilling. He remained in Canada, well beyond the reach of the U.S. laws using his "Monroe Directional" in Canadian oil fields.

With Brush out of the picture, Lindy, whose mental competence came and went, summoned Mom to California to meet with a judge. Judge Malby had grown up across the street from Lindy, had eaten her cookies, and had been her lawyer for years before his judgeship. When he found out from Lindy's housekeeper that Brush was taking Lindy's money, Malby had the Bank of America appointed as her guardian. This infuriated Brush who was in Canada and couldn't do anything about the court order.

During a hearing, Lindy sincerely wanted Edith to have the ranch. Lindy said to Judge Malby, "Edith should have the Two-Bar since it's the place to raise five boys. Brush has never been a rancher and will just sell the Two-Bar. Besides, he has no family." As a result of Lindy's statements, a judge issued a court order to change the will again. Since Mom was to inherit the ranch, I stopped worrying for a couple of years.

When Lindy actually passed away, Brush had returned from exile in Canada, and spitefully had buried Lindy before Mom and Dad arrived in Long Beach for the funeral. Later he exploded when he saw the will and learned that Mom was to get the Two-Bar. Because of the changes in the will that gave him only three houses, Brush actually brought a lawsuit against the folks.

My parents feared the value of the ranch would be taken by court costs and lawyer fees in an upcoming legal fight. However, Judge Malby assured them that his court order would stand up.

Then, of all things, Judge Malby died. Still worried about the cost of a legal battle, Dad and Mom settled, paying Brush $16,000 in cash to balance the value of ranch against the houses. Finally the ranch was ours, but Dad had a mortgage on it from paying off Brush and from legal expenses. I rested much easier when I knew that our name was on the ranch deed. Once again Lindy Monroe, even after death, had protected Mom and her great-grandsons by keeping us on the ranch. I again settled down with my brothers, enjoying the ranch, trying to find something to protect us from that was intruding on our empire-the Richard ranch.

Looking back on all that today, I marvel how way out in California a former neighbor kid, and then a judge, could get wind of an old ladies affairs, step in to make things right and assure our life continued on the Two-Bar. What a wonderful happenstance protecting us and my childhood.

Growing Up Wild

Map of North Park ranches worked by the Monroes and Richards. Illustration by David Hartman

Across the Two-Bar, three times a week, that smoke-belching train invaded our place. It roared across our ranch spewing smoke, cinders, and sounding its whistle as it pleased, making it a logical boy target. I'd place pennies on the track and marvel at their flatness after the iron beast's wheels had rolled over them. Often I planned to put objects on the tracks to derail the train. When I realized that because of our record of attacks on the iron horse, I'd be the first suspected, my nerve failed. South of Walden someone did place spikes on the rails and upset a putt-putt car. A worker who was injured, later died. I was afraid someone would blame me for the wreck, but no one did since I'd never raided the train off the Two-Bar.

Once, after I had helped a section worker push his putt-putt car back onto the steel tracks, he rewarded me with a ride to the second bridge. I thrilled as I sat high above the rails and sped along across the Two-Bar. Yet, I still needed to adventure against the enemy train to test my skill.

One summer, a huge crew of dark-skinned workers replaced the rails and installed larger ones across our place. I watched the gandy-dancers, as Dad called them, and noticed that nearly all of them were Indians with red and blue checkered bandannas around their heads. I was thrilled to see fifty "real live" Indians for the first time. They told me they were doing an Indian dance that night on Main Street. I begged Mom to let me go see the performance. With her permission, I went. The drums and round dances aroused my spirit, leaving me breathless. To see real Indians at last was a thrill, but seeing them as workers on our enemy's tracks was hard to stomach.

Using today's perspective, our attacks on the railroad train were not in the least bit logical, but at that time boy-thinking prevailed as we thought we were defending against something foreign on our soil. To us boys, it was exciting raiding the iron horse.

Over time, we protected our place in many ways, and guns were not always our weapons nor our friends as events unfolded on the ranch beside our small town.

For example, beyond the railroad tracks, Post's sheep continued being interloping enemies, eating our pasture grass. Dad was often trying to get the neighbor to repair her fence to keep them off of us. In retaliation, Bob roped them from his young saddle horse for practice but stopped his roping after he broke one sheep's neck. He never told Dad.

I got into the act each fall, protecting against sage grouse hunters who crossed our fences and shot near the cattle. Dad, who objected strongly to the hunters, had me run them off and anyone else shooting on the Two-Bar. I could use a gun while defending our borders, hunting, target practicing, and "plinking around," since I was family, but Dad didn't want outsiders shooting on our property.

Once when Larry was small, he took our .410 shotgun and pointed it at the light fixture on the kitchen ceiling. Bob came in and told him, "You're too young to be fooling around with the shotgun." Bob grabbed it and slammed it down in the corner where it belonged. Instantly, it discharged and blew a hole in the kitchen ceiling, sending Mom into scolding all of us over gun safety. Over the years, three other guns went off in our house. Once when I was unloading my rifle, it went off accidentally and hit Mom's kitchen sink.

We were fortunate when the guns had fired accidentally inside, but not so lucky outside. Bob got shot in the leg and Jimmy in the arm, neither wound fatal, but lots of blood, doctors, and drama were involved.

One summer, I got into the act by running around with the hired man's son, John, also a gun nut. Since Bob had gotten shot, Mom wouldn't let guns out of the house as easily. So when I asked to use our .22 rifle, she refused. Later that day, when she went to town, John and I sneaked the gun outside. We thought she wouldn't notice. We figured we could sneak it back in later.

John and I were both shooting down on the Post Place and blasting everything that moved. Suddenly I spotted a pair of buteo hawks, circling high overhead. Because we thought that to watch one of them fall would be great, we blasted away. John emptied his rifle and had to reload. I was still blasting when John slammed his bolt shut. His .22 rifle accidentally went off. When I turned and looked at him, his eyes were big as dollars.

"What's wrong with you?"

"You damn fool. I just shot you," he stammered in a soft tone.

Sure enough, there was a hole in my shoe. Although I could feel wetness, there was no pain. I removed the shoe, pouring out the blood, ripped up my handkerchief, and wrapped it around my foot. The hole was clean through, just at the base of my second toe. And, since there was no pain, I decided to head home, return the rifle, put a better bandage over the wound, and never tell. Being shot didn't seem a big deal since the guys in the picture shows I saw up town recovered almost instantly.

Halfway home, however, my foot started throbbing like mad. When I got to the house, I had to tell Mom what had happened. She rushed me to Dr. Morgan who ran a long needle with cleaning gauze through the bullet hole several times. The procedure hurt so badly I cried. He told me that I'd have a stiff hammer toe, whatever that was, the rest of my life.

To protect him, I never told my parents that John had shot me. The story was that I had had the muzzle of the gun on my foot and was bouncing it up and down when the gun went off. John didn't want to get in trouble for shooting me. He had a mean father who would have beaten him terribly with his razor strap. After such accidents happened, Mom and Dad took the guns away, gave lectures on the safe handling of guns, and issued just punishments.

One day a bunch of high school boys from town headed out to hunt at the duck ponds behind our red barn. Although those big ponds were not actually on our place, I considered them and the birds there to be ours. All spring and summer, I had watched the ducks hatch their young and raise them in the cattail-lined ponds. I didn't want anyone to bother or to hurt them. Besides it was not duck season.

I yelled from behind the barn atop the hill, "Get the hell off and stop huntin'." They ignored me and started shooting. Aaron Dove, our hired man's younger brother, and I ran into the big red barn.

Inside, Aaron said, "Hear the buckshot hitting the barn. They're shooting at us. It's a shoot-out." He ran to a saddle in the tack room, took his brother's .22 rifle out of the leather scabbard, and opened a small window on the side of the barn facing the duck ponds.

Below him down the hill were four guys who were standing near the railroad tracks shooting into the cattails at my beloved waterfowl. With the lever action 22 rifle, Aaron opened up towards them. The first few shots into the railroad gravel sent them running. Two guys jumped the barbed wire fence and ran west for the Illinois River. Long legs flew.

The other two hid behind the railroad tracks. Aaron kept them there. If they looked over the rails, Aaron would shoot a few feet from their heads, to keep them down. After about twenty shots, Aaron grew tired of shooting, put the gun away, and we left the barn. Those older guys stayed hidden behind the railroad tracks until dark, when they decided they could safely sneak home.

Although I hadn't done the actual shooting, I had been the one to yell the warning. The next day I had to face those upper classmen in school. It was very unfriendly. Bob stuck up for me and prevented my getting beaten up. Nobody, especially my parents and the duck hunters' parents, was pleased with the incident. Dad banned Aaron Dove from the ranch, and he chewed me out for my being involved. The only good outcome was that the ducks, which I treasured, were protected and kept safe that day.

Once earlier, Harry and I were hiding in the feed rack and shooting around the corrals with our BB guns. We had been plinking at the bulls and milk cows, when Jay came out to saddle Blackie, our quarter mare, for Dad. Harry and I watched Jay as he was about to catch the mare in the six inches of mucky manure. We decided to hit Blackie just at that moment to see them both jump. Jay had one rein around Blackie's neck, when our BB's hit the mare's rump. Unexpectedly she whirled and with both hind feet kicked Jay in the chest, flopping him into the mud and manure. We watched Jay slowly get up, hobble to the feed rack, and lie down. His back was dirty brown and covered with manure. We stayed hidden, terrified.

Then Dad walked by and saw Jay in the feed rack. He said, "Send you out to do a little chore for me and you end up sleepin' in the feed rack." Disgustedly Dad walked on, caught the mare himself, and left to do his riding. Jay hurt so much that he couldn't answer Dad. We then helped Jay to the house, and Mom took him to Doc Morgan who wrapped Jay's broken ribs. Later that afternoon when Dad came home from riding, he saw Jay on the couch and said, "What are you doing there? Don't you do anything but sleep?"

Dad felt foolish after he learned what had happened to Jay. No one ever knew the total story because Harry and I didn't breathe a word. We had stupidly protected ourselves, nothing to be very proud about. Everyone supposed that the young mare, feeling frisky, had whirled and kicked, accidentally hitting Jay. We sadly kept silent to protect each other.

Sometimes people got hurt when using other kinds of weapons. Jimmy threw a hunting knife and hit Warren Rosenfield in the foot. Tony Zangari stuck a throwing tomahawk into my foot. With an arrow, Jimmy shot a hired man's daughter in the hand. These wounds all hurt, bled, and left scars as did those from the rocks and the sticks we flung at each other. Usually, our hurts resulted from accidental hits when we were aiming to come close, not actually trying to hit the target, so we said in self-protection.

Since I enjoyed perfecting my shooting, I was always searching for something to hit. I blasted at fish in shallow water in ditches, gophers in the pastures, and insulators on telegraph lines along the railroad tracks. To hit an insulator was great sport. The green glass flew in all directions and a humming song went down the line. If Dad saw me do it, I was in big trouble. He contended that the railroad would have me arrested. Careful not to be seen, I listened for the train and section crew before I fired. Birds' nests, window glass, chimneys, dead animals, and even perched birds came into my .22 rifle sights. I wasted ammunition at hawks on the wing, but I didn't shoot toward town or our cattle.

"Guns and boys don't mix--they worry me to death," Mom used to say. Yet she put up with our having guns.

As if our having guns didn't worry Mom enough, certainly our ancient fascination with fire did. Mom's parents' ranch home on the Paulk place had burned to the ground, smoldering for days, when she was a small child. Never having forgotten that troubling event, Mom had a phobia about our house going up in flames and was alert about fire protection. One year the Allard ranch house five miles to the north of us burned, consuming everything our neighbors had, including every photograph. It upset Mom terribly, something we rarely saw in her.

Later, one fall I watched our big hay pile burn slowly, resulting in the loss of fifty tons of prime hay which had been trucked in from the Norris place. Dad never knew who was responsible. He ordered that there be no more playing in tunnels in the hay piles. Yet, later each spring when he removed the stored bales, he saw secret chambers and tunnels galore built by his wayward sons, who may have ignited the flames when the pile once burned, scaring the wits out of Mom and the rest of us. For in those days when something caught fire, it usually burned to the ground before the local fire department arrived at any ranch.

One wet morning following a hard night's rain that halted haying, a stray dog appeared at the ranch. I immediately wanted to help this dog, a beautiful Collie. Wet and trembling, it stood outside the bunkhouse and watched the men leave to fence haystacks.

Before they departed, Dad told me, "Chase that dog off. We don't need stray dogs."

The poor thing was shivering and seemed so alone and helpless. Up the bunkhouse stairs I took it, wanting to warm the Collie by the pot-bellied stove. Seeing that the stove fire was out, I found some dry wood. Since I couldn't get the wood to catch fire, I got a can of gasoline from Dad's tank outside. After I had poured about half of the gasoline into the stove, and before I could strike a match, the gas suddenly ignited and flashed at me from hot coals. Blowing the lids clear off the old stove, I jumped back and flung the half-empty blazing can across the bunkhouse. The can landed on a bed. Using a blanket, I smothered the bed flames. By this time the stove was blazing, but my cold dog had high-tailed-it. During an unsuccessful search for the dog, I forgot about the bunkhouse and wandered down to the river, knowing haying was cancelled.

When I glanced back at the ranch buildings, I saw a huge column of smoke rising above the bunkhouse. Afraid to go back, I wandered further down the river into the dense willows. After awhile I saw that there was no more smoke. I waited until dusk and then slowly walked back, ashamed of myself. Although I decided to go home, to own up, and to face the music, I knew I'd get a licking from Dad.

When I faced him that evening in the shop, he was stern and told me of his great disappointment in me. He told me several ways he expected better behavior in the future. He stressed, "You have to help with this outfit and protect this ranch and family, not do things that hurt us."

That long talking-to hurt far more than a hundred lickings ever could. When he did finally punish me with a small short stick, I hardly felt the strokes at all—it was sort of symbolic. I had gotten the message to do as I was told and help better in protecting our ranch and livelihood. Never again after that evening did my father spank me. I had come of age at thirteen.

Chapter 8

ROAMIN'

"That dog loves you as only a dog can."

Looking around me as I sat there on the old 1950's rusted rake seat, I couldn't help recalling how wild and free I had been, being allowed to venture out as much as I pleased in these river valleys before me. My mind fondly keyed back in time to my roaming kid days.

I looked at my ranch realm's offerings. Vertical rocky bluffs, cattail-lined marshes, sage-dotted hills, sloughed pastures, densely tangled willows, winding crystal streams, and damp wide meadows provided variety. Our nearby town of Walden with all its kids beyond our huge ranch buildings was a boon, too, giving nearby opportunity.

At the ranch house, we Richard brothers sometimes slept outside. The wrap-around ranch house porch was open to the east and had a roof held up by stately white Greek-shaped wooden pillars. Out there, we could hear Two-Bar animal sounds and giggle and talk far into the cool summer nights. We were on the opposite end of the house from Mom and Dad's bedroom.

Late one cool spring night I heard Smokey barking far down the ridge and, judging from his barks, I knew the big blue dog was in close contact with something nasty. We brothers dressed, grabbed a few weapons, and rushed toward Smokey along the ridge on the two-tracked dirt road in the semi-darkness of the moonlit night.

Although badgers were mostly on our minds as we investigated Smokey's barks, our imaginations were rich with visions of bear, mountain lions, or lurking criminals. Somehow, I wanted to be attacked to actually see how it would be. But, alas, no attacks took place, and Smokey came running when we reached the far end of the ridge near the swimming hole.

Mom later told us that she had walked through the house and peered onto the expansive front porch. Blankets were scattered at random in the bright moonlight, but no boys were present.

She rushed into the bedroom, "Willard, Willard, they're gone."

"What did you say?"

"The kids aren't on the porch. They're all gone."

"Well, maybe they came back to bed in the house."

"No, I looked. Let's get dressed and find 'em."

Dad groaned as he dangled his legs over the edge of the bed and coughed that cigarette cough of his, but this time he didn't spend ten minutes sitting on the edge of the bed doing so. Quickly he put on his shirt and shoes, while peering out the window into the moonlit night. At two in the morning, it was nearly as light as day outside.

"I wonder where they can be this time of night,"

Dad said, "You check the other house, bunkhouse, and shop. I'll do the barns, corrals, and meet you here in a few minutes."

No one was found in the quick search of the ranch buildings. "Maybe they went to town or something," said Mom, increasing concern showing in her voice.

"Let's get in the pickup and go there, then." The quick trip up the deserted streets of the small sleeping town yielded no clues.

As the pickup pulled up in front of the house, Dad said, "They must be on the ranch someplace."

"No, I think they have been kidnapped," replied Mom, in a frantic voice.

Dad paused a moment, then said, "Who'd want 'em?"

Mom burst into tears and Dad quickly placed his arm around her shoulders.

"I'm sorry. Let's drive down to the meadow and look."

"Listen."

They could hear the distant barks of Smokey.

Pickup lights came down the ridge as we returned up the shadowed road. We stood in the approaching headlights and the pickup halted. Seeing it was the folks, we tossed our rocks aside.

"Why didn't you tell us where you were going?" demanded Mom out the pickup window.

"We just didn't want to wake you up," said Bob, who was the oldest of our group. He held a hatchet in one hand. He continued, "We just knew Smokey had a badger or something.' It was just a bunch of skunks, and Smokey really stinks, Mom."

"You kids scared the wits out of us. We have been looking all over for you. You know better than to go off like this in the middle of the night."

"Why didn't you just ring the dinner bell, Mom?" asked Larry.

Mom fell quiet and Dad said, "Get in back and let's get to the house. Keep that dang dog out of the pickup! He can just walk home the way he smells."

Smokey was free and wild in his own way just as we boys were. He was probably the happiest dog ever to live. His life was centered around five active ranch boys and he had all the room any dog could want, 2,029 acres.

He had a big black spot on his rump, and his face was a mixture of black, white, and blue. He was a handsome dog with a long thick coat, a short bobbed tail, and big brown eyes. His color was typical of many dogs of his breed, except his eyes were both the same color. Many Australian Shepherds have one brown and one blue eye. Smokey was a striking dog. He was tall and weighed nearly fifty pounds when fully grown. He seemed to radiate dominance. Yet he was not condescending or obnoxious as if he was top quality and knew it.

If we were too rough with him, Smokey would just move away and avoid us all for a while. A few times he even left us and went to the house, teaching us a lesson.

He developed into a very efficient watchdog as he defended the borders of the Two-Bar. Off the ranch he was friendly and played with other dogs. Yet when they reached our gate and came onto Richard property, Smokey would turn on them, and run them off. He knew what was his and was willing to fight rather than share it.

But, Smokey was a lost soul when we boys were in school. He would walk out of the yard towards town and wait under the big square Two-Bar gate until he saw us coming. He would then race up the road, zip around us in a circle, jump, and bark.

Fear was a stranger as he fought badgers, attacked packs of trespassing dogs, and took on what we boys set him after. Badgers were Smokey's deadliest adversaries. In one of his first badger encounters, he was bitten through the top of his nose between its tip and his eyes. This small hole in his nose bone never healed closed, remaining all his life. His hatred of badgers, and his attacks against them never subsided either.

We once built a small, two-wheeled cart and harnessed Smokey to it. All was going well until we headed down the rocky ridge road toward the railroad track, and he spotted a huge badger. In a flash, Smokey raced up the hill after the carnivore. In the chase and fight our cart was upside down and left behind. We rushed to Smokey's aid with rocks and sticks. The vicious badger hissed and charged us with flashing teeth and long sharp claws, ignoring our rocks.

Bob yelled, "Get on the fence!" We bounded up on the buck-and-pole fence while Smokey battled below. We yelled encouragement but were afraid to get on the ground.

Smokey's tactics against the stoutly built animal were maneuver, chase, and be chased. At the opportune moment, Smokey would lunge at the badger and grasp it behind the head by the loose skin. The badger was helpless in this position and could neither bite nor claw well. Smokey shook the animal furiously then dropped it and retreated. Again and again he performed the same maneuvers, until at last the badger ran and escaped into a burrow. Around the supper table that night we told and retold of Smokey's bravery when the badger had us all trapped up on the buck fence.

Smokey was injured several times during his night roaming excursions, without the incidents being witnessed. His nose and face bore scars from such battles. Had it been a badger, bobcat, bear, mountain lion, or another dog? Those secrets would always belong to Smokey for he seemed to own the nights on the ranch while we slept in the stately log house.

During Smokey's third summer with the family when I was in the sixth grade, he started courting the female dogs in town. He would be gone all night, coming home to sleep during the following day. By night, he was ready to begin carousing again.

One day at noon, Smokey came dragging down the road to the Two-Bar. Dad watched him come in the yard. We were all having dinner at the kitchen table with the hired man.

"Jim, will you help me cut that dog?" asked Dad. "He just won't stay home."

"Sure," replied Jim, our tall hired man.

After dinner, Dad slid his chair back from the table, took out his pocketknife, sharpened it, and poured a little iodine over the blade. Soon he headed for the door. As the screened door slammed shut, he, Jim Parker, and several of us boys followed. We caught Smokey in the yard.

Larry, Jimmy, and I watched the castration. The smallest boys didn't understand. Dad hadn't explained what was going on. Ranchers didn't talk details of such cuttings.

After having cut Smokey, Dad said to Jim Parker, "Let's go cut those two pigs while we're at this."

Two young male hogs were being fattened for butchering later in the summer. The entire bunch of us followed to the hog pen and watched the hogs get cut, too. Dad knew this would eliminate fighting between the two and would produce better meat for the haying crew.

Larry's reaction to this hog cutting business was immediate. He ran from the pigpen and went bursting into the house bawling to Mom.

"Now stop that crying and tell me what's the matter."

"Mom, I don't see why Daddy had to cut those pigs, too. They don't ever go to town."

Later on that summer, Smokey was following the car to nearby Walden. Dad had driven through the ranch gate with Smokey in hot pursuit. Larry saw Smokey following, rolled down the window, and yelled at the top of his lungs, "Smokey, you had better go home, or Daddy will cut you again."

Everyone in the family claimed Smokey as their very own dog. Even Mom called him, "My dog." We all claimed him but he treated us as equals. He was a free roamer and none of us could lay a genuine claim on him.

Thousands of small rodents were living in holes along the ridges and roads of the ranch, and Smokey spent hours digging for them. He would be soiled chocolate brown after his digging episodes.

Smokey was more of a water dog than anything else. He'd stick his nose under the water, blow bubbles, and fish alongside

Growing Up Wild

us. Often he captured small water birds and brought them tenderly in his mouth, never hurting them.

Smokey stuck with me and never asked for more than a pat on his blue head. He showed me that he loved me more than he loved himself. He was my alert companion, protector, and friend. As a little ranch kid, I could always count on him as we freely roamed our domain.

Along our rivers, three sharp dog barks in a row repeated three times was my secret boy call. Bob's was an echoing Tarzan call when he was out of sight. Larry's was a long howling wolf cry. We used our specific cries to call each other from a distance. Jimmy, Larry, and Harry were easy to identify from the wild calls we used back and forth. None of us wanted to be yelling names across the ranch. Wild roamers never did such things! Bob made my call best, and I always knew when he was searching for me in the dense willows.

I practiced imitating animal voices. I mooed at cattle, bleated at sheep, neighed at horses, barked at dogs, crowed at roosters, clucked at hens, whistled at gophers, cawed at crows, quacked at ducks, cried at hawks, and uttered the primitive "booock" at great blue herons. I had lots of practice hearing the animals, calling them repeatedly, and many times they'd answer me. I enjoyed keeping a town rooster crowing back to me much of the way to school and delighted setting off a wave of dog howls across Walden when I howled my hurt dog call.

One early morning Smokey and I were searching for gophers along the ditch adjacent to Walden when I gave several dog barks toward the slumbering neighborhood. Immediately, a dog answered my barks. During the next few minutes, we exchanged a number of very good barks. Then all went quiet as my dog and I headed past several blocks of shanty-like houses to the Rosenfield's to see if Harry was up yet.

A half block from Harry's place, a man smoking on his porch said, "Did you see a big dog down the way you came?"

"No."

"Well, he must have been down there somewhere because I barked back and forth with him for a long time."

"That was me barking, thinking you were a dog up here."

He smiled and then laughed with me. We each sounded off our barks to show each other. We departed feeling good about our barking and knowing a bark wasn't always what we thought.

With my usually silent dog and my noisy brothers, we roamed all over the ranch and sometimes adjacent to it on other people's property. With Smokey at our side we'd load up with ammo, our pockets bulging with rocks. With enough ammo, we felt safe and could take on the whole world. If we didn't have rocks, we felt naked and unable to attack or defend.

As a kid I had a rock in my hand most of the time, much like the early humans did before they learned to put handles on them as tools and weapons. We heaved rocks into the water-filled ditches, sloughs, and rivers just to see splashes. We skipped flat rocks on water surfaces to count how many skips a rock produced. We threw at the livestock and soon learned the types, sizes and, usefulness of our ready weapons. Rocking was always a contest among us to see who was the best. We used small rocks in our regular rock fights so we wouldn't injure each other. And we were careful to avoid throwing near windows, fearing Dad's wrath if we broke one.

Livestock was off limits when Dad was around. We were in serious trouble if he saw us heave a rock at milk cows. We would get a sound licking to impress on us that he didn't want his animals abused or made spooky wild.

I hated getting the milk cows from the pasture and would chuck rocks near their heels to take out my frustrations. It was always done out of sight of Dad and the buildings. I knew I shouldn't be doing it, but I resented the freedom the cows took from me. It seemed that just about the time something interesting came along to do, I was sent to drive in the danged cows to be milked.

Often when throwing rocks, we boys competed just to prove our accuracy. Heaving rocks close to a forbidden target, like Mom's chickens, and not hitting them was a joy. That way we could claim we were not throwing directly at, but to miss the feathered birds. If we made a hit on one, we were disgraced. We did the same when throwing at each other. Rocks were always flying when we were roamin' around.

Mom's chickens congregated behind the house and below the hill out of her sight providing safe targets. If I was lucky enough to hit one, the rock usually glanced off, as the chicken flock raced up the hill towards safety in the chicken house. Once my throw hit an old hen smack in the head, killing her dead on the spot. Larry and I were worried that Mom would count the hens and discover one missing. We got a spade out of the shop and buried my victim in the sagebrush just as criminals would. For weeks I feared Mom would confront me about the missing hen. She didn't, but I had dreams about her doing so, waking in the night, sweating in the darkness, but afraid to own up to my foul deed.

I had great fear of mean dogs. Dogs at the neighbors had bitten my older brothers when they were small boys on the prairie. Each carried the scars on his cheeks from the German shepherd attacks, marking him for life.

I recall walking to town alone when I was in elementary school. Our winding paths crossed dirt streets, alleys, and vacant lots leading to the main drag in Walden. A huge black shaggy dog baring its teeth and emitting a God-awful growl charged me from behind a trash barrel as if wanting to rip me apart. I froze. Snarling and daring me to run, the unwashed animal came within a foot of me. There it kept me in heart-pounding captivity for what seemed like ten minutes. It walked a few paces away, whirled, and rushed back at me, seeming to show more rage with each charge. Finally, it trotted across the street to a vacant lot. Only then did I dare move. I felt as if I had no breath in my body.

After that incident I always loaded up on rocks when approaching town. A good offense usually sent dogs high-tailing it. I had little to fear when Smokey or a group of us were together. We then relished any attack.

Often Harry Rosenfield was at my side to help fend off roving town dogs when we roamed the north end of Walden. His throwing arm was great in scattering stray dogs. Harry was the best, able to surpass me in running, shooting, throwing, tracking, and sneaking up on wild things on the ranch.

Often I wondered why he bested me at everything if I was some special person as Mom had said. On the other hand, my talking, planning, and leading were stronger. In my bossy and optimistic way, I lured Harry into many things that his shy nature would have avoided. The two of us were a good match in our ventures. I would do the talking while Harry would often back me up with his outdoor skills.

Thank goodness I had Harry as a chum from the fifth grade on. He took the place of Bob, who after he reached fourteen spent much of his time alone. I felt he had other fish to fry and considered what I did "kid stuff." Although I never ceased trying to win his favor and companionship, Bob largely ignored my efforts to include him in running around at the rivers on the ranch.

One mid summer day I made plans to roam a couple of miles north of the Two-Bar to the Col. Davis Place where, Dad had said, "There's blood on the upstairs wall where a man killed himself with a shotgun. Blew his brains all over the place."

Since I had never been north to the old Davis buildings, I was anxious to go there and see the death scene. Larry, Harry, and I gathered a lunch of bread, butter, and sugar sandwiches and apples and headed northwest with Smokey with our bows in hand. We took off our shoes and waded the Illinois River behind the corrals in the green willows.

We decided to wander over to the old tin-roofed slaughterhouse on our way to the ridge. Looming over the tall sage, the forbidden two-storied rusty tin building seemed to lure us. It was locked up and unused. We'd seen lots of rabbits outside but had never entered. Hundreds of bank swallows had stuck earthy-colored nests under the eaves. They darted swiftly about, filling the sky as we approached.

"It's locked from the inside just like before. I told you it was crazy to come clear over here," said Larry.

"Look here," yelled Harry from around the side, "this little door is open a crack."

"If both of us pull on this, you can slip inside Larry," I said.

"Why me?"

"Cuz you're littlest. Are you afraid?" Harry asked.

"No!"

"Take off that quiver and get in here," I said as we pulled with all our might allowing Larry to squeeze into the old slaughterhouse.

"What do you see?" Harry hollered.

"God, it's dark. Give me a second for my eyes. I hear something movin' up above."

"Get to the door an' let us in," I yelled, then rushed around the side with an arrow notched, as did Harry. The door squeaked open.

In one dank corner was a table sized square wooden lid. We dragged it off, and a strange odor nearly knocked us down. It came from a well of some sort.

"That's the worst stinking crap I've ever smelled," said Larry, gagging, as all of us reeled back from the opening.

"It's got a sweet smell about it. Dad says dead people stink like that," Harry reported. Harry's dad knew all about such things, and we never questioned his knowledge.

"Look at all this old dry crusted blood. It's stained all this cement floor, and here's some that is more recent," I said.

"Do you think something was killed here?"

"Well, I can't see a thing down that stinking place," said Larry," an' we don't have a flashlight."

"Let's light something an' drop it in," suggested Harry, who always carried matches. He soon had brush burning and floated it down the stinky shaft. It went out before it reached the bottom, but it allowed us to see the reflection of water in the bottom of the pit far below.

"Boy, is that deep. Let's try again with more brush," suggested Larry. On the second try, we saw the bottom water clearly and a mass of something dark with hair resting against one wall.

"Looks like a dead body to me," Harry whispered. Larry and I couldn't be as sure, but sharp-eyed Harry was seldom wrong.

"Let's close this up and go tell someone," I said. We replaced the lid and exited as we'd entered, locking the building with its horrid secret.

Harry talked us into not rushing to tell right then saying, "It will still be there tonight." He wanted to head on to the Davis Place. We agreed reluctantly and took off.

But first we rocked the mud-dobber nests, knocking down a few before moving north across the sagebrush towards the river bottom. I fought the urge to dogtrot home with the hot news.

Just as we hit the meadow, a flock of forty sage hens flew across the river. We put arrows to our bowstrings as we spread out twenty feet apart, and hunted at a slow walk. We took four shots at rising birds and hit none. Hitting a flying bird was a dream that seldom came true. Far behind us we saw the fading rusty building and to its left Post's sheep as always venturing onto our property. They could be chased another day.

A few Richardson's ground squirrels avoided our shafts and popped back underground as we reached the river where it knifed into the bluff. It was the highest point on the Two-Bar. We struggled upward to get a birds-eye view of the ranch below and to the east.

Two fishermen, fishing where they shouldn't be, were secluded among the willows on the Michigan. On the north in a depression and hidden from view from the Two-Bar buildings was their vehicle.

We slipped under the west fence onto the Taylor Grazing Land. Larry and I uncapped the valves to the tires and Harry used a matchstick to release the air, flattening all four. Feeling satisfied, we dropped back down the bluff to the river, knowing these men had hid their car in that spot intentionally sneaking in to fish. It would be a long walk to town for the trespassers.

In the next bend of the creek, there was a black mass of fish in a deep clear hole. As we watched hundreds of massed suckers on the muddy bottom, Smokey spooked two great horned owls out of the willows near the cliff face.

Forgetting the suckers, Harry said, "I think maybe they have a nest."

"Damn right, I'd like some owl feathers for my headband. Maybe we can ambush them when they return," said Larry as he headed toward the sandy colored outcrop jutting behind the willow tops.

"Hold your horses, Larry, and wait for us. We need to plan an ambush," I said.

Larry snapped, "You always have to have some big plan. Let's just do it." It reminded me that I always tried to be in charge like some general or chief, and Harry usually went along. This time I couldn't get mad and send Larry home or he'd tell about the body in the slaughterhouse pit.

"OK, let's find the nest, if there is one."

We scoured the tangled willows along the creamy sandstone wall but we couldn't spot a nest. Yet, Smokey, looking upward, continued to bark.

"I can't see what he's seeing," said Harry searching the treetops, "bet it's in the rocks and not the willows." We finally spotted a hidden opening in the shadows facing northeast about eight feet up.

"Maybe you can stand on my shoulders and look in, Harry," I said.

Harry climbed up and stretched to look into the hole. He turned and said, "Reach up and I'll give you something." He handed Larry a half-grown owlet saying, "Don't grab it by the feet. Its beak won't get you, 'cuz they don't peck!"

"God, it's really soft and listen to it snap that bill," replied a wide-eyed Larry as he took all three young owls gently to the ground one at a time. They had giant big yellow eyes and clicked their bills as if to bite us each time we touched them, but they didn't. They crouched on the ground as we played with them for some time.

"There are your feathers, Larry," said Harry.

"I'd never take them from a baby owl! I can find a dead one sometime and get all the feathers I need."

"Let's put 'em back and let 'em grow up. I do want an owl foot, but not from a baby one."

"Dad says they eat a lot of mice, so we'd better let them live," I said. Soon we had them back in the nest hole.

"Let's not tell anyone about the hidden cave," pleaded Larry. We agreed to it on a blood brother oath. None of us wanted town kids coming down and killing our owls.

Our path took us to a deep gully and a favorite sandstone fortress in a walled area where, hidden from all eyes, we paused. In the sand, peering out at the world to the east and the sand dunes at the base of the mountains far across North Park, we rested. We talked of how we could defend this place against thousands of attacking enemies and slip out at night and escape. Larry and Harry thought themselves great scouts capable of sneaking through any enemy lines.

Trying to observe everything on both creeks snaking below us and in the willows hugging their banks, we continued on. Crows and red-tailed hawks often glided by us as they cruised the dead air seeking opportunity along the rivers below. Ducks and cackling kingfishers flew up and down the streams low over the water below.

This time of year few cattle were in sight on the ranch. Our meadows were cattle free and growing wild hay. Most of our cattle were on summer pasture at the Norris Place or the La Rand Pasture.

At last we stood on a knob of sandstone and could see a flattened rock in the creek sixty feet below. It was our "steamboat rock" where we sometimes swam secluded under the protection of the cliff and alder trees. Its flat top allowed half a dozen of us to sit, dive, and talk as the slow current glided by on each side. No swimming for us today, for beyond lay our towering Point Of Rocks, the yellow sandy formation that gave the name to the town before it was called Walden.

We helped each other between the fence wires on the steep slope and descended to the grassy river bottom below. It was pockmarked with gopher and badger holes. Our path took us along the river in the short willows and chest-high slough grasses as we neared the meeting place of the Michigan and Illinois.

The two creeks were strikingly different. Fast and hurried, the Michigan carried much water in its narrow twisty channel while the wide and slow Illinois lazed along. Apparently her waters, void of trout, contained only the suckers and creek chubs native to the Park. The blended waters formed a wider and slower Michigan that descended north to the North Platte.

We rested on the banks, watching the three distinct bodies of water, knowing that more critters passed here than any other place on the Two-Bar.

Soon, Harry sent Larry with Smokey ahead to scout and report back. Larry loved sneaking and spying ahead.

Harry and I sat in the damp grass below lance-shaped willow leaves and watched over the magic waters. Trout jumped, clearing the water to take flying insects, leaving rings behind. Munching gnats and mosquitoes on the wing, five-inch darner dragonflies zoomed up and down the banks in front of us. Only rarely did they alight on a twig or grass tip and allow us to see their green, yellow, and blue colors in full glory. When seining for minnows, we had caught their immature spider-like forms on the bottoms of sloughs and deep river holes and knew that ugly could become gorgeous overnight.

The tall grass quietly parted and Larry and Smokey were back with us again.

"We saw a flash of something move back into the big middle cave, and Smokey stiffed all up like he does when it's something big."

"What you think it was?" asked Harry.

"It's big like Smokey here. Wish we hadn't spooked it so you guys could see."

I said, "Well it won't probably come out now for a long time. Anyway, let's check out the rocks." Single file, we followed Larry back to his scouting spot.

Our rocks stood at the tip of two east-pointing ridges, anchoring their bases with forty feet of erect yellow-green sandstone. Wind and water had been at work on them, carving out caves and holes aplenty. It was a magic place where we knew Indians would have watched, hunted, and camped since the river valleys to the east, south, and north could all be observed from its top. We waited a few minutes, feasting our eyes, before moving toward the opening near the caves.

"Look at this," whispered Harry, dropping to his knees. "No claws, has to be cat tracks." His dad had taught him signs. There in the soft dirt the tracks of the cat stared up at us. Harry checked their size and stood up.

"Bobcat."

"Wow," whispered Larry as we all moved towards the rock base with arrows on our bowstrings.

Smokey growled as we peered into the dark sandstone openings. The big opening had a path of bobcat tracks leading up into it. The other openings were littered with woodchuck, fox, or coyote droppings outside the entrances.

After we had stuffed a huge pile of willow branches into the opening that led upward into the bobcat den, Harry set it ablaze with his trusty match, priding himself for always starting a fire with only one match. We had our best hunting arrows ready for the beast and waited for its exit. We waited and waited until the fire was half burned. No rushing cat. Finally, I backed up and saw a plume of smoke flowing up the bluff from a small hole a dozen feet up the cliff face.

"Damn, there's a hole letting the smoke out, Harry," I said as we all backed up and lowered our arrows.

"Bull, I thought we had 'em for sure," grunted Harry.

Butter-and-sugar sandwiches hit the spot as we grumbled about our rotten luck and feasted in front of the caves.

"Maybe we could set a trap and catch it later," said Larry.

"They are really leery, and we'd have to come down here twice a day to check it," said Harry whose woodsman code wouldn't allow setting a trap and not tending it.

"At least we know where it is, and maybe on the trip back we can come from the top and sneak up on it," I said.

"With all this smoke, I doubt it will be out again until tonight," retorted Harry.

"Wish we could camp here and blast that cat in the moonlight," said Larry. "Want me to scout ahead to the head gate and see what's there."

"Naw, let's all go since it's on the way," I replied.

As we approached, two green herons lifted from the sandy bar below the head gate. Our arrows touched only dark blue sky as they streaked north past the herons and stuck into the pasture sod beyond the big ditch. Suckers and small chubs in a drying hole had attracted the wading birds with their dagger beaks. Our arrows danced and zigzagged when they struck suckers in the fish school, stirring up bottom mud and blackening the water. Harry used a long willow branch to retrieve our shafts and the fish. We didn't want to have wet feet as we marched on north to the Davis Place. We discarded the suckers in the grass, collected our arrows, and we sneaked on, following the declining sagebrush ridge dotted with smaller sandstone outcrops.

After a mile hike we neared the Col. Davis Place buildings. I had a feeling of impending doom. We shouldn't be here, and I wanted to leave quickly. I feared that something awful was going to happen. The Allards, who had the place, were good friends with our parents, but that didn't ease my bad feelings and worry that the house may be haunted.

The entry into the house was easy compared to that of the slaughterhouse. Our footsteps echoed in the vacant dusty downstairs rooms where we found nothing but emptiness. Warily we took the stairs to the death scene. In the second bedroom, we found a light red stain with a few pellet holes in the wallpaper. We stood aghast in disappointment.

"Is that all there is?" I asked.

"Rats!" Harry snorted. "Someone must have cleaned it."

"There isn't nothin' here," complained Larry while he looked out of the flyspecked window whose ledges were thick with the dead bodies of hundreds of Miller-moths and huge houseflies.

"This trip is a bust," complained Harry who must have been expecting the same gory mess I had in mind.

"Let's try the attic. I thought there was a noise up there when we came in," I said.

Although it wasn't much of an attic, Harry crawled into the small hole after we removed the lid. He yelled his findings to us below in the closet. There were ups and downs in the place where the attic followed the contours of the ceilings and steep roof. Holes produced enough light for Harry to see hundreds of empty whisky bottles and other junk.

"Guys, there are a lot of shiny things in a nest on the ledge below the chimney. Looks like coins and jewels."

"Throw 'em down!" yelled Larry.

"Hold your shirts on, I've a tangle of boards to move."

Dusty, cobweb-covered, and coughing Harry exited the attic with a packrat nest filled with broken glass, tin, and other bright objects. He did have two dimes and a quarter to show for his efforts. When he offered to share the loot with us, we refused, knowing he seldom had money and didn't get an allowance in his large and poor family.

"You keep it, Harry. You earned it eating all that dust," I said.

"It could have been gold coins just as easily, and we could buy all the new arrows we want," Larry lamented.

Harry replied, "If we ever need old bottles, I know where there's a ton of 'em. These people must have been real drunks. But, why would the bottles be in the attic?"

"Maybe somebody was hiding his drinkin' like our haymen do in the bunkhouse," I said.

As a parting gesture we sank three hunting arrows into the weathered front door, then removed them after they stopped vibrating. We headed on south toward the rocks, deciding to cross the pastures and meadow rather than following the ridge back. We chose this shorter route to avoid going the same way twice, always seeking new territory when on a roaming expedition.

Greasewood plants and alkali soil dominated the first pasture and whitened the bottoms of our shoes. A white-tailed jackrabbit jumped up and with its erratic running pattern escaped our arrows. However, Harry's shaft grazed it.

Our meandering then took us across the big Davis meadow in tall wild hay. We didn't know whether they were going to hay or pasture the field with lease cattle. Dad would have punished us if it had been his meadow for we didn't dare tromp down hay that could later be cut. If the Allards did cut it later, our tracks would be as clear on the meadow floor as uncut prints.

Soon, Larry spotted what appeared to be a saddle horse coming from the willows to the east. As it neared, we saw it was a Brahma coming at a lope. It was gray, tall, and horned. Allards must be pasturing the "crazy things" as Dad had referred to them. He had warned us how dangerous they were, even taking a man on horseback.

"Run like hell," yelled Harry, taking off in a sprint.

Since it was way too far to beat it to the meadow fence, we raced for a wire stack pen as fast as we could in the tall hay. The cow was a hundred yards behind, gaining on us fast.

"Harry, shall we stop and shoot it, or try for the pen?" I yelled in panic, seeing Larry was trailing behind.

"Doubt if we can stop it. It's probably crazy or it wouldn't be after us like this," he shouted from ahead, always being the fastest runner.

As we neared the stack pen, I glanced back, seeing blood below the cow's left eye and her protruding giant horns. I knew we couldn't make it, and she was going to really hurt someone. Maybe I could divert her and jump aside quickly, I thought, as I stopped and turned. Larry whizzed past as I notched my arrow and drew the bow. Before I could release, the cow suddenly went down in a heap. Smokey had launched himself at her, hitting her neck and falling into the front legs and tripping her. Amid the pileup was his familiar fighting growls. We instantly fled on to the stack pen, sliding under its wires just barely ahead of the panting, crazed bovine with Smokey gamely barking and snapping at her heels. She hit the six strands of rusty wires full force and by some miracle the ancient wire held her outside.

We called Smokey and held him back as we watched the snorting cow race about outside the stack pen seeking a way at us.

"Let's shoot her," Larry roared.

"No," I ordered, "she must belong to the Allards."

"The hell with the Allards! She tried to kill us, and would have except for Smokey," said Harry forcefully.

"I'd like to kill 'er too, but Dad would skin us."

The crazed Brahma continued racing around and around outside the stack pen. She was in a frantic charged-up state I'd never seen before in a cow, crazy wild, snorting, pawing the ground, and wanting to gore anything.

"What's the deal with her eye?" asked Harry.

"Guess she had a cancer-eye removed. We had one at the Norris Place. Dad and the vet cut it out. They couldn't get her out of the willows for days, and she was totally nuts," I replied.

"Maybe that's why she's on the prod and took us," said Larry. "God, she came a long ways after us."

Harry answered, "We were probably the only thing she saw moving. And she still wants us."

Around and around the wire enclosure she raced. Good thing Allards hadn't opened the stack pen for haying as Dad always did on our place or we wouldn't be safely inside. For thirty minutes she wouldn't leave. We pelted her with rocks. That made her determined to stay. Siccing Smokey on her produced the same result. So we hid, laying down out of her sight in the tall grass, praising and petting our dog for his valor. Eventually the cow left. Until we reached Richard land, three wiser boys hustled on across the hay meadow with a keen eye out for more cow danger.

Crazy cows were always more dangerous than any of our bulky bulls, I thought after once seeing one take our hired man. Dad had put an on-the-fight cow in the corral without letting Kip know. When Kip came out of the cow barn with his bucket of milk and was strolling along to the far gate, this crazy cow raced after him. He saw her out of the corner of his eye charging him at a dead run. Leaving milk bucket in midair, he grabbed the top of the six-foot-high board fence and cleared it all in one motion, just avoiding the cow's one sharp horn.

Back at the ranch house after our brush with the mad cow, Dad was more upset about the crazy cancer-eye being in the Davis meadow than he was about the body in the well. He thought the Allards should have let us know about such a threat. He talked with Mr. Rosenfield who called the county sheriff asking him to check out the slaughterhouse well. We got no reward. It was a dead dog someone had dumped down the waste well.

Later Dad told me in no uncertain terms, "You had no business being in other people's meadows and buildings, and you guys should keep out of them in the future."

But on the good side, Mom was thrilled with Smokey, saying, "He's the best dog in this country. That dog loves you as only a dog can."

Smokey, a prince of a dog who lived a beautiful
and free life. Illustration by David Hartman

Dejected by Dad's rebuff but not detoured by what came our way, we continued roaming with Smokey.

Once we roamed with gasoline from Dad's storage tank to the river intending to get at a huge rainbow trout by burning out a giant dry beaver dam. We thought the flames would scare out the huge rainbow trout. We'd seen it trapped behind the dry willow tangle of the dam. We craved arrow shots at it. But, no such luck. Mom saw light reflections off our tin gas cans, followed us, took away our fuel, and marched us back to the buildings, ending our grand plan to garner a huge trout.

Later she also put a stop to Jay's teaching us to smell fumes from gasoline. Using little tin cans, we'd sit against the highboard fence and get zonked. In our dazed state, the sky would spin and produce patterns of wild variety. Having Dad lock the gas tank and give Jay a sound licking probably kept us from brain damage, according to Mom.

She couldn't, however, keep Jay from leading us in smoking as we roamed around the buildings. In our old log barn, we tried smoking coffee, cow manure, horse manure, and leaves. Horse manure was the least gagging. Tobacco was the best, but it was hard to come by since nobody in town would sell it to kids. I concluded that smoking wasn't worth all the effort Jay put into it.

When I did something terribly bad during our wild roaming, Mom would quickly tell me how I was a Richard and that she didn't want me growing up to be an awful scoundrel like her uncle Brush. He'd done unpardonable deeds like squandering away the Buffalo Ranch he'd been given and cheating everyone by taking advantage at every turn. Her uncle Brush had even assumed the name "Colonel" when he was a big-time gambler and traveling singer although he had never been in the military. Brush had been married four times, had hid illegal big-horned sheep heads at her Dad's place, had bilked oil companies by stealing their scientific devices, and had pretended to be their inventor. He'd also been a slick real estate salesman, often fleeing to Canada to avoid the law.

At the ends of such scoldings, Mom usually said to me in no uncertain terms, "Paul, I expected better from you than this.

You're special, not like my uncle Brush. Go think twice about how you're supposed to be."

Such reminders kept me on a sane pathway in my ranch wanderings, preventing me from really doing something dastardly awful that would hurt someone or our ranch. I still had vast freedom, but was always nudged toward responsibility letting me figure out how I really wanted to be.

Chapter 9

RAIDIN'

"What the hell are you kids doin'? It's against the damned law to stop this here train!"

Far across our meadow, I could see the second railroad bridge, reminding me of some of the boy raids we made there from the Two-Bar. From my perch on the old rake seat, I pondered if we had had too much freedom in going after supposed enemies. Still, I chuckled to myself about some of the wild things we tried to do.

Some people on nearby North Park ranches made hired men of their kids. Not my parents. We had daily chores, and we helped during the busy times of haying, cattle drives, and branding. Otherwise, our time was our own. I had vast acres, wide-open sagebrush range, mountain wild country, and a small town nearby. But to what avail would wild country and freedom have been if I hadn't had enough spunk to use it to test my fiber?

I didn't much fancy being known as the little brother of Jay and Bob Richard. Going the outdoor route offered the most hope of showing my differences from my older brothers. I knew Larry had guts, but at times I was not so sure about myself.

Our raids might have brought serious trouble with the law had we been kids in some big town. However, we were descendants of pioneers and sons of a well-respected rancher in a small community. Also most everyone looked out for us and excused our adventuresome ornery behavior saying, "There's never a dull moment with those five boys around."

One day while Jay, a high school freshman, and his friend, John Clark, were hanging around our log cow barn, we smaller brothers started throwing rocks at them. When the rock fight ended, the train whistle sounded down below the hill behind the gray high-board fence.

"I'd sure like to ride on that train," said Jimmy.

"You're too little to even jump up on it," Larry said.

"Maybe we can just get Jimmy a ride. It's too late today, but next run, John and I'll stop the train and get you a ride," promised Jay as he took a long drag on a horse-manure cigarette.

"How are you going to stop the train?" asked Bob.

"John and I'll make the plans. You guys get out of here, and don't say anything about smoking, or I'll say you were doing it, too," threatened Jay. We younger brothers assumed that Jay knew what he was doing, and we were all excited to ride along with Jimmy to the train depot in town.

A few days later, Jay and John had us pile old railroad ties on the tracks to stop the slow moving train. We made a five-foot pile of twenty old heavy used ties placing them across the double iron tracks. Then we sat atop the pile to wait for the late afternoon coal-burning train.

At long last we heard it. The old steamer rumbled as it crawled along the tracks from the north. Black smoke belched from the engine's single stack and hung stagnant above the train. A chugging sound filled the air as did steam and screeching brakes once the engineer saw our barricade. Just a few feet from the pile of ties, the engine jerked and halted in a cloud of white steam.

Jay didn't get a chance to make his request. As men climbed from the noisy engine to the ground, the dark-faced engineer said, "What in the hell are you kids doing? It's against the damned law to stop this here train. You could have caused a wreck with those damn ties. Don't you know a damned thing? Help us get those ties off of there, now!"

All of us, with the help of the railroad men, turned to and removed the ties. Before climbing back aboard the firemen turned to us saying, "You've done it this time. We have put up with your throwing rocks, but now you've gone too damned far. We're going to call your Dad. Don't you dare ever stop this train again."

We were disappointed as the train eased off toward the depot half a mile away. That we might meet unfriendly men hadn't entered into our heads. The encounter put a bad taste in my mouth toward the train and its crew. We all grumbled, as we walked up the rock-strewn ridge to the house.

All five of us were crowded around the table the next morning when Dad said, "Bob, Paul, Larry--I mean Jay, stop that kicking under the table."

The phone rang. "It's for you, Willard," said Mom.

"Yes."

"Oh, yeah, Cliff." Upon hearing that name, we boys looked at one another in dismay.

Dad was silent as he listened. Then, "Oh, the heck they did." Dad said.

Again he listened and finally responded, "I understand, Cliff, and I'll talk with them. Thanks for letting me know."

"Good-bye."

He sat down at the head of the table and started sipping his coffee while Mom cooked extra pancakes to go along with the eggs and bacon on the table. I wondered what was going through Dad's mind. Since all of us knew who Cliff was, we realized that we were in trouble. Dad was very quiet. We all fell silent and kept on eating.

Finally Dad spoke up. "You guys had better leave that train alone. That was Cliff at the depot. That's three times this year.

You're going to get yourselves in serious trouble if you don't stop it."

Nobody commented, even though some of us hoped to explain to him how we had just wanted to get Jimmy a ride. But we all got the message. When Dad told us something important, we heeded.

Although we stopped the train raids for a while, we sought revenge for them being so mean to us. They should have provided us a ride since the train was, after all, stopped. They could have easily given us a ride were they good men. We became more cunning with later attacks on the iron beast. We raided and rocked the train from positions where the crew couldn't actually spot us. We used large rocks and targeted the engine's smokestack. When we stood behind willows or at a distance from the high cut, we were sometimes able to throw our rocks right down the stack without the crew seeing us. It was great hearing the rocks hit the iron engine and to know the train crew was scanning wildly trying to locate us. Since no one had spotted us, we could always say it was probably some other trespassing kids from town doing the rocking. I felt like part of the Jesse James gang, having so much fun in attacking what Indians called the iron horse.

I could sometimes get Harry to stand on the tracks as the smoking train approached. Upon seeing Harry, the engineer applied the brakes with flying sparks and screeching coming from the rails. At the very the last moment Harry would step off and run. We were safe since they hadn't seen a Richard. Usually Larry, Jimmy, Harry's brother Warren, "Wart" to us, and I were all crouched in the big sagebrush up on the ridge. From there we would watch the train nearly stop and then continue on to the depot. We'd tell Dad that none of us had stood on the tracks.

Sometimes, with rocks in hand, we'd hide on cross-timbers extending outward from the Michigan River railroad bridge.

To hunker there only inches from the giant rumbling steel wheels took some guts. Once the caboose passed, we'd spring up and loft rocks onto the caboose roof from the rear. The train crew never caught on to where we were since they could only see out of the side windows.

Richard boys testing their courage by rocking the iron horse on the Two-Bar. Illustration by David Hartman

We had a jolly widow woman neighbor to the south who didn't cross our property three times a week as the train did, but her animals violated us. Rose tried to run her tiny ranch on the Illinois River by herself, having an awful time getting anything accomplished. Dad urged her on, but his patience sometimes gave out.

"Rose, this is Willard. I locked your sheep up in the shed here on the ranch," said Dad on the telephone. "You'll have to talk with Sheriff Norm Woodruff before you come get them."

"I see," she replied.

"Those sheep have been on us for years, and we can't have it anymore. Our half of that woven-wire fence has been up for two years now, and yours needs finishing to keep 'em off our grass."

"I'll get on it, Willard."

"Thanks, Rose."

Dad sat back down at the table. I knew he wasn't really angry with Rose Post. But enough was enough, and he was forcing the issue.

I just knew she wouldn't do anything to keep the woolies out, and decided to punish the sheep. Those sheep had been back on our place, grazing again even after Dad had them locked up. So many times during the summer, Dad had sent me down to run them out that I was sick of doing it. I decided to run them out once again and shoot one. I had never shot anything that large before. But I could justify such a shooting. After all, it was trespassing. I figured to throw the dead sheep into the river. The current would carry it downstream. I would escape the possibility of blame.

I organized a big raidin' party--the Wilsons, Jerry and Kale; the Rosenfields, Harry and Wart; plus Larry, Jimmy, and I. Armed with bows and arrows, we descended the big hill toward the Illinois River with intentions of punishing Post's sheep. Before we could get into arrow range those spooky woolies saw the seven of us coming and raced for the fence and home territory. We unleashed our arrows, but they were too far away.

We milled about and shot our arrows nearly straight up into the air to see who could put one out of sight in the blue sky. Then we wandered over and pulled our arrows from the pasture sod where they appeared to be growing as an upright-feathered crop.

In the willows between Post's ranch and ours, we stopped to talk. Since this was the biggest war party I'd ever led, I couldn't disband it now. We agreed to cross the fence onto the neighbor's property and from there administer just punishment on the wayward sheep. Dangerous though it was being off Richard territory, we decided to keep in the thick willows as Apache would. After advancing some distance along the willow-covered banks we peered into an opening. There standing on the far side of the clearing was a bunch of horses. Among them were a mare and a young foal.

"Shall we shoot a horse?" asked Kale, youngest of the Wilsons.

"Shut up, stupid," whispered his older brother, Jerry. "I need a horse myself. Maybe we can catch that colt."

"What would we do with it?" asked Larry, knowing Jerry was a town kid whose mother ran a café in Walden.

"Maybe we could take it down on the Michigan and make a pen for it," replied Jerry.

Since he wanted a horse so badly and had never had one, we decided to put our bows and arrows aside and to capture the foal. We spread out, charged the horses, and forced them into the willows and towards the river. The older horses forded the thirty-foot stream. Because the foal was afraid to jump off the tall bank into the water, Larry and Jerry caught her. With a belt around the foal's neck, Jerry led and we pushed the animal a mile to the thick willows below the railroad bridge.

"What will we feed it?" asked Kale.

"I can get milk from Mom's cafe to feed it in the evenings. Maybe Paul could get milk and feed it in the mornings," said Jerry.

Why not? We had captured Jerry a horse. Now we had to raise it in secret.

Larry and Smokey trotted to the house and returned with spikes, baling wire, hammers, and a saw. We constructed a small corral for the young filly in the dense willows using big willow branches as cross rails. We fed her cow's milk, and she learned to drink well from a bottle with a nipple. Jerry named the beautiful little filly "Bess." She was a bay with a white blaze the length of her face. She had three white feet at the ends of her long gangly legs.

All went well for some time. I kindled an early morning fire in the dense willows to heat milk from Mom's refrigerator. In the evenings, Jerry did the same with milk from his mother's cafe.

Then our secret was discovered. A game warden was trapping beaver along the Michigan River and heard Bess whinny. After he had seen her, he informed Dad that the animal looked underfed. Dad summoned Jerry and me into the dining room, looked us over in his quiet way with unblinking cold blue eyes and said, "You guys are keeping that colt down in the willows, aren't you?"

"Yes," we nodded, knowing when it was time to own up to the truth.

"Well, taking someone's horse makes you guys horse thieves, you know. And they usually hang horse thieves," said Dad in his low, stern voice.

"What shall we do?" asked Jerry in a panic. My heart was sinking and I was just speechless, thinking of the terror of being hanged.

"I suggest you take it back to its mother. It belongs to Charlie King. He thought the mare had lost it."

We made a race for the Michigan, took Bess and returned her to the mare at Post's Place on the Illinois. Although the mother wouldn't pay any attention to her offspring, we left her there anyway. Feeling terrible about having to give up Jerry's filly, we expected to be hanged any day, but we young horse thieves escaped the noose. Bess, raised on a bottle, grew up to be a beautiful mare I saw a few times years later in Walden's

Growing Up Wild

Rodeo Parade. Charlie King nevertheless called me " horse thief" for years, as did Jay and Bob, thinking how funny they were. They never realized that it wasn't my idea in the first place to take the foal.

Mom also hurt my pride when she told me, "I don't want to be raising some horse thief in this house." I couldn't tell her that Jerry had wanted the horse and that I had just helped.

Way back then it seemed that we had to have some raiding adventure going all the time. We needed to be planning ahead in our raids, giving us something to look forward to. To be sure, we didn't share our plans with the folks since they might have toned down our raiding.

Mom once told me how her dad, Jay Monroe, so angry after his ranch had been stolen had said, "I'd like to go there and burn down all their haystacks." I could see the hurt and sadness in her eyes, and her hate, as she remembered her dad's vengeful words.

Harry and I planned a Kiowa attack on the ranch whose people Mom detested. In revenge for them having stolen the ranch from our grandfather, I wanted to burn down their buildings, using fire arrows at night, and torch their haystacks. Since that ranch was a long dozen miles from ours, no one would have suspected us of the fire. Fortunately for us, the ranch was too far away. Because we didn't have transportation to get there and back without the folks knowing we were gone, the ranch thieves four hundred haystacks never burned-- except in our own vengeful boy minds. Nonetheless, just in case, we made fire arrows and stored them and gasoline at the Rosenfield's boys shack.

In the dark dead of winter, we talked about our dream of catching the main ranch thief in the sagebrush and torturing him Apache style. Larry and I had read how the Apaches would cut a man's Achilles' tendons, slice off his eyelids, and leave him to crawl until the sun maddened him. Pure justice, we thought, for the dastardly scheme he led in stealing our grandfather's beautiful hay ranch.

I even tried to get my brother to help. My efforts to get Bob to hang out with us at the Rosenfield's place where we planned such raids were unsuccessful. He seemed to drift along as a loner, doing his own winter projects in our ranch shop. Perhaps he felt we were too much into kid stuff, or perhaps he felt too old for such activities. His lone ranger style puzzled me when he turned down our invitations to honor our family's grandfather with a revenge raid.

Harry's grandmother lived in one of three rough-board logging shacks located in the sagebrush on the north end of the Rosenfield half acre. As an old age pensioner, she seemed to be sour, enjoying only her pipe smoking and chewing tobacco. The weathered prune of a tiny woman who didn't get along with Harry's mother, existed there in the little shack, all alone. Bessie, Harry's mother, however, made sure the old woman had water and wood, which Harry and Wart supplied. Mr. Rosenfield did most of the errands, caring for his mother. I longed for a grandmother, too, who I would surely want to be in our house.

We kids had taken over one of the adjacent shacks beside the grandmother's as a hideout. There in the six-by-twelve-foot room, heated with a little wood stove and lighted with one dangling bare bulb, we told stories, read comics, played games, wrestled, and dreamed the winter weekends away, awaiting spring.

On Big Chief tablet sheets we drew maps outlining campaigns and indicating prime camping spots on the ranch. As we planned our forays, Jimmy's eyes would bug out in excitement. He couldn't sleep at night. Harry and I made everyone swear to secrecy on an oath of blood never to reveal our summer plans.

In the long winter's darkness, we whittled arrows from pine boards and schemed summer raids. We dreamed boy dreams and planned to live down on the river and to attack trespassing fishermen and other undesirables. Arrows filled our quivers. We prepared knives, sharpened them, and laid them away in a cache under the shack's one single bed.

We ordered other essential Indian items by mail. I sent away for an Indian wig, complete with long braids. Black and shiny it was, made of horsehair. Once the wig was in place, all of my blond hair was totally hidden. Well equipped with clothing and Indian weapons, we were just waiting for what the Utes called the "never-no-spring thaw" in North Park.

On a little radio, we listened breathlessly to "Straight Arrow" and "The Lone Ranger and Tonto." Buster Brown telling dog stories filled our ears, too. We saved cereal box tops and ordered secret message decoders and rings in which to hide messages. We assembled small mirrors to enable us to flash signals to each other across the willows.

At long last, spring with its warm weather arrived. It was time for the great uprising in the willows. The first attack was to be quick and effective. I thought if we convinced our first victims they had actually been attacked by "real Indians" our fame would spread. People in the county would be terrified, just as rumors of Utes in 1879 had caused ranchers to flee to the blockhouse at Pinkhampton in the north end of the Park.

With intentions of attacking the railroad section crew, Larry, Tommy Gray, the hired man's boy, Jimmy, and I made for the river. Harry and Wart couldn't come. There were five men working at jacking up rails, digging holes for new crossties, and pounding spikes. Larry scouted them out and reported back, and I devised a plan of attack.

I set things up by warning the section crew. They were busy installing ties near the trestle at the second railroad bridge near the northeast ridge below Linsdy Coe's tiny log cabin. The section crew listened with some interest as I said, "You guys should be pretty careful when you're working down around here."

"Why?" asked the section boss?

"There were real Indians seen in those willows over there last winter."

"I have some Indians on my crew," he replied.

"My dad said the ones in the willows are dangerous. I just thought I would warn you."

"OK, kiddo." Other men grunting or laughing seemed to take little notice of my warning.

Larry, Tommy, and Jimmy were preparing our attack. The three boys in catalogue-acquired moccasins were naked except for breechcloths, which consisted of a belt around their bare waists and a brown decorated cloth draped under and then over the belt. The three savages were well painted with yellow, red, and green patterns on their bodies and faces. Jimmy wore the black wig since he was the lightest haired of the raiders. They all had their weapons ready. Each with a war club or a tomahawk, a knife, and a bow with plenty of arrows. I moved back from the trestle and vanished into the willows.

Larry who moved silently to the high hill above the trestle began to shoot arrows near them to divert their attention.

Screaming war cries, Tommy and Jimmy raced across an opening between the willows and the railroad tracks. To attack the section gang, they waded a shallow slough and raced toward the tracks, yelling and whooping. Fully armed and decked out in paint and feathers, Tommy and Jimmy gave savage screams as they advanced. Larry, who was still at the high point above the tracks now released more arrows, which stuck in the ground and ties near the section crew. Tommy and Jimmy had some difficulty getting across the last ditch full of irrigation water. The ditch was deep and had a soft, muddy bottom. Its chest deep cold water slowed the war whoops of the two semi-naked boys.

When they were finally across, Jimmy and Tommy screamed and waved their war clubs at the section gang. The attack broke down, however, because the section crew didn't run. The men, while ducking Larry's arrows, were getting a big laugh out of this frontal attack. But most of all they were laughing at one of the two stark-white attackers who had lost his breechcloth and was dancing and chanting around them in total nakedness while waving his Sioux war club and yelling, as green war paint streaked down his white skinny body.

Upon discovering his condition, Tommy raced back for the willows. Jimmy soon followed, as did Larry after the release of his last arrow. Eventually, we had a meeting in the willows to discuss our failure, to plan another attack with Harry and Wart along, and to modify the Indian breechcloth.

Often unexpected events just happened without us boys planning anything, keeping things exciting on the ranch. One July day Smokey and I tagged along watching the men fix fence along the ridge top above the Illinois River. We spotted a lone fisherman emerge from the willows in an open bend across the pasture on the Michigan River. He was fishing alone, trespassing, and enjoying himself. We were over a half-mile away from him and would have had a long walk and the Illinois River to cross to run him off.

He was in the pasture with our two hundred steers. Frisky yearling steers are often playful and run as a group right up to a person, stop, look for a few moments, then playfully bolt and run off.

While this man was merrily fishing, I watched the large bunch of our steers round a river bend and in a playful run head his direction. Some were bucking, others running half sideways. Most of them were kicking up their heels as they thundered along. When the fisherman looked up, he saw the group of over a hundred Hereford steers only a couple hundred feet away, running toward him and closing in fast. Had he ignored them, they would have stopped, looked at him a minute, snorted, and raced off. Making a quick decision, this greenhorn fisherman took off on the dead run through the willows and toward the pasture fence. In his rubber wading boots, he ran for all he was worth. Running like a scalded dog and looking back only once to see the steers still coming behind him, he approached the fence and in one motion threw his fishing pole and himself over the five barbed wires. Catching the toes of his boots in the top strand, he was left hanging upside down until he finally kicked free. The steers stopped at the fence, watched the man, then bolted and ran west in the pasture.

The hired men laughed and wondered what kind of story the man later told. He probably related how a herd of wild bulls had charged him and he had narrowly escaped with his life. It seemed that our livestock were helping run off fishermen, too. Sneaking onto our ranch could be a hazard since our cattle even protected it.

Much of the time we ventured along the rivers totally hidden from would-be enemies, hoping for some action. Most often we had to find adventure on our own, using our imaginations and choosing up sides and having kid battles. As much fun as raids and our make-believe battles were, we spent most of our time messing around and enjoying being out of doors in our own empire.

Amid the tangled interwoven web of willow branches, corn-like stems of standing cow parsnips grew six feet tall. We cut the side branches off and used them as green spears. And beneath the shifting canopy of alder leaves, we lazed at Camp Big Chief that was hidden deeply in the dense willows near the railroad trestle.

Beside the magic flowing waters of the Michigan we chewed and sucked on sweet timothy stems and mint tea leaves. The chest high grass hid us, and the tin sheeting on the railroad bridge banged to tell if anyone was crossing to our side of the river. We gathered the nearby wild onions and gleefully ate their stems and roots. On the soft carpet of riverbank grass, we carved and whittled willow branches making arrows, war clubs, flutes, and spears.

Our boy sounds muffled by the continuous gurgling river riffles and our movements concealed by tall grass and willows, we basked in safety and dreamed our dreams of courage. Nature was our companion as we slipped away from our worries of growing up and of making something out of ourselves. We thrived in our dense willow river bottom where only boy-time existed. It all belonged to us.

We scouted, kept our eyes peeled for interloping fishermen, listened for barking from trusty Smokey. We searched the river gravel bars for good flat rocks that we attached to willow branches with wire or string. We made tomahawk heads and spears from willows by attaching sharpened bones from old carcasses of dead animals. To make fish spears we drove nails in the ends of willow branches, cut off the flat heads of the nails with pinchers, and then sharpened and barbed the tips with files. Guards, sections, and ledger plates from old mowing machine sickles were used as spear points, hatchet heads, and arrowheads. Such weapons were ever present in our play, during our raids, and in our hunting wildlife along the Two-Bar's pure streams.

Since enemies were so hard to find, we exerted much of our energy in mock battles among ourselves. With six-foot cow parsnip stalks as spears and their lower ends as knobby rooted war clubs, we engaged in combat. After having chosen sides we battled up and down the willows beside the deep waters of the creeks.

Although Dad was always warning us about falling into the rivers and drowning we took risks and sailed on makeshift rafts to view the beds of the creeks for fish. One spring evening, Freddie Arnold, a kid from town, was helping pole one of our rafts along the Illinois River. His pole got stuck in the bottom muck and when he tried to yank it free, the raft went out from under him and he probably would have drowned in the deep water had not Bob finally thrust out a long willow branch and pulled him ashore. None of us could swim well enough to rescue anyone else. North Park's river waters were too cold to encourage anyone to become a proficient swimmer.

Later that summer, Bob accidentally stepped off into the deepest water at the ranch's old swimming hole on the Michigan River. It was just as Dad had said "deep and dangerous." In the ten-feet-deep water, none of us dared attempt to rescue Bob. We stood paralyzed. Bob had recently seen a Tarzan picture show in which Johnny Wisemiller was bound by evildoers and tossed into the Congo River. Using his legs to spring up and down, Tarzan was able to reach the shore. Bob did essentially the same thing. He would sink to the bottom, spring upward, take a breath on the surface, and sink again. I seemed to take forever to cross the deep water until Jay was able to get hold of him.

Never had we brothers been so happy to help dry off a brother and welcome him to a quickly started willow branch fire to warm up. Bob shivered so violently that it scared the dickens out of all of us. Finally, we got him warn. That event alerted us to the dangers of getting caught in deep and icy cold water in the river holes of the Michigan, sometimes sixty feet across and over our heads in depth. Dad had often warned us about them, but we still didn't inform him about Bob's escape for fear of punishment. He could ban us from the rivers, and we did not want that.

Bob told us that when he nearly drowned he'd seen the giant trout "Grandpa" in the depths of our swimming hole. Many times we had done our best to catch this monster trout. He was nearly a yard long, and on occasion during our so-called swimming we'd glimpse him in the deep water. Our constant challenge, Grandpa gave us reason to head for the old swimming hole with its crude diving board. I became incensed when people fished without our permission in the swimming hole for I feared some stranger might catch Grandpa, who I knew was at least a dozen pounds of German brown trout.

All of my growing up days we schemed to get that giant fish, devising and planning new ways to net or hook him. Devil-pitchfork barbed spears, lines with numerous hooks of worms, and set lines of minnows all proved fruitless. Although thwarted, we never gave up getting him since he was large enough to win the weekly big fish contest of the *Denver Post*. The prize was a real rowboat, something we all craved. Eventually Grandpa became a ghost-like myth since we knew for sure he was there but never clearly seeing our elusive prey.

At Camp Big Chief we had a tree house atop a huge alder tree since we wanted to see all we could along the railroad tracks. At the base we constructed a lean-to. From there we'd climb spikes driven into its trunk to our platform fifteen feet off the ground. Sometimes we'd camp overnight at Big Chief whose location allowed us to spy. Usually, when we were small boys we'd get spooked by animal sounds, rained out, or get too cold, we'd end up walking and carrying our blankets the half-mile back to the ranch house.

Being on Richard territory, however, provided security. This was my place. I loved it, and I felt the need to protect and defend it with all my might. My brothers and I guarded what was ours, but we freely shared it with friends and with those who asked our permission.

We sometimes assembled in the dense trees to throw cow chips and to ambush cars on the highway as they crossed the Michigan River Bridge near town. It scared the heck out of drivers when we rose up along the bridge and pelted windshields with big chunks of dry cow dung. After having dunged a few cars, we'd vanish into the willows. Sometimes from our hiding places deep in the thick willows we'd watch the sheriff's car drive down by the bridge, stop, and then slowly cruise back to town. Even tall and scary Norm Woodruff couldn't catch us in our familiar willows. Our raids were hit and run, then hide and watch, and then strike again in another place where it was least expected.

Larry who liked to fight was a real tough scrapper. In times of boredom, we'd head to town to raid, sic Smokey on the dogs and Larry on unfriendly kids. Larry feared nothing and nobody. We had lots of kids who would rather join us than fight Larry and have Smokey, who was also a fighting champ, put their dog on the run.

In the middle of Walden on a fighting raid, we met one of the Hughes who claimed he knew how to get some easy candy. I thought he was just spoofing, trying to keep us from having Larry beat up on him. The Rosenfields and Richards followed him to Teen-Town Building behind the courthouse where he slid open a window and let himself inside. Not wanting to chicken out but scared to death of getting caught, I entered after he had opened the door. Never had I seen so many candy bars. We took handfuls of O' Henrys and Babe Ruth and fled across to the county shed area. I felt guilty but didn't have the courage to do the right thing.

We hunkered down, hid among the parked heavy equipment at the county sheds, feasted and watched the comings and goings of the Jackson County road crews. Such information could be important for future raids.

Finally, I sent brave Larry with a big stick to pound on Lillian Kiner's door. Today, I still remember that woman as a mean, nasty, fat ole thing who always cussed us out if we said anything to her on our walks past her little house.

Earlier her son, Chuckie, and daughter, Phyllis, had sicced their dog after us while Lillian stood on her porch and didn't even try and call the dog back. We had fought off the dog but hadn't forgotten. When Lillian came roaring outside with her big ugly dog, Larry shouted as he ran, "Shotgun Annie with a six-barrel fanny."

She set her dog after the swift Larry. Before it closed in for a bite, we rose from behind a road-grader blade and rocked the hell out of the dog. Smokey then caught her retreating dog just outside her gate and gave it a sound thrashing. She yelled, "I'm callin' the goddamn law on you white trash." Our revenge had been heartening. We departed Lillian's knowing that we'd be safe at Rosenfield's within minutes.

But first, we sent fifteen rocks high in the air; they were soon dropping from the blue sky and pounding onto another hated neighbor's roof. It was not Richard-like to pass an enemy stronghold without a host of Rocky Mountain rocks raining down on his roof.

We finally made it a day by also bombarding the new town dump-boss Grease's place, just a tar-papered squatter's shack on log runners in the sagebrush. Dad had said, "He had no right to be there since he didn't own the land. And the only way the man could be any dirtier was to be bigger."

Harry and I were determined to drive him out since his shack blocked Rosenfield's view of the highest mountains to the west along the Park Range. Grease finally dragged his abode to another location on the other side of town after we started pissing on his door while he was away supervising the dump or swamping up at the Elkhorn Bar in the evenings.

But that evening, afraid Lillian or Grease might come after us, we hotfooted into Rosenfield's yard and headed for our kid shack to plan our next raids.

Later, Lillian Kiner did call Dad. He listened patiently and he asked her, "What do you expect after you set your dog on my boys?"

One dark August night we raided people's gardens to test our courage and stealth and to see if we could get away with goodies and avoid dog detection. If dogs were alerted, Smokey could spring into action and repulse them. None attacked this night. Eating great tasting raw turnips and carrots, we march down that old rutted, dirt road back toward the Two-Bar's faint lights. But in the darkness we always stopped and bombed Herman's place one more time just for good measure, then ran like the night winds for home.

We usually got away with it. With most everyone saying, "It's just those Richard boys being boys." I think we had the devil-in-us as we looked for reasons to be violated in order to test and try and prove ourselves. Looking back on it today in my maturity, we seemed to dwell on the extreme edge of risk-taking. Perhaps we did our raiding simply because we could.

Chapter 10

HAYIN'

"Do as we say, not like we do!"

I looked over the green leafy treetops on the Michigan River to my east, scanning our huge flat meadow, reflecting on the biggest family effort in my growing up days. Haying season always started with the excitement a new big job brings. But it also ended with the great relief of having done what I was supposed to in a setting that was never the same two years in a row. Haying was always riveting and full of new people, work adventures, and the unexpected. But, I remember as a little kid I often thought haying lasted forever.

The Two-Bar soil dutifully nourished us. We watered the soil, fertilized it with cattle manure, while the sun shone on it across our meadows and pastures. Plants fed our cattle, and our cattle provided us with food. How we cared for our soil determined the quality of our ranch lives. While we appreciated the soil's productivity, we were still the ones to bring in our own hay crop. And as a kid I had to help as part of the harvest, enjoying the newness haying brought to each summer, but deep in my heart sometimes I was a bit resentful about how my August freedom vanished.

Draft horses provided the needed energy in our hay fields. We North Parkers were still using horses in the 1950s and 1960s to harvest the wild hay, two decades after people on the Colorado plains had switched to tractor power. Our harvest took only a month. To own tractors when they weren't used year around, according to my dad, would be too expensive.

A few days before haying, Dad and some of us would ride down on the Illinois River to drive in the workhorses, which had been free and wild since haying ended the previous September. As we approached the herd, they whinnied and raced off with a cloud of insects at their heels. Big chunks of green sod and black mud flew skyward from their hooves when the herd crossed soft places as they ran to escape us. It was as if they sensed the time of year. After we'd turned the herd, it was a swift horse race through wet sloughs, over humpy ground, and across soft pastures into the big corral up on the ranch hill.

I could feel my horse's sides heaving in and out as I stopped inside the gate and watched. The workhorses thundered into the outer corral, ran up on the big manure pile, and milled about. Their eyes were wide, their ears forward, and their muscles tense. Some jumped sideways. A few bucked and kicked. Such wild appearing beasts they were, compared to the gentle herd of horses we'd turned out at the finish of last year's haying.

There were browns, blacks, whites, roans, bays, and sorrels in the bunch. Some weighed over 1,700 pounds, other were as small as 800. All of them had names and personalities, and each worked as part of a team. Having to rope a few, we talked gently, letting them know we meant no harm. Eventually, we caught and haltered all the horses.

Teams of Richard draft horses pulled clanking iron mowing machines that circled the fields and cut the standing wild hay with sharp-toothed iron blades. After letting the hay cure for a few days, we then used horse-pulled rakes with curved steel teeth to comb the ground and to form the hay into long rows. Next, we got wooden-toothed sweeps powered by huge teams in place. Straddling the long rows of hay, the sweeps swept the hay up into large green piles. The piles were then put in front of a tall inclined plane of slanting poles. Up the sloping poles, a square-headed pusher powered by our most hefty horses pushed the hay, until it dropped onto the haystack twenty-feet below. There men with pitchforks called "stackers" arranged the hay into haystacks. Once a ten-ton haystack had been completed, we moved the equipment on to the next field and repeated the operation. Although haying usually lasted until the end of August it sometimes continued well into September. To cover all of our meadows and to make nearly a hundred rounded haystacks, took time.

Stacking wild hay was done each late July and August in a family effort. Illustration by David Hartman

Each July, Dad hired men for our big hay crew. New haymen, machines, and horses came together around our workshop and big red barn in our dirt yard. All of the activity seemed to revolve around Dad.

I could see in his dealing with men how he reflected his quiet leadership with dignity. I yearned to be in charge like him. Each of us boys wanted to be bosses at times. I was the worst with the "Big Boss Complex," Bob was right behind me. Jay, who never showed much interest in leading, was more interested in doing mechanical things.

Although Dad had the nucleus of a hay crew in his five sons, he needed additional haymen to work our many horses. Manpower for haying was scarce in North Park with its small population. In order to hire a dozen haymen, Dad would go to Denver or have men sent up on the local bus from skid row's McMillian Employment Agency. He'd have to be exactly on time to meet the bus in Walden or other ranchers would hire our men away.

One afternoon Dad was at the bus depot to pick up some haymen while my fifth grade teacher, Jill Peterson, was moving boxes and luggage to get to the newspapers for the drugstore where she worked that summer. A gunshot rang out on the sidewalk. The bullet from a gun inside a suitcase went through both of her legs knocking her to the ground. Dad helped get her to the doctor's office where it was determined that she had only flesh wounds, with no bones broken. Dad said it was the only case he'd ever seen of a suitcase shooting someone.

Some haymen when hired on would tell Dad, "Willard, I can drive a team of horses right up a telephone pole." But they couldn't even harness their horses after reaching the Two-Bar barn. Dad would promptly fire the men, for he wouldn't pay grown men to work for him if they didn't really know the first thing about working horses.

Often older fellows in their fifties, most of our haymen wanted some seasonal work at a place where they could escape the summer heat of the big city. Although the majority were winos from Larimer Street in Denver, they were a special breed of men from an older horse-working class of an earlier era. None of them had been too successful in life. Some had tragedy in their backgrounds. Most had drinking problems. With little hope for the future, they were usually broke, alone, and single.

Not lacking in talents, many of them had fine skills and experiences enough to earn a good living. Their main problem was alcohol. Dad and Mom had a saying about drinking, "It destroys people. The only way to enjoy a drunk is to be drunk yourself."

As long as our haymen stayed busy working and away from the bars, we couldn't have asked for better help. But if they couldn't work because of bad weather, they would go to the bars in town and drink. I saw it bring a total change. When they were drunk they became worthless, falling all over themselves, some having the blind staggers and the dry heaves around the bunkhouse. Many stayed sober until haying was over. Afterwards they went on a binge of drinking until they reached Denver or until they had spent all their wages. Booze made them crazed, and I just couldn't understand their attraction for the same rank stuff we boys had sampled from Dad's few bottles in the dining room cupboard. It tasted as bad as gasoline.

I recall seeing one hayman, lying in his own puke and urine, passed out on the gravel outside the bunkhouse. On another occasion, one had fallen backwards and had passed out in his wastes, unable to make it on to the outhouse. There he lay half undressed.

Haymen, however, showed affection for our horses and adopted them as their own. They talked to their teams with kindness and took special care to see that they were properly grained, harnessed, and worked. They talked about their horses as if they were their own kids.

The men showed respect for Dad, too, and treated him as top dog. If a man didn't like the boss, he quit and found new work. For men to stay around a ranch and work while backbiting and criticizing wasn't dignified or proper to the horse-working man.

The workingmen also treated us kids great. They probably treated us better than we treated them. They helped us, liked us, kidded us, and teased us. I loved listening to their tales of the big city life--wine, women, cars, work and the world. They were our summer friends who looked after us. By being around them, I gained insights into what it was like to be a man. Mom and Dad, who tried to tell us not to be too caught up with the workers because they hadn't done much with their lives, both advised me to take what haymen said with "a grain of salt."

The haymen reserved their very best behavior and manners for Mom. Hard working men who enjoyed eating big meals always found a good plenty at her table. They cleared their dishes, called her "Ma'am", and complimented her on the food. Very dedicatedly, they followed the rule of buying Mom a box of candy if they had forgotten to carry their dishes away from the table to her sink.

Mom expected the men to come in from the hayfield on time. Her grandmother, Lindy, had taught her that a woman's work was as important as any man's. By coming in from the field anytime they darned well pleased, men had no right to tie up a woman's day. Mealtime was set, and that was it. Mom was as strong on the subject as her grandmother had been. And Dad clearly respected her wishes.

For what seemed an eternity, I waited to grow big enough to help hay. The day finally came. Although someone had to help lift my harness onto the tall draft horses, I was puffed up with pride about being able to drive my own team. Jay seemingly had always been old enough to work, even drove our one green-and-yellow John Deere tractor to mow hay. Bob had been raking and even scatter raking before my turn finally came. But of course, he was older.

My first job as a hay hand was to rake downed hay into long rows. Our most popular field team was Red Shorty and Babe. She was a shiny black mare with a bright blaze face, a good worker, but was very high strung. Babe often jumped up and down, threw her head high in the air, and had a complete tizzy when excited. She often kicked and bucked in an empty-headed manner. I hated having to ask someone to help me bridle her when she held her head so high that I could not reach it. What kind of teamster couldn't bridle his team? To bridle her, I tried tying her head down low to a fence post at the stack, but Babe reared back and pulled the post out of the soft sod and still remained beyond my reach. How I wanted to grow taller so that I wouldn't have to ask for help. Eventually, by tying her halter rope low on a pole on the plunger head, I could get up high enough to put the bit in her mouth and bridle her.

Red Shorty, her teammate, was a stocky dark sorrel. Easy going and absolutely lazy, he was a perfect mate for the wild, empty-headed Babe. We said that Red Shorty did little more than hold up his side of the rake tongue during the haying season. His tugs were often slack as he trailed wild Babe. If I slapped Shorty with the lines, Dad would say, "Lines are for driving horses with, not for hitting them." If I used a switch on lazy Shorty, Babe heard it and went nuts, often pulling twice as hard and leaving Shorty far behind. I designed a sharpened willow branch with which I poked Shorty in the rump. Shorty responded appropriately, but Dad frowned upon my using a sharp stick. How to get Shorty to pull his fair share remained a problem my raking days.

I needed to learn fast and not let Dad down, so I wouldn't be thought of as some kind of "dummy" raker by my brothers. I tried with all my might to use good judgment on when to turn and avoid obstacles, how to keep from bending a rake wheel while turning around near small ditches, and when to dump my rake. I had to keep slack out of lines and to press the hold-down lever with my foot. It was a job that first taxed a boy's mind, but driving soon became routine. To learn hay raking, all of us Richard boys took our turns driving lazy Red Shorty and wild Babe.

I had difficulty sleeping at night because I was still wound up about work. I wanted to do a good job, to feel that I was carrying my share of the workload, and to not lose face. For me the inability to handle a team of horses would have been failure. I now felt a part of the haying operation and was no longer just a little kid who hung around and ran errands. I wanted to show Dad that I was capable of doing the job he assigned me. Driving a hayfield team was scary because it required more skill than just holding the lines as a team walked along some wagon road or across the meadow. I had a job to do, and the crew was depending on my doing it right. That my work was there for all to see, to praise, or to laugh at, was frightening.

At first, my raking was a mess. Sometimes I'd get too interested in driving and forget to dump the rake. Sometimes I'd get carried away with operating the rake, and the team would wander. Thankfully, Dad had great patience with me.

Many a night Mom and Dad could hear me talking in my sleep in the bedroom saying, "Shorty, get-up damnit, Shorty, Shorty." Even in my dreams I expected Shorty to do more than he would.

At the end of a long haying day, we Richard boys would hop on in a line on old Red Shorty's back. He was generally in a big hurry to get to the barn for his grain. The slowest loping horse on the ranch, Shorty would kind of jump up and down as he moved across the meadow. His gait was extremely smooth--like riding in a rocking chair. What a fitting end to a hard day's work.

After that first year, I was in competition with my brothers. We jockeyed to see who got what jobs in the hayfield and which horses Dad assigned. Although I lobbied Dad, I never knew whether I was to be advanced to a new job or would be stuck with the same job I'd done the past summer. As a rule, Dad kept us at the same jobs for a couple of years. We all wanted to move up faster, of course, and to prove our worth.

I worried that Dad lacked confidence in me. I could never tell what he was thinking, and he didn't talk a lot about plans. He and I were opposites. While I planned everything and told everybody, Dad seemed to keep all the future plans tightly in his head.

At school I bragged, telling kids, "I hayed this year..." as if I'd always done so. There was keen competition among ranch kids regarding what kind of equipment we drove. In swapping stories about runaways, haymen, and our jobs, we tried to make ourselves seem more important than we actually were. I did care and wanted ours to be the best hay crew in the Park.

Just like real men, we boys were paid a wage. I usually planned to spend my wages on hunting arrows and knives. My brothers were the same way in that they had already mindspent their money well before the first hay was cut.

Early in the haying season before leaving the fields to go home for our dinner at noon, we removed the harnesses from the horses when the insects were at their worst. Without the harnesses the horses didn't get tangled up and break straps while fighting flies.

It was a ten-minute ride to the house in our jeep nearly covered over with kids and men in coveralls. We sat on all the fenders, on the hood, on the top, and in every possible seat.

At dinner, the food quickly passed from one man to another around the big red-and-white oilcloth-covered table. Hungry men and hungry boys gulped potatoes, gravy, creamed corn, bread, roast beef, sliced lettuce, salad dressing, milk, iced tea, coffee, and chocolate pie. I loved having Mom's pie every dinner and special deserts for our supper.

"Old Maude about went nuts one time from those bad flies. I was sure she was gonna run," said Rudy, "Sure don't want a runaway with my mower."

"We had a few good ones with mowers," said Dad. He put down his fork, gave his little smile, and launched into the tale, gesturing with his thumbs as he talked.

"One year this Jack, an old circus hand, mowed. He always said, 'I can drive a team clear up a tree.' He was a real muleskinner, but had his bottle in the mower toolbox. We were mowing right below the house here, and Jack stopped his team behind the spring wagon, opened his toolbox, got his bottle, and was standing taking a nip.

"The team, Turtle and Myrtle, turned their heads, and saw Jack's eyes were off them. They gave a sudden jump forward and jerked Jack off his feet. One of the lines was pulled away, but he held on to the other as the horses dragged him. Jack couldn't hang on long. Then, Turtle and Myrtle tore off across the field.

"Runnin' top speed, they raced through the gate below the house here and headed toward the railroad track. When the mowing machine wheels hit the rocks near the railroad track, it spooked them worse. Then the wheels hit the first steel rail. The mowing machine went high into the air and came down smacking the second rail, breaking big chunks of iron out of each wheel. That slowed Turtle and Myrtle, but they didn't stop. They dragged the broken-wheeled mowing machine along in a big cloud of dust clear up on the ridge beyond the railroad tracks.

"Rocks flew. That bar holding up the cutter broke; it fell down and hooked the fence. They ripped off at least ten yards of wire and finally stopped, all tangled in fence posts and wire.

"Those two mares had run away the week before and I had just put them on that mower to take some vinegar out of 'em and work 'em down so they wouldn't want to run. Sure didn't take any spunk out of 'em either," chuckled Dad.

The folks encouraged talk at the table. I watched the men and listened as they rambled and boasted. Although there were some big windbags among the crew, there were others who didn't deal so fast and loose with the truth. Because we boys were discouraged from dominating the conversation, we listened and learned how men talked.

Holding the belief that a man had the privilege to quit the job any time he wanted, Dad also felt that it was a boss's privilege to fire someone whenever he saw fit. Whenever a man was not making us money, it was time to get rid of him. When Dad fired a man, he would simply say, "I'll give you your time," pay him off, and take him to town without explanation. Conversely, when a man quit, Dad never asked the reason why. Dad always felt that one's reason for quitting was a personal matter. I always thought things should be talked over and people given a second chance. But, I was not the boss.

Rosy-faced Dave looked up from his heaping plate and said, "Over to the Big Horn Ranch they're apayin' mowers ten dollar a day. That's a damn site more than anyplace in the Park." After swallowing a mouthful of potatoes he again burst out, "Willard, you know a stacker can earn twelve dollars over there and get in more work days."

Dad replied, "Well, if they are paying that kind of money, that's where I'd be."

"Funny thing about the Big Horn. It never rains over there, and you can work all the time," said Jay, winking at Bob across the table. Dad gave Jay a stern look, and he ceased his comments.

The men sat in the shade of the tall white bunkhouse until the boss came out. Then they either rode new teams to the hayfield or led them by saddle horse. Some rode the jeep down to continue the haying operations all afternoon.

The aroma of cut wild hay refreshed my senses as we passed over where Jay and the mowers had been. It was the perfume of my summer. Our hay was beautiful when it stood waist high and moved with the slightest breeze as a shallow sea in great waves. But when it was cut it clung to our socks and clothing like dried needles seeking revenge for our having destroyed its youth and beauty.

Crows, magpies, brown cowbirds, and blackbirds would often fly behind our equipment to catch moving insects, frogs, and mice. When we reached the field each morning, nearly every stack pen fence post was topped by hawks, black crows, or black-and-white magpies waiting for us to stir up a day's meal for them.

The blood seeking insects made it difficult for teamsters to handle their animals. On several occasions horses threw themselves while fighting biting flies. One horse would be standing and the other flat on its back on the ground. Often Dad had to go right the situation with downed horses.

Because of his "know how" Dad could do it all with our teams. He understood horses. He could get fallen, stubborn, and balky ones going and drive them. If someone was having trouble getting a team to pull, and the horses were seesawing the doubletree back and forth, Dad would sternly take over. Just by the way he spoke and held the lines, he told the horses something I never could. The horses would get down and pull their hearts out for him. The regular driver was usually impressed when Dad calmly handed the lines back. Dad could get horses to move objects we kids knew were impossible to move. He was always kind and firm with little margin for nonsense, yet he was never mean or unreasonable with animals. I was amazed at my Dad's keen sense of what could and couldn't be done. He didn't take chances, either. If the job looked too big, he'd use two teams of horses.

I constantly watched the sky and hoped to heavens it would rain as I rode my rake back and forth across the hay fields, dumping and dumping. Rain was our best hope for a day off since we worked seven days a week. I became an excellent forecaster of North Park weather patterns. Watching potential rain clouds to the north and west, I prayed for rain. When a rain headed our way, I raced to the stack to tie up my team.

We usually hayed until about six o'clock each evening. By that time, our horses were tired, and everyone, except Dad, was hungry and anxious to leave the field. Sometimes I wondered whether Dad would ever tell me to unhook and stop raking. We unhitched the horses and tied then together for the ride to the huge red barn.

At suppertime everyone gathered in the ranch kitchen for the biggest meal of the day. Seeming to talk more, the men spent a longer time around the supper table.

"Sure that rain cloud was gonna get us today," Pete said.

"It just barely missed; went off across Brownlee's place. They really got rained out bad," Jay added.

"Jimmy sure got fooled. Did you guys see him come on the trot to the stack with his rake teeth up and tie up his team? Thought you had the afternoon off," said Pete with that twinkle in his eye.

"I wasn't the only one, Pete. I seen you and Jim come down off the stack and get your coats, too!"

"We will soon be in green hay and will need a day off because of the slow mowers," said Bob, knowing that Jay would react.

"All you'll see is our dust tomorrow," said Jay who was driving our one tractor and mowing a fast seven-foot swath instead of the horse-drawn mower's six. Mechanically inclined, he proudly cared for his tractor as if it were his baby.

Dad spoke up saying, "We've really been making good time. If the weather leaves us alone, maybe we can finish the big meadow next week."

"I'm always glad to get across the railroad tracks," said Larry.

"That's so you can hide in the willers better and eat gooseberries," said Pete.

"No, sir."

"Me and Jim seed you last year. Didn't we, Jim?"

"Big as life! Your team was tied up half the time to those willows back where only we'd see you from up on the stack," teased Jim.

"Bull."

"Larry does have a few neat tricks," said Bob.

"Paul does too. I always see him off that rake chasin' some animal in the willers," said Pete.

"I'm usually after a snake to get you with," I replied.

"You bring another one of those squirmin' things around me and it'll be your last, sonny!" We all laughed, having seen Pete in his baggy bib overalls and high-topped work shoes race out from under his hat, off across the meadow at top speed each time one of us sneaked up on him with a harmless gray garter snake.

Chuck said, "Let me tell you about the snakes we had when I worked over on the Drowsy-Water Ranch. Well, it's the only place I've ever worked where I saw snow snakes."

"Let's hear about 'em," said Jay.

"Snow snakes get about three feet long and live in snow banks. Because they're albinos, you know, they have red eyes and the rest of them is pure white--white as hell. 'scuse me Mrs. Richard. They are real tough to see in the snow. The red eyes give 'em away.

"Where they live is interestin'. During the summers, they're in the snow banks high up in the mountain peaks. Usually those banks don't melt all summer but just become littler and littler. This bunches up them snow snakes 'til they're crowded thick. Snow banks above timberline are just alive with the white critters. You can see red eyes peering in all directions.

"It's during the winters they get you. When snow covers the mountains, they move out in all directions doin' evil. On ski slopes, they lurk in soft snow and leap right 'tween the ankles of skiers. Along sidewalks and stairs, they dart out of snow banks and ram their slippery bodies between people's feet and ice. It's like stepping on grease, and people get bunged up. On icy highways they lay themselves flat and just let one tire strike their slick bodies causing cars to spin. Thousands of people die each year from 'em. Most people never see 'em or know what they do 'cause snow snakes are so white, sneaky, and lightening quick. So, next time you have a winter accident, look for those beady, red eyes Pete," said Chuck unsmiling.

"The heck you say," said Pete.

"Up here, we also have hoop snakes like they do in Utah, Pete," Jay said.

"You'll like these since you're so afraid of snakes, Pete," Larry said.

Jay continued, "Hoop snakes are strange. They roll down hills to capture their food."

"We were fixing a stack pen over below the Illinois ridge, when I spotted one rolling down towards us. It was in a big circle-like hoop, spinning down that steep bank headin' right for the fencin' wagon. It was goin' so fast I didn't even have time to shout a warning. At the base of the hill, it let go its tail and stretched out like an arrow. With its mouth wide open and fangs showin', it shot across the wagon toward our hired man. Luckily, he bent over to pick up a hammer just as the hoop snake sailed clean over his back and hit a tree. Its teeth stuck in that bark. Instantly, all the leaves fell to the ground; hoop snakes have the worst poison known. It's a good idea to keep an eye out for them hoop snakes when you're around here, Pete."

"You better stay up on the stack to be safe, Pete," Larry added.

"It could happen to you, Pete," added Jay from across the table.

"Horse feathers, you can't scare me with that kind of stuff," Pete said, pushing his chair back from the table.

"Why are you leaving then?"

"Got to get those plunger horses turned out. Thanks for the good supper, Mrs. Richard. I loved that lemon pie."

In the evenings, the men and Dad often played poker in the bunkhouse. How I dreamed of the day when I could play cards with them and maybe win some money. Eventually I got to. They all passed at my first hand, letting me win a pot. I grabbed the money, quit the game, raced to Harry's and took us to see a Durango Kid picture show. After that first card game they let me lose and taught me the hard game of men's poker.

In the hayfield meadows, I moved through a hay raking apprenticeship and got savvy enough to hold my own with the men in conversations. My third year of raking Dad gave me a beautiful team of roans. I was thankful to be emancipated from Shorty and Babe who had tested my patience. I showed everyone I could rake some serious hay with my good team, Bob and Maude. Strikingly beautiful red and gray mixtures in colors, Bob and Maude never slacked a tug and seemed to enjoy pulling the rake and me endlessly across the hay fields.

Once, however, I was on foot leading them and trying at the same time to open a tough gate, straining with all my might while holding their halter ropes over my shoulder. Bob moved closer and stepped on my foot with his huge hoof. I grabbed his halter to urge him to move backward. The big roan moved every foot except the one on my foot. He pivoted on mine, grinding it into the ground. My foot turned blue-black, and I hobbled for about a week. But I could never be mad at my wonderful Bob horse the most beautiful animal I ever drove.

The following year Dad bought a new tractor for mowing and transferred the old one to pulling a new twenty-one foot scatter rake. That summer on the old tractor I followed horse sweeps all over the ranch and cleaned up the hay they spilled. Although I covered every inch of the ranch meadows on the tractor, I didn't love tractors as Jay and Bob did. I asked Dad if there could be a horse job for me the next haying. I missed taking care of my team, talking to my horses, and singing to them. I hated hand cranking that old John Deere, siphoning gas, and listening to the thing pop, pop, pop all day long.

On North Park's many rainy days, our hay hands joined those from other ranches and congregated in Walden. They stood on the street corners, leaned against buildings, gabbed, and flocked back and forth between the Elkhorn and Corral Bars on Main Street. Some passed out in the gutters and against buildings. Public drunks gave a skid-row appearance to our small town.

Sometimes after the dishes had all been done, Mom and Dad would take us up town and park our car on Main Street between the two bars. We would sit in the car and watch the people go by. Somehow this activity fascinated Mom, but Dad preferred to wander off, have coffee, or visit with other ranchers.

One evening Jay, as a teenager, witnessed six fistfights in Walden. Our town marshal, Charlie Snow, calmly leaned against an automobile on the street, watched, and waited. He never broke up a fight that evening, and no one was seriously hurt. When the fights were over, back into the bars the fighters and spectators would go. Pretty soon, out they'd pour again to witness another fist battle.

On the peaceful side, I remember a lot of hay-hand characters who worked for us over the years. In 1944, before I could rake, we had a pair of hay men, Eddie and Willis. Willis would interpret for Eddie, who didn't stutter but talked so fast no one could understand his gibbering except Willis. Both stacked hay for us. If Eddie asked for exact placement of a load of hay on the stack, no one could understand him unless Willis was nearby to clarify it. Both men were extremely dirty and stayed that way. Hay seemed to poke from all the pockets, cuffs, and other openings in their clothing. They never cleaned up all haying. These seedy and destitute haymen took care of each other as though they were brothers.

I recall seeing Willis staggering down the road from town after having apparently spent all his drinking money. After he got some more cash, Mom took him back to town in our car. On the way he started telling her his troubles, and he had aplenty. She parked on Main Street. He started sobbing and spent nearly an hour crying. We kids were seldom aware of the hopelessness of these men's lives since we had never heard any man cry.

One haying, a tall skinny man called Rett had a fit in the bunkhouse. Everyone was calling it "Saint Vitas Dance." Dad began to wonder how Rett could drive a team if he were to have a seizure in the hay field. One evening a terribly fat lady, claiming to be his wife, showed up in a beat up old car. Seeing her get out of the car was a shock, as I wondered how anyone that size could fit inside a car. Finally, Dad had to fire Rett in order to get rid of him and his immense, pushy wife. As they were leaving, I heard one of the haymen shockingly say, "Fatty and Skinny went to bed. Fatty rolled over and Skinny was dead."

Desperate for help one season, Dad hired this strange-looking fellow with one wooden leg. He worked a day or two. Then a real downpour came, holding up the haying operation. Drawing what money he had coming, Ole One Leg, as I called him, hobbled down the muddy road to town and the bar.

He drank up all the whiskey his money would buy, but he sought more drink. "Hey, barkeeper, how about advancing me another drink?"

"I can't give you anything without security, Mister," replied Bert Quinn from behind the bar, "Do you have a watch?"

"No," answered Ole One Leg.

"Well, I can't very well let you start a bar bill without something in hock. If I did that, every hayman in here would drink my whiskey, quit the county, and I'd be stuck. I've been nice before and always got stung," said Bert as he looked across the bar. Bert's bloodshot eyes were half hidden by bushy unruly eyebrows.

"You make a killin' in here. So ya' don't really lose."

"I lose enough money in this here place just from broken furniture in the fights. Last week, I see'd a man hit over the head with a full beer bottle. Should have killed him dead, but I don't think he even blinked. Had a hard head that one."

"You've probably seen some tough ones," muttered Ole One Leg.

"You betcha! Last summer a man bit off and chewed up the glass top of a beer bottle in here just to win a bet. I saw it with my own eyes. It wasn't no trick either. I still can't get over that one. If you can do that, people will bet against you and you can earn a few bucks." There was a long pause.

"Would you loan me $5.00 on my wooden leg?"

"Hell, yes, that's good collateral. You won't leave town without that," replied Bert as he turned to the cash register and picked up a crisp five. The wooden leg and money were exchanged across the bar. Soon the money was back in the cash register, and more firewater was numbing Ole One Leg.

I recall seeing a strange car drive up in front of the house and two men climb out. As if wounded, one hopped toward the house. I noticed it was Ole One Leg without his leg, being helped by a fellow drunk. I got Mom who called to Dad.

"Willard, go see what those drunk fools want! I don't want them in my house."

Dad went into the yard and talked with the two men for a few minutes. They then helped each other back to the car and headed towards town. The water and mud flew high to each side as they obliviously hit all the mud holes in the road at top speed. Dad came into the kitchen.

"What was that all about?" Mom asked.

"Bert Quinn has a five dollar debt against that man's wooden leg," said Dad as he moved towards the telephone to call the bar.

Dad talked to Bert and agreed to pay him the money. Bert gave the wooden leg back, and Ole One Leg was able to work the next afternoon. After a couple more days, Dad let Ole One Leg go because his eyes were glazed over and his mind was on town and booze, not on haying. Sometimes our Two-Bar was just too close to Walden's bars.

One summer a drunk hay hand of ours stumbled across town to the east late at night and entered the Hampton Ranch house. He must have thought he was in our bunkhouse since it was also tall and white. He staggered upstairs, crawled into bed with one of the Hampton kids, and fell fast asleep. When he awoke the following morning, the man tried to slip out of the house. Howard Hampton, the father, saw the man leaving and asked, " What the hell are you doing in this house?"

"I'm one of Richard's haymen. Guess I got lost last night."

"Guess you did."

"I better get back where I belong."

"Guess you had."

Howard called Dad and teased him about keeping our darned haymen where they belonged and out of his house. Mom was horrified, but Dad just laughed.

When hundreds of hay hands came into town to join the already rough local population, Walden had real problems. To allow youngsters on the street alone at night was not safe. One haying season a man killed several dogs in town. This guy was a peeping tom, too. After peeking through the windows, he would catch the woman's dog outside the house and cut its throat. When the sheriff finally caught the offender and no one could prove anything, he was given a bus ticket out of Walden. To put them on that next bus was the way to handle many criminals and strange men in Walden, Colorado. Put them on a bus and let someone else deal with their problems. Our town and county didn't want the expense of holding suspects in jail, much less of feeding them.

Going to town on weekends was a big thing in my boyhood hayings. In addition to the hundreds of wino haymen in small Walden, there were timber workers from Missouri and Arkansas, oil-well drilling crews, construction workers, and a host of other hard living men. When the local residents were added to the mix, Walden was a wild and exciting place, especially on Saturday nights. All of the action took place on the one city block of Main Street.

Our haymen often told stories about their nights in Walden and their long winters in Denver on skid row. Their stories usually dealt with wine, women, and fights. Along with my brothers I took it all in, although I didn't really understand the appeal of that kind of life.

As the summer slipped on by, the newness of the men wore off, and the thrill of the early days of haying waned. I'd dream, watch the tree lined rivers, and wonder what was going on with all the animals there. I could hardly stand it. At every work stoppage or rainy days I sought the river bottoms. It puzzled me why the men sought town rather than fishing in their free time.

Pete was a good example of one who spent his free time in town. A good man, he had one big problem--a craze for wine. One year he came to hay for us in real bad shape, very skinny and washed-out appearing. Thinking he didn't look well Dad asked him, "How'd you winter?"

Pete told Dad, while I listened, that he and three other fellows had pooled a hundred bucks each, bought $400 worth of cheap wine, and rented themselves a small room in one of the flophouses in Denver. They went in some time before Christmas with their wine and stayed there four months, drunk, crazed, and dulled.

Near spring when the wine supply was depleted, they drew straws. The loser got a gunnysack, went down the back alleys of Larimer Street, and picked up enough empty wine bottles to trade in for a full one. After that bottle was gone, the next loser had to go bottle searching. Pete lost forty pounds because he never ate a solid meal. He also told us about his having seen caterpillars and big biting snakes on the room's walls during those months.

"I don't see how you do it, Pete," said Dad, shaking his head.

One day we were haying down in the small meadow near the Michigan River. The stack was about three-fourths finished as we neared the end of haying. Bob and I climbed up on the stack and visited with Pete and his buddy, Ole Jim. Things were slow since one sweep had broken down and the other was making long hauls for hay.

"Lookie yinder, the big meadow is all up and soon we'll be finished here," said Pete as he leaned on his pitchfork and gazed across the river at all the stacks he'd built with Ole Jim. The most recent ones were bright green, but older ones had sun-faded until they were a straw brown.

"Wish it wasn't so damn cold up here or I'd stay and feed cattle a winter or two," said Jim. He removed his hat, showing the many scarred puncture wounds on his forehead.

"Hell, Jim, you couldn't stand being away from Larimer, The Rescue Mission, and the bars," retorted Pete who always said exactly what he thought.

"Yeah, guess I'm too old for it, but you guys aren't. I suppose you boys could stay up here and feed cattle for your Dad the rest of your lives, couldn't you?" asked Jim.

Pete butted in, "Hell, Jim, they don't want to do that all their lives. Don't tell them that! It's a big, big world out there with thousands of places to work and things to do. There's more to life than staying in one place."

"I think Pete's right about getting out. But the safest thing to do is stay here and take over from your Dad when he gets too old to run this ranch," said Jim.

"There are five of us and this ranch can't really support more than one family or at best two," said Bob.

"Some of you are sure enough havin' to leave and do somethin' else. I think getting some education would really do you a lot of good. I didn't have a chance to. Did you, Jim?" asked Pete.

"No, there was nine of us kids and I've worked since I was thirteen. Had to quit school. Only job I ever stuck with was the railroad. That's how I got my little pension I live on each winter. I think learnin' something would be good for you boys even if you stayed on the ranch. Just makes you see better and think different," said Jim as he leaned against the backstop and spit rusty tobacco juice over his right shoulder. Thigh deep in hay, Jim was a leathery hatchet-faced man. Tall in his bib overalls, he was crowned by a brown city style hat, greasy around the band from his own sweat. His long sleeved shirt was buttoned to the top to keep hay out of his neck. Jim was a rather quiet man who seldom gave advice.

"What do you know about education and learnin'? You're like me, Jim--you ain't never been nothin' but a drunk."

"I wasn't always a wino. And I've learned a lot by listenin' and livin'. I've been all over these United States and did a lot before I lost my family," replied Jim.

Pete spit tobacco juice over the edge of the stack and continued, "Probably the best piece of advice I can give you guys is get the hell out of here for a while. Then come back, but at least find out what's outside these mountains. This isn't the entire world, you know."

"I think you boys better be careful with your drinkin'," said Jim.

"You're damn right! Look what it's done to me and Jim. A preacher can tell you drinkin' ain't no good, but he's sober and successful. Look at us, we're hay bums and have let liquor get aholt of us years ago. What a mess we are. We haven't hardly anything beyond the clothes on our backs. Everything goes to wine, and we ain't got no future or ever gonna have one. We'll end up knifed in an alley or frozen in a doorway. You want to be like us? Aren't we a fine pair?" roared Pete, his face getting beet red.

"You guys aren't that bad," I said.

"Don't kid yourself, Paul. If you'd knowed the stuff Pete and I've done and been through, you wouldn't even stay on this stack with us."

"We haven't seen you do anything bad."

"But you see us at our best, sober and putting out a day's work. The rest of the year we're usually staggering drunk, grubbing around, and doin' stuff you couldn't respect us for. We're fifty-year-old bums. Real winos," said Pete.

"Pete's right, and I hate to admit it."

"You damn right I am, and you guys had better take some advice from someone who knows. Don't let the liquor get aholt of you. It'll wreck your lives," advised Pete.

"Here comes a load up the slide. You better watch out," said Jim.

When the hay had all fallen off the pusher head and settled on the stack, Jim and Pete stabbed their forks into it, arranged it towards the sides, and smoothed it out. Bob and I started across the deep hay and toward the slide ladder leading to the ground.

Pete turned to us and barked, "Think about it. Do as we say, not like we do."

"OK," Bob said.

After my raking days, Dad put me to work as the plunger-driver, driving the largest horses in the field, Pet and Ribbon, a pair of 1700-pound white mares. Their muscles and a battering ram plunger pushed the hay up the wooden inclined plane slide allowing the hay to fall onto the growing haystack below. No longer one of many lonely rakers off in the distance, I was now in the center of the action with stackers telling me where to dump hay on the stack, Dad was close by sweeping hay loads in, and watching my efforts. I loved my big towering mares that pulled their hearts out for me, a skinny kid. It was a great year when I built confidence, and Dad allowed me to make tough pulls instead of taking my lines. I relished pulling the huge pole slide to the next stack pen, moving the plunger, and laying out the size of next haystack with Dad and the stackers. Although I had these tasks to perform, Dad still gave me messages to deliver and errands to run while the plunger team stood idle, hooked to a thirty-foot log pole. No plunger team ever had nor could run away with such a contraption.

Before heading home at noon, we'd unhook our horses and water them. At a big slough watering hole Mac told me, "Watch me get up on Ribbon's back while she drinks. No horse can buck me off in this much water."

Larry said, "Dad claims that she is like a zebra and can't be rode."

Mac slipped his foot onto her harness tug and slid onto Ribbon's back while she was gulping. As he grabbed the brass-capped upright hame, the huge cream-colored mare with a roman nose came unglued. Her entire body rose and twisted out of the water like a jumping trout. After only three hard shaking jumps Mac was up to his neck in slough water and sitting on the muddy bottom while Ribbon resumed drinking.

"Great ride, Mac," shouted Larry as he lent a hand to help the grizzled rider, "Dad knows our mares."

"Rodeo's over," said Bob as we led our teams to the stack pen and unharnessed them.

A big blue truck entered the haying operation the next season. The long plunger pole was attached to the truck's front bumper, replacing the horses. I drove the truck and used Pet and Ribbon only when the ground was too soft for the truck.

Once when I was driving the plunger with daring Larry on the top of an extra tall sweep load of hay, Larry fell off the hay and over the plunger head about half way up the slide. He became wedged between the poles and a cross brace on the slide. By the time I finally got the truck stopped, a big steel plunger roller was on his chest cutting his wind. The roller had to be backed off. A few more inches, and he would have been crushed. This close call scared the liver out of everyone. We ceased the load riding up the slide and we never mentioned the event to the folks. The thought of a brother being killed while I was driving was terrifying. I thanked God that the Chevrolet truck had quick brakes.

My dad was a fair boss and the only family member who didn't tease. Never unreasonable, he always gave me the benefit of the doubt and taught me how to do what he expected.

Mom fed well and treated the haymen as equals. They weren't just hay-bums to her; she liked all people. She did errands for them and provided an atmosphere they liked. It didn't take much to capture the hearts of men who had been kicked around a lot in life.

Finally, that next year Dad decided to drive the plunger truck himself in order to be at the stack where he'd have more time to help with repairs. I thought that he was just tired of sweeping every year.

That move thrust me into driving Topsy and Daisy, Dad's special sweep team. They had always been as steady and no nonsense as Dad. According to him, these big, jet black, and hard working horses had swept hay so long they could do most of it without a driver. Although I wasn't happy giving up my soft plunger job, I enjoyed having a new team to curry, harness, and pamper.

My black mares were by far the most wonderful team I'd ever driven. Quick and strong, they never slacked a tug. I never had to yell or slap one with a line, for they never lazed like Red Shorty. I used my ninety-six pounds mainly to counterbalance the sweep teeth up and down, moving back and forth on the long tailboard. Topsy and Daisy knew exactly what we were doing. Several times when I wasn't on the sweep, the mares would take off by themselves and head to pick up a windrow of hay. I'd race pell-mell and get aboard. The men said Topsy and Daisy were keeping me from goofing off. With my newfound friends, I moved a lot of hay that summer. Although they couldn't be ridden back and forth from the field, they were otherwise as prefect as Bob and Maude had been when I raked.

The following year Dad bought a fast, orange Allis Chalmers sweep tractor for moving hay. I drove it the entire year, sweeping most of the hay. Topsy and Daisy were there to sweep the soft ground and to prepare the loads for me to haul the long distances to the stacks. The stately mares worked, but the job wasn't as hard on them as before. I felt sad watching them standing idle around the stackpen and working only part-time. That noisy tractor moved a lot of hay, but I couldn't love it as I had my mares. I took more pride in our horses, decorated them, curried and groomed them.

In the years when we used exclusively horses, haying was a quiet operation as the machines glided over the soft meadows. We haymen could talk back and forth. The man on the stack could shout down to the plunger driver or sweeper to tell him where to put a load on the slide or stack. In later years, noisy machines shattered the peace I associated with haying.

After the last haystack was built, seeing the last of the crew leave the Two-Bar always left a void in my heart. I knew I would never see most of our haymen again. They had all said, "I'll be back next season," but I knew they wouldn't.

Haying had stolen most of my summer, but we had gotten our hay up. I was proud of my efforts and now free and had my wages to spend.

There were no mosquitoes after the late August frosts. The meadows had turned brown. The days were long with clear soft blue skies, cloudless. "When the hay was all up this fall," was a happy phrase to me. I looked forward to this quiet and clear time along our rivers when once again I could explore and be away from work.

The hayings of my youth were the times when I had to buckle down and grow as a kid. There was no hiding along the rivers or getting out of my job. During haying I, along with my brothers, had to measure up, doing the kinds of things city people think ranch and farm kids do every day. From late July to early September, I had to catch my horses in the corral, halter them, grain them, and after my breakfast harness them. I had to find a way to get them to the hayfield, hook them to machinery, drive them all day. Then I had to get my team back to the house at days end, caring for them on my own. It was a working, helping, and learning thing for a kid to do, building discipline along with family pride in being a serious part of something important to our survival. During haying, I was a part of something far bigger than myself.

Chapter 11

DOIN'

*"In this here shed, I'll have forty hounds.
Meaner 'an hell they are..."*

There I sat, scanning the country of the haunts of my sometimes foolish youth. Striking mountains rose up beyond the shanty buildings of town just outside the Two-Bar's gate. These reinforced how my life had been a combination of interactions with town people in those varied houses and my rural wanderings in the Park, exploring all the huge mountains encircling me. How lucky I had been being able to learn from our mountains and our Walden neighbors. My mind flashed back to the end of a haying season.

Walden, Colorado viewed from the Two-Bar Ranch
with the Medicine Bow, Never No Summer, and
Rabbit Ears mountain ranges rising beyond.

Paul Willard Richard

By the end of summer, Smokey would be following my haying machine hoping to get at the mice I uncovered when the rake removed the protective layer of hay. Then he'd pounce. While he enjoyed the hunt, I would be working and scanning the lofty mountains, wanting to go. As school and September neared, I craved to flee to the nearby mountain peacefulness. I was sick to death of haying, and probably most ranch kids across the valley felt the same. The 8,100 feet at the ranch wasn't high enough when 200 miles of mountains, towering up to 12,000 feet, offered nearby escape after the harvest work. Several of the escapes still stand out in my memory.

My very first camping trip to those steep mountains happened after one haying. My cousin Kenny Rae from Brush, our hired man K.C., Bob, and I headed to Red Canyon Falls in an old Model A Ford. We tossed our bedrolls in the back, rounded up our fishing gear and food, and headed off on the dirt road west of Walden late one cloudy afternoon.

Soon it started raining a steady drizzle. By the time we passed the Delaney Butte Lakes, the road was muddy and slick as snot. K. C's old Ford kept sliding sideways until a stretch of clay, slick as grease, finally stopped us. The car ended up with two wheels in the deep barrow pit. We couldn't get out by ourselves in the deep mud, so we walked down the road in the pouring rain to get help.

There was a set of buildings on the south side of Delaney Butte. An old red Farmall tractor stood in the yard beside a squat dirt-roofed cabin and low tan-colored log out buildings. Cow manure and clay mud had been used to chink the spaces between the logs way back when they were built in settlement days. The log buildings reminded me of our old cow barn.

We knocked at the screen door. Someone yelled, "Come in!" We entered, relieved to be out of the downpour. After we introduced ourselves, Mr. Yoder and K. C. went to see if the tractor would start. It wouldn't. They headed to the nearby

Manville Place to get some help. I waited in the kitchen with Mrs. Yoder, Kenny Rae and Bob. We boys were soaked.

"I've known your mother since she was a kid, and her parents, too, and even her grandparents for that matter. Guess I've known the whole Monroe, I mean Monroe-Richard outfit," said Mrs. Yoder still sitting and knitting, not offering a chair or to take our coats.

"Thanks for letting us come in out of the rain. It's really coming down," said Bob.

On the back of Mrs. Yoder's ancient rocking chair sat an old white chicken. It was just sitting there as the old lady rocked back and forth. Over on the kitchen counter I spotted two more hens standing by the sink. Six friendly dogs were milling about on the floor, seeking petting. A cat was on the warming oven of the wood-burning kitchen cook stove, another on the window ledge, and a third on Mrs. Yoder's lap. Six half-grown sheep, probably bum lambs, came out of the bedroom and jumped out the half-opened kitchen window. Soon they leaped back in a bedroom window, raced through the kitchen, and leaped out the kitchen window again. This tag game, bringing in mud, went on while we stood dripping wet and talking with Mrs. Yoder.

The leathery-faced woman was in her late sixties. She dressed in full black and resembled someone I'd seen in a painting holding a pitchfork with a somber old man. She worked in the Walden Post Office and knew everyone in North Park. She had a small house in town where she stayed during the long winters, since the roads were impassable to reach their tiny ranch. She loved cats, according to Mom, and during the winter months purchased a gallon of milk every day to feed them. Sometimes she had as many as thirty cats in her back room in town. She also took in every stray dog she could find.

Mrs. Yoder finally got up and put some wood in her cook stove after chasing two cats off the wood box. She then brushed the two red hens off her kitchen counter and started getting ready for supper. They squawked as they hit the floor amid the sheep and dogs. She asked us if we wanted to have a bite to eat. We assured her we were anxious to get camping as soon as the men could pull us out.

We soon left with K.C. for our camping spot. We made it to Red Canyon about dark, set up our tent, and spent one of the coldest, most miserable nights I ever remember. There weren't enough blankets and the ground was granite hard. Lumpy rocks and pinecones under the tent made it impossible to sleep.

The next morning's sun warmed us and dried everything. Fishing was good and we enjoyed the twenty-foot Red Canyon Falls. It was cloudy and chilly until the sun came out in late afternoon, but we caught lots of fish below the falls which were surrounded by striking red rocky formations. We could hook two rainbows at a time under the frothy falling water and land most of them.

We were in an aspen-filled wonderland with woodchucks, chipmunks, and deer. Despite the rock hard ground under KC's teepee tent on those rainy nights, it was a great first experience camping away from home territory, one that remains vivid in my mind as boyhood firsts seem to.

The next camping trip developed after seeing some 24-inch brook trout caught above the Rogerson Ranch. Dad, Doc Morgan, and John Riggen had caught them at Kelly Lake high up on the east side. The sight whetted Bob and the hired man's lust for big fish. Jay and I went along, too, toting bedrolls and cooking gear uphill to the timberline lake. A seven-mile hike up the narrow canyon took most of the day and wore us out. Carrying bedrolls was hard, heavy work since the canyon was so steep. K. C. was carrying two water pails of food, one in each hand, up the sharp narrow trail.

Growing Up Wild

Wrapped in my thin green army blanket I nearly froze again, but I did catch a 25-inch eastern brook trout below a big rock at the south end of the lake. Bats darted over Kelly Lake in the evenings as the cony rabbits, or pika as we call them, made sharp bleating tones from the jumbled rock piles below the canyon walls.

That night something prowled around the camp in the short stands of twisted pines, killed a bird in the brush amid a lot of thrashing, and scared the wits out of us. Bob knew he saw glowing green eyes across the dying campfire and sneaked the hatchet into bed while K.C. held his loaded pistol. I shivered in my army blanket all night. Sunshine and the morning campfire warmed everything at dawn.

Exploring was always more interesting than pole fishing and after catching the biggest trout of my life, why fish more? The next day I climbed the rocky wall on the west side of the lake and got myself stuck on a ledge out of shouting distance from those fishing below. I was afraid to go up or down for fear of falling. I clung to the cliff face deathly scared until I got courage to use finger-holds in the cracks of the rocks to slowly descend. It put enough fear into me that I vowed not be so stupid again. But from high up there, I had spotted an old tumbled down log cabin hidden in the timber below the lake.

Once back down, Jay and I searched the old cabin whose roof had fallen. The place had been infested with packrats in the rafters and woodchucks under the hand-hewed plank flooring. A jar full of papers and letters had tumbled from the packed dirt of the roof where it had been imbedded and now rested on the decaying floor. We dumped the papers out and Jay blasted the jar into a thousand pieces with KC's pistol.

Later, I learned the cabin had belonged to "Crazy Kelly" an Irish hermit who was rumored to have had gold. Kelly Lake and Kelly Canyon had both been named for the little man who lived alone. North Parkers thought he was crazy because he talked to visitors about living in heaven and didn't give a hoot about ranching. I thought the spot was so beautiful that maybe he was in heaven. Towering mountain peaks rose upward on three sides of his cabin near the large beautiful lake in its box canyon. He could see evergreen trees and open parks spreading downward in the canyon below his meadow for several miles. Weeks later when we learned more about Crazy Kelly, Jay and I wondered if we'd missed a treasure of gold by not reading the papers for clues, codes, or maybe even a treasure map.

The next day, Bob was fly fishing along the big rocks on the west side of the deep lake while Jay and K. C. built a small raft from the logs they found in the evergreens on the east shore. Near dark, Bob was casting his white miller fly at the circles left by rising giant brook trout on the water's plate glass surface when he hooked something, which abruptly took off up in the air. It flew wildly around and around as he reeled it slowly inward. On the end of his line was a little brown free-tailed bat. He took it back to camp to show Jay and K. C., knowing they wouldn't believe him unless they actually saw it. Then he released it, squeaking off into the night.

For supper, K. C. prepared two blue grouse he and Jay had killed with rocks along the trail. The meat was great, and we talked around the fire of all the big trout we'd catch from the raft the next morning. Finally, we crawled into bedrolls and watched the fire turn to red glowing coals, captivating all of our eyes. That night under my cold blanket how I wished to be back on the Two-Bar instead of this strange place.

That next day, K. C. and Jay caught all the two-foot-long eastern brook trout they wanted from their raft. Trout as long as a man's leg floated aimlessly in the greenish water of the timberline lake. How happy we were for the huge fish when we walked out and started home in the ranch pickup.

When we passed the Rogerson Ranch buildings, Jay told us a too weird story he had overheard Cecil Arnold tell our folks.

"Cecil was doing remodel work out here with the fighting Rogerson's. Mom told me they battled like a couple of cats. They had earlier gone to town leaving Cecil alone. He ate lunch, flopped down on their couch, and fell asleep. They apparently thought he was gone when they returned. First thing he knew there was a lot of screaming and yelling. Cecil peeked over the back of the couch that separated the living and dining rooms and saw Ole Lady Rogerson dart out of the bedroom buck-naked with Bob right hot after her. Both were cussing and hollering up a storm. Poor Cecil watched him chase her around and around the dining room table kicking her in the butt every time he got close enough. Finally, she got out a door and escaped into the yard. Poor Cecil stayed all hunkered down on the couch until he could escape," related Jay. I thought that tale showed a sharp separation of natural peace in the wild from human happenings of no beauty.

After hearing our stories of freezing in bedroll blankets at Kelly Lake, Dad bought World War Two army surplus mummy sleeping bags. I had to try one on our next trip with Harry. I thought I'd died and gone to heaven with the difference it made in comfort and carrying weight.

We took the new sleeping bags on a late spring trip to Roxyanne Lake. We used bows and shot a dozen beautiful cutthroat trout with blood-red sides. There were hundreds of these native trout making easy targets as they spawned among the rocks. We put them in a nearby snow bank for safekeeping.

That evening, we watched the bats fly low over the water catching white miller moths while the fish leaped from the still water also grabbing the moths. Most of the time the surface of the lake was patterned with bull's-eye rings from jumping cutthroats and feeding bats.

That cloudy night something clawed on Harry's sleeping bag and awakened us. We remained frozen, trying to figure out if it was a bear or mountain lion. Finally, the moon appeared in a small opening in the clouds allowing us to see a fat porcupine licking and scratching the tarp covering Harry. He scared it off, and we figured it was getting salt from the tarp.

We returned from our camping trip refreshed and primed for more since backpacking with light sleeping bags was such emancipation from the old heavy bedrolls. We were better for the experience, and the mountains were little the worse for wear.

Looking back on this and my myriad of other camping trips, I loved them so much in spite of the difficulties. Later, as a teacher, I took my students on such camping field trips, teaching them natural science and biology while we shared the experiences of outdoor life and beauty that had so captured me as a kid.

On other trips in my youth, I took some big and unwise risks, learning more about the wilds and non-ranch people. I took Larry, Harry, and Tony Zangari to Rainbow Lakes the first week in June to catch big spawning trout in the inlet. We wanted to enter the Denver Post Fish Contest. We were still after that rowboat. We had rushed the season and struck deep snow in the dark timber. For over the last two miles it was chest deep and we often fell through the crust, finally arriving at the lakes wet to the waists, and finding the lakes totally frozen over. A thirty-foot snowdrift rose between the two lakes and we luckily found a bare outcrop of rocks to sleep on that night.

Squaw wood was gathered from the trees after we decided to dry our clothing and stay because it was too late to leave. It was a bitter night on the rocks as the icy winds roared across the snowscape fanning our fire. Crouched inside my sleeping bag, I was up on my knees most all that eternal night seeking body warmth above the frigid granite rocks below. What absolute misery. Yet, I dared not complain since it was my idea to come.

Hurriedly the next morning we were readying to leave when Tony discovered his shoes had been too close to the raging fire. The front halves were shrunk and wrinkled not allowing his toes entry. Harry finally cut off the portion ahead of the laces. The morning's retreat was awful for Tony as his shoes just fell apart. We ended up wrapping his feet in shirts and assisting him the long four miles back. He had big blisters and no big trout like I had promised. There was no chance of getting that boat.

That fall after haying, I again talked Tony into visiting Rainbow, Slide, and Roxyanne Lakes with me, and this time he brought along extra shoes. Fish and fun were our goals as we took along three packhorses and two young hay hands, Jim and Derry, who had worked with me in the hayfields. On a crisp September morning, we walked out of the Norris Place with the horses carrying everything and arrived refreshed at Rainbow Lakes. Gigantic trout could be seen cruising the shores in clear water, but they wouldn't bite. That night two horses spooked in the timber and broke loose, heading for home. We chased them for half a mile through the shadowy timber clad only in our underwear before luckily capturing them.

All during the trip we had to worry about and baby-sit the horses, which I hated doing. I had had to bring the nervous horses along or the two former hay hands wouldn't come. They didn't want to carry gear on their backs uphill seven miles.

We adventured around and climbed the adjoining canyons leaving Derry behind. As it turned out he was a big eater, in fact "a human garbage grinder," consuming our stores at an alarming rate unbeknownst until we reached Slide Lake the third day. There, Tony and I concluded the move to the next lakes could only take place if we lived on the trout we caught. That night it snowed eighteen inches, burying us in a world of whiteness and scaring the dickens out of the others. My sleeping bag was the only one not soaked and I stayed in it while the others attempted to build the fire. Finally I had to get up and gather squaw wood from under the snow covered branches and get the fire going. All three neophytes campers thought I had saved them from freezing to death.

Thinking the snow might melt quickly and still wanting a crack at the big cutthroat trout ahead, we spent most of the next day drying sleeping bags around the big fire.

Jokingly, we sent Jim out with Tony's .22 rifle telling him to get us some deer meat so we could eat. He surprised us by coming back dragging a small doe. We had fresh deer meat thanks to Jim, but little other food, thanks to Derry.

The next day I couldn't find any trail markers in the much deeper snow above timberline. So we turned back. We spent more time hunting for the snow covered trail and trail blazes on trees than moving that long day. Eventually, we fumbled our way seven miles in the deep snow to the Norris Place in the cold twilight carrying the half deer we hadn't eaten.

The other three were all afraid that we would get arrested for killing a deer out of season. Paying no attention to their worries, I told them, "No game warden in his right mind would be out in this much snow."

When we reached the Norris Ranch, Tony, who was nearly snow-blind told me, "I don't think I want to risk more camping trips with you. Each one scares me a little more."

Despite my companion's misgivings, I was pleased to have had the trip, but Derry and Jim didn't share my delight and had had enough camping. So, I decided that from them on I wasn't going with non-ranch people, except Harry. These guys couldn't cook, couldn't build a fire, couldn't gut a deer, couldn't handle a horse, and couldn't be tough when things went sour. I didn't want to nursemaid people any more. However, I planned to use my head better in checking the weather and using horses that were more trouble than they were worth when trying to enjoy peace in the high mountains.

Old Harold Rosenfield, who had lived like a mountain man often said to me, "Paul, campin' can be your best friend or your worst enemy." Harry and I were camping buddies and at ease with what came in the wilds.

Camping trips after haying was over were about as close as most of our neighboring ranchers came to actual vacations. Many headed to the hills when the hay was up, when the mosquitoes were gone, and when the fish were really fat from having feasted on hordes of insects all summer. But mostly we ranch people needed a break between haying and the upcoming winter.

I seized every day I could before school started, exploring the hills and freely taking of nature's offerings. While camping I was rich without gold and happy without wealth. The wild and pristine places around North Park where I camped seemed to become a part of me.

I camped a lot with Harry and my brothers. Our tonic was the peaceful wilds where we kids were refreshed. There we also learned self-sufficiency far away from our comfortable Two-Bar. There, in the wild mountains, Richard boys better understood themselves and sensed their true fiber. As in a cold winter storm, North Park wilds revealed one's true character for all to see.

Many years later as a teacher of biology, I was able to get my students out into the natural world on many camping and exploring field trips to enrich their lives. My growing up years had allowed me to see how young city people needed such growing experiences, not scary ones like some of mine as a kid, but ones to develop a comfort, understanding, and love of the natural world. Such trips had allowed me to grow and later made a terrific impression on my young students, mainly because I was at ease in leading them in outdoor ventures.

After Labor Day, however, North Park school captured us all. Every morning on our walk through town to school, we barked at the dogs, crowed to the roosters that people had in their yards, and threw rocks at town dogs, cats, and rusty trash barrels along the snaking alleys. We were full of "the dickens," looking for something to use our youthful energy on after school.

In seventh grade, one day we were walking home from school and saw a strange man at work constructing a small new house and shed between the Rosenfield's place and town. At my urging, Larry boldly approached the man and sought to find out what he was up to.

"Hi! What are you buildin'?"

"A shed, if you'll use your damn eyes," said the man, who was a squat and wiry fellow with bushy dark hair and snappy brown eyes. He appeared to be in his forties. Not a large fellow, Herman Pittington was less than friendly, unsmiling, a banty rooster of a man.

"Are you going to live here?" I asked.

"What the hell does it look like? Are all you kids blind like you, four eyes?" he asked.

Suspiciously and disdainfully, Herman answered a few other questions. Finally he proceeded to elaborate on the half-built shed nearby and its future occupants.

"Inside this here dog shed I'm gonna put forty hounds, meaner'n hell, they are. And if you snot-nosed kids get to messin' around here and stealing, I'll set the whole damn lot on you. They'll rip your asses apart!"

I said, trying to be brave, "I don't much like hounds and don't think you have any call to name me Four Eyes." Instantly leaping at me, Herman forced me against the half-built building, shoving his forearm under my chin and drawing his clenched fist back to hit me.

He yelled, "I don't much care what you goddamn like. I'll knock all your teeth out if you ever sass me again. Understand!"

"Understand."

Slowly he lowered his fist and let me go.

Speechless, we ran. We clearly saw that he had no dogs, yet. We also recognized a challenge since he had humiliated me. We made plans as we watched the unfriendly dirty little man do his shack building. He talked nasty to us each time we spoke to him calling us "White Trash." Continuing to threaten, he finally said, "Stay the hell off my damn property!" Then he set posts to mark his land and to block our narrow path that had once led through his place to school. All of these were slowly making us his enemies.

One Saturday morning Larry, Jimmy, Harry, and I decided to see whether Herman would make good his promise. We walked up the road and ran on our old path across his property. He dropped his tools, scrambled for rocks, cussed, and in vain sent a stream of tennis-ball-sized rocks after us. We sought refuge several hundred feet away in the Jackson County road equipment storage area. Among the rusty yellow road graders and old trucks, we planned our reply to his barrage. Armed with slingshots, we hid there behind the machinery that surrounded the south side of Herman's yard and waited.

At last, Herman came out from behind his shed to use his newly constructed privy, which had posts set deep in the ground to prevent us from pushing it over. At least, that was what he had said, "No damn kids are ever going to upset my damn toilet."

When our antagonist was in his new house-with-the-half-moon, we sent a hail of small stones onto the outhouse roof and raised puffs of dust where our rocks hit the parched ground. We remained hidden and reloaded. The privy door soon flew open. When we launched another volley, and made a few more hits, Herman took cover behind his hounds' shed.

He soon emerged to hurl big rocks towards us. Herman had a good arm, Zipping out, throwing three or four rocks, and then darting back behind the shed. He'd then throw a few big rocks over the top of the shed in our direction to keep us pinned down. Next, he would peek around the side of the shed to confirm our location. Finally he would fake and bolt out of the opposite side of the shed, blast us with rocks, then seek cover and repeat his attacks.

"I'll get you damn kids, and when I do I'll knock the holy hell out of every one of you shits," Herman screamed. He seemed to be getting madder by the minute. His yelling was scaring us, making us think he was crazy mad.

Harry bravely yelled back, "Herman, you mustard brain! If brains were gasoline, you wouldn't have enough to prime a piss ant's motor scooter!"

As his screaming became more loud and nasty, we decided to get out of there and run for the ranch. We had covered the first hundred yards rapidly when from behind us came Herman at a dead run, heaving big rocks. He screamed, "I'll get you little shits, sure as damn hell I will."

We ran through the ranch gate, turned left, and raced into our big red barn, sliding the door shut behind us. Through the darkness within, we ran instinctively to the ladder leading to the hayloft. Once we were up the ladder we made ready to flop hay over the loft opening. Herman's cussing broke the silence which had prevailed below. Herman shouted vile threats and talked loudly to himself. We easily heard his movements as the sound of heavy boots echoed on the plank floor. He searched for us below in the main horse stalls and slammed the doors to the grain bin and tack room. At last he found the ladder.

Except for Larry, we were all terrified. I prayed that Dad or Jay would come to the barn and save us. As Herman's foot found the second rung of the ladder, Larry blasted his upturned face with five gallons of dusty oats. Herman half fell and half jumped backwards to the floor with a thud followed by gasping, coughing, and more awful cussing.

"That's just a sample of what you'll get if you try coming up, you mustard brain!" shouted Larry.

"We have pitchforks up here too," yelled Jimmy.

Herman fled the barn. We descended and ran into the dazzling sunlight after him. His feet moved even more rapidly when we stopped and shot small rocks at him with our slingshots. Trotting, he left little puffs of dust at each step as he retreated. We continued the chase and closed in behind him. Frequently he stopped and loosed a rock or two at us, and we returned a volley from our slings.

The chase lasted until Herman was within a hundred yards of his house. We then stopped our pursuit and fell into the soft dirt and sagebrush along the shoulder of the road, where we laughed and tried to catch our breaths. We played in the dirt and boasted of our great victory. We discussed time and again our personal feats and maneuvers. As we talked, we made boy battle maps in the soft North Park dirt with our fingers.

After the barn skirmish, Herman began to construct a six-foot board fence along both sides of his property facing our ranch and the Rosenfield's place. Along the top of his wall he laid two strands of sharp barbed wire. Atop the flat posts and boards, he also placed broken glass and roofing tacks. The other sides of his property had already been securely fenced with high barbed wire. In our boy minds, the fortified appearance of his property showed us that Herman intended to keep us out and defend his evil fortress against our attacks.

So, at night, we used a gunnysack to brush the broken glass from the fence top. Then we folded the gunnysack over the sharp tines of the barbed wire to render the wire tines harmless. We would boost cunning Harry or daring Larry over the fence to spy on Herman, to swipe his good wood for our arrow making, or rob his carrot garden. In the blackness of the night, we'd steal silently away like Blackfoot horse raiders.

The road from the ranch to town now meandered between Herman's place and the county shops. When Herman constructed the board fence, he created a blind corner. Herman then built a large sawhorse blockade across the road to force us outward from the corner. Soon after Herman erected his barricade, Jay moved it aside. The next day when Herman put it back, Jay, who was now driving, ran through the center of it with our Willy's jeep. Although Herman produced other barricades of various descriptions, Jay, in the little Richard jeep, promptly enjoyed breaking through them. Herman finally put up steel pipe and cinder blocks to block our path, forcing us to drive away from his fence.

Dad had finally had enough and talked with the sheriff. After the sheriff had sized things up, he told Herman that he couldn't block a county road and that Dad could take him to court over it. That ended Herman and Jay's battle of the barricade.

We boys were in awe of our Jackson County Sheriff, Norman Woodruff. To us he appeared as one of the old-time lawmen of Dodge City as in the picture shows. Tall and quiet, Woodruff wore a wide-brimmed hat above a glistening badge. The revolver on his belt impressed us and gained our immediate respect. We knew who was in charge of the law in our county. At six-foot three, his size and his authority made us all a bit fearful of doing anything really terrible.

The war that ensued after the arrival of the Pittington family as neighbors was a thrilling endeavor for we wild boys. After supper, we usually received permission to go and play at the Rosenfield's. Mom and Dad were unaware that nightly we were carrying out battle maneuvers against Herman, our archenemy.

We met at the Rosenfield's where we drew up detailed battle plans. Each boy got a different assignment and orders. Our goal was to force Herman to move, make peace with us, or to shape up. Since he didn't know how to talk peace, didn't depart, and wouldn't change his unfriendly ways, he brought onto himself total kid warfare.

One favorite plan of attack was bombing. We would load up on rocks and sneak to the southwest side of Herman's property close to the fence around his fortified house. At the same instant, we'd all release our rocks as fast as possible. The trick was to see how many we could have in the air at one time. Then we'd disperse into the machinery as the heavy stones bludgeoned his roof. We could hear the bam, bam, bam as all those rocks pounded down.

Herman and his wife reacted instantaneously to the barrages. They'd issue from the house and start throwing rocks in various directions. Herman heaved rocks and shouted threats and cussed. He always threatened to call the law and have us all thrown in jail. When exhaustion or lack of targets forced them to retire back into the house, we'd again arm ourselves with rocks. The same performance would be repeated, and we'd then run like the wind for the Rosenfield's.

Late one night, we all were going to the picture show up town. Of course we loaded up on rocks, as was our general procedure before we passed Herman's. We bombed his place and ran for town. Sheriff Norman Woodruff had been sitting in his car near the county sheds, watching us do our rock and run.

He pulled up under one of Walden's few dim streetlights beside us and got out of his car. Towering, he strolled over to us three Richards and two Rosenfields. He looked us over with an unsmiling face, placed his hands on his hips, and said, "Will you boys please leave Herman alone? You know the man's crazy."

From under his western hat, his unsmiling face and eyes looked in turn at each of us. We said, "OK." Then he got into his car and drove away. We decided to leave Herman alone since we didn't want to be on the sheriff's bad side. There was no action for a couple of weeks as unwelcome peace prevailed.

After school several weeks later, Larry, Harry, and Jimmy were walking past the Pittington place. Herman leaped on top of his chicken house roof and threw rocks at the unsuspecting trio. One big rock hit Harry in the back, another hit Larry in the leg. Jimmy escaped injury as all three, under a shower of rocks and cussing, made it to the Rosenfield's.

Outraged, we decided to disregard the sheriff's warning. If we were leaving Herman alone, why should he be allowed to suddenly attack? For Harry and Larry, who had both been hit, we sought revenge. At first we voted to burn his place, but we decided that kind of action was a bit harsh and could land us in jail. Finally, as revenge for injuries, we settled on Indian warfare against Herman.

We hid in the sagebrush and used arrows, spears, and rocks on the Pittington fortress. We made nightly raids, using a ladder to scale his glass-and-wire fortified fence. We made arrows from his wood, then shot them into his house the following nights. By day we avoided walking close to his place. But at night we quietly attacked from the dense brush. After we had launched attacks, we'd fall flat in the sagebrush. He could never spot us in the darkness.

One night we directed a major arrow attack at his house. We shot about a dozen arrows into the front. One arrow broke a window and entered his kitchen. Herman didn't come out. Later that evening, we returned for our second arrow attack. Larry had made fire arrows by putting rags behind the tip of the arrows and soaking the cloth in gasoline. He crawled close to Herman's house, lighted his arrow, shot it into the front door, then withdrew, leaving the arrow burning. The rest of us fired a few arrows into the door and then withdrew.

The next day Sheriff Woodruff came down and talked to Dad and Mr. Rosenfield. Woodruff and Dad agreed that no adult with good sense would fight with a bunch of kids. But we kids were going way too far when we started shooting fire arrows into Herman's front door, riddling his house with arrows. So Dad, in laying down the law, made his point that we were to use no more arrows. We stopped the Indian arrow raids, yet a low-key war still simmered.

Near the Fourth of July we purchased firecrackers, including two-inchers, five-inchers, and cherry bombs. On our way home, we couldn't resist lighting a few five-inchers and tossing them over Herman's fence. After all five-inchers weren't arrows. Of course we ran for home. By the time we arrived, Mrs. Pittington had called and told Mom that we had blown up one of her chickens with dynamite. We denied using dynamite. We readily admitted using firecrackers, but we hadn't tossed them near her chicken yard. I felt falsely accused of having killed a chicken.

Larry and Harry sneaked up to Herman's place and investigated. They found no sign of a dead chicken and no trace of feathers scattered about. Dad wasn't home, but we knew there would be big trouble when he heard about this one two days later.

We decided that since we might be punished for killing Herman's chickens, we had better really kill some. The next day, we gathered glass coke bottles, five-inch firecrackers, and sneaked through the sagebrush to Herman's chicken yard. We lit three firecrackers, dropped them into coke bottles, and threw them in with the chickens. Glass flew in all directions, but not a single chicken was killed.

When Dad got home, we explained everything to him. Taking our side, he too believed no chicken had been killed. We were glad and promised not to throw any more firecrackers near Herman's.

While we usually moved in groups or pairs, I was walking home alone toward Harry's a few days later. Herman waited in ambush and chased me by the county shop. He was obviously trying to catch me to beat me up. Luckily, I saw him in time and just barely outran the man. I was scared to death, for this attack was different from our usual long-range warfare. Later Mom told me that it was illegal for an adult to hit a minor. I didn't think Herman would care whether I was fourteen or twenty-one.

Soon we acquired the ultimate weapon against Herman. We designed a firecracker cannon. The principle was that of high angle fire. We elevated a six-foot piece of water pipe to the proper degree and tied it with bailing wire to the Rosenfield fence. Pittington's place, which was half a block directly southeast of Rosenfield's, was within easy firing range for the cannon. We put a few round stones, bolts, or marbles into the muzzle end of the pipe. We inserted a large firecracker into the barrel end of the cannon. The fuse extended out of a small hole that we'd bored into the side. We then bolted the back end of the pipe closed. Before long we artillerymen were making direct hits on the Pittington house. Herman couldn't match the range of our new weapon. The firecracker cannon was effective since we could blast Herman from safe territory. For more than a week we bombarded him. Finally, we exhausted our supply of five-inch firecrackers.

After the firecrackers gave out, we used the same principle with BB-guns. We wired them to the Rosenfield fence at the proper angle and sent copper BBs onto Herman's house anytime we pleased to pester him. We kept the pressure on the mean little man.

His family was composed of two sons and a wife, Peg, who was so skinny she looked like an escapee from a concentration camp and was just half there mentally most of the time.

One day Mom and the hired man's wife were driving around the blind corner when our car clipped a black pup. The little dog half-dragged itself under some county road equipment. Of course Mom stopped to see how badly it was injured. Peg came out and joined them. The pup looked as if it would to be all right. Mom said, "I'm sure sorry we hit the puppy" to Peg, who she had never before met.

Peg, the "Stick Woman" as we boys called her, opened her mouth and blasted, "That's OK, but it wouldn't be if it had been those Goddamn Richards. They come by here a hundred miles an hour an' don't care who the hell they kill."

"Really," Mom replied.

"Yeah, and you know they have the law under their thumb being ranchers and all."

"Thanks for tellin' me. I'd better get going."

We boys knew the Pittingtons were "on the county dole", and we all looked down on that since Herman was able-bodied, but seldom worked. He faked some sort of disability. However, we knew that he could run like the wind, work on his own place, and throw rocks like crazy.

Many a morning we spied on them, watching Peg, dressed in only a sheer nightgown, stagger from the house with a steaming hot frying pan in one hand. She'd cuss and corner a female goat against the fence, milk into the pan enough for gravy, and then return to the house. My oldest brother, seeing the wretched woman half-clad, would say, "Twenty-seven, twenty-seven, and twenty-seven, wow, that's enough to drive all the men insane."

She did call once to complain that Mom's sons' attacks on Herman and our tantalizing were "spoiling their romance."

The Pittington sons, Ben and Joe, were half-baked too and often joined in rock throwing. The whole lot was a bit "off their rocker" as Dad said. They surrounded themselves in summer with visiting gypsies in tents and other transients who stayed in small trailers and parked in their fortress yard. Herman's War often involved some of these others throwing rocks on his side. It dragged along off and on for years.

As we older Richard boys drove more and walked less past Herman's place on our way to school, we didn't bother Herman as much. He mellowed a bit and stopped a good deal of his rock throwing, too. Still, on occasion, we would loose a rock attack, beat on his fence, and pound the nearby empty fuel storage tanks at night just to remind him of his self-created war.

Having an outside enemy just past our gate who could be truly dangerous made us cunning and alert. It also contributed to our kid unity in our doings.

One topper was the championship of our dog. No matter what kind of canine Herman came up with--and he had a parade of many--our dog, Smokey, always trounced his dogs. It stuck in Herman's craw to see his dogs run for their lives and his front porch, whimpering every time we came by with our proud Smokey. We, in our arrogance, felt like we were kings of our end of town since we had such a wonderful dog at our side and had taught Herman a lesson.

Today, when I think back on what we did, I smile to myself knowing that most of the time we had been proud ranch kids, living in our dream world freely doing as we pleased. Two wrongs in our misdeeds never made it all right. But as an adult, I now realize how our dealings were way out of line as we behaved in such dangerous ways. I often shudder, thinking of what we got away with in our battles with Herman and others. But, those times and days were far different from today when such things in any city would probably put us into serious trouble with the law. That time and place still doesn't excuse how we pushed our freedom and sense of superiority beyond sane limits. It was, after all, a time when we considered ourselves brave Indian warrior boys.

Yet today in my adventurous heart, I am glad to have survived those times of combat, misdeeds, and camping that helped give me such strong confidence in myself as a grown man.

Chapter 12

HELPIN'

"Paul, there's nothing wrong with those cows."

I walked back east on the sage covered ridge. Rocks, rounded and colored, were scattered amid the tangled blue sagebrush. Pausing to sit atop the buck-and-pole fence that faced the bunkhouse, I again sat remembering my few ranch duties and those characters having worked for us as hired hands.

Our ranch helpers were many and similar to unhatched eggs under an old setting hen. When they first started working, we'd watch and wait for them to hatch and develop into great helpers. Those who didn't hatch were "rotten eggs." We had plenty of them. Some cracked early, never having left the shell before Dad fired them. Those who developed and made it into the later stages of helping the Richard family were worth watching.

A host of hired single men came before us and ate at Mom's big table. Hired hands never lived in the house with us, always the bunkhouse or nearby cookhouse. At times Dad seemed to have one man coming, one going, and one working. The folks had little patience with problem help. When Dad spotted the rotten eggs, he quickly sent them down the road talking to themselves. He tolerated, and I enjoyed knowing, a passing parade of ranch helpers.

The folks often talked of someone coming along and planning to stay and work for years. For a hired man to do that, however, he had to have some money to invest in livestock as a personal stake in our ranch. Few did. Usually, after a year or so a ranch family would move for one reason or another, often involving kid problems. Single men didn't last even a year. They had itchy feet once the newness wore off and usually wanted to seek their fortunes elsewhere.

K.C., who lasted an entire year, came to us after the big Hitler war. The bald, blue-eyed, square man would spend hours telling sea stories. Dad, who had grown up with K.C. in Brush, Colorado, knew him well. K.C. was strong as an ox, a hard worker, and good with kids, but, "he had a screw loose in his head someplace," Dad said.

K.C.'s U. S. Navy service during the Second World War hadn't helped. He told of sea battles in the Pacific Ocean after which his job was to shovel the dead bodies, guts, and severed parts of dead people off the decks of ships into the churning ocean. Never having heard such gory stories, I listened intently. Mom didn't like to hear them, but we boys encouraged K.C. to talk and talk. He was a jolly good storyteller with a wild look in his eyes that fascinated me.

His problems had increased because of his stay in the U. S. Navy. He had a total hatred of navy doctors. He told how they experimented on all kinds of navy men, including him. K.C. told of seeing a sailor swinging around on the lines of the ship's superstructure one day. His conclusion: the doctors were experimenting on the man and had given him a shot of monkey blood.

All of his problems could be traced to the doctors or to his wife who had left him while he was in the service. He told Dad one day that he had wilted on our haystack because the navy doctors were after him. They had flown over the haystack and activated the tubes that they had placed in his body during the war, causing him to wilt flat in the hay. Since he didn't want them to gain total control again, he had to quit and move someplace else. Without question, Dad paid him off and K.C. escaped the evil ones.

Later he came back after having worked in a lumber camp up by Gould for most of a year. During his visit he was the same old K.C., full of stories and fun. At night he said he could see the faces of navy doctors inside the flames of the lumber camp stove each time he opened the door to put in more wood. Now he was fleeing again. They were after him and had caused sawdust to come out his chest while at the Gould lumber camp.

He told us he had tried to escape the devious doctors. One day, he drove his jeep without a top the nearly hundred miles to Fort Collins. He frostbit one ear on the trip, since he didn't wear a hat that December day. The trip to Fort Collins had thrown them off of his trail for a while, he said. Soon he ended his visit with us and moved along to keep ahead of his pursuers. Years later he passed away in a mental hospital in Wyoming.

On our ranch there was always plenty for me to do, but most of the jobs didn't pay me anything. On the ground of our five-acre rambling ranch yard, seemingly millions of old square nails had accumulated over the years. My first opportunity to earn extra money came when Dad offered cash for picking up nails. I gathered nails by the can full and sold them at a dime a can to Dad. Larry got my cans and sold them back to Dad. Then when Dad mentioned how well Larry was doing picking up nails, Mom told him that she had never seen Larry picking up any nails. Larry lost his profits, had the seat of his pants warmed, and we all learned about the value of working.

Dad placed the nails and other scrap iron beside the log shop. He would sell them to a Jewish peddler who sold fresh fruit and purchased horsehair, animal hides, and other junk from us twice a year. Mom said, "Willard would rather argue and trade with that old, tight Jew than eat when he was hungry."

When we boys were at loose ends with nothing to do, Mom would shoo us outside saying, "If you're bored, go do something, but get out from under my feet. I've work to do."

With my brothers I often spied on our hired help, even watching through windows when they milked the cows. Dad paid them from $125 to $175 a month, furnished electricity, provided meat, eggs, and milk if they juiced the cows for us. We'd get up in the mow of the cow barn where we could watch and listen. Often hired men cussed or talked to themselves and the cows. Sometimes they had a snort of booze from a bottle that they had hidden while getting the milk to split between our family and theirs. Bob and I often tried their hidden booze until we drank from a whiskey bottle that one of them had apparently urinated into. We spit and gagged on that salty swill and swore no more nipping on someone else's opened bottle.

At the cow barn I walked on the tall corral fences with my brothers. The highest pole was at least six feet off the ground. Seeing who could walk the most poles without falling off, I practiced walking around the several acres of corrals. Sometimes I walked poles while waiting for Dad to finish milking his cows.

As a kid I always enjoyed hanging around the hired men while they worked, providing conversation while giving me insights into how they did different jobs on the ranch. I learned there were many ways of doing every job, and some were better than others. That even applied to milking our cows.

On a summer evening after a big rain, while I was walking the slippery pole fences, I planned to climb on top of the milk barn to look for baby birds in the swallow nests stuck to the gray logs there. I tried to be careful not to make sudden noises and spook the cows the hired man was milking below me. I needed something to hoist myself up onto the roof. There were two bare copper electrical wires leading into the old 1880 barn.

I touched the first one. When I grabbed the second to pull myself onto the slanting roof, it knocked me off the pole fence. I dangled in mid-air as the electrical current raced through me. Finally, I came loose and fell to the ground. There I sat a long time in a fresh pile of cow manure, unable to move, and breathless as if all the air had been sucked out of me. When I was able to walk and talk, I told of everything, including the sky, having turned blue-white as I had hung on the hot power lines. My brothers kidded me about my getting a "large charge" out of climbing on the cow barn.

Mom scolded me when she heard about it. "You could have given yourself a heart attack doing that. Don't you know anything about electric lines?" I didn't.

Even though I learned to milk those cows, I couldn't measure up to Dad's skill. He could milk a cow fast without a hitch and put a three-inch head of foam on a bucket of dirt-free milk. At thirteen, I always got dirt in the milk, no matter how well I had brushed the cows, and I only got half a bucket from cows that wouldn't give down their milk. Often the bovines kicked me and my bucket, seeming to dislike my slow milking. I hated those milk cows, and they knew it. I would have rather died of rickets than to milk them. But Dad kept sending me back, again and again.

My problems with the milk cows were not totally my fault. One evening earlier as I was slowly milking, Larry, Jimmy, and Harry had made a running attack on my cows. They threw rocks as they raced past the open door of the barn and hit the cows. My cows, thinking I'd hurt them, immediately kicked me and my bucket. Milk was all over me. No matter how cute my brothers thought the raid had been, from then on I had big cow problems.

The milk cows didn't trust me. They kicked at my slightest error and swatted me with their tails while holding back milk the family needed. Wondering why the cows were giving so little, Dad would do it himself, returning with a full foaming bucket saying, "Paul, there's nothing wrong with those cows." The next day I'd get half as much if I escaped alive from the deadly kicking. How thankful I was whenever a new hired man milked all the time.

During my teenage years we had a continuous line of hired help. They were as interesting to me as any picture show I ever saw up town. All were unique in some way, giving me something to think about.

Way back when I was just a toddler, Mom and Dad had a sheepherder who milked for them. The Mexican, Fermin, had worked many years and always had handcrafted items he wanted Mom to sell for him. The items came from his son in prison, of whom Fermin said, "Fine boy, fine boy; killie only one man."

Dad told me that as a young man, Fermin had found two men branding his boss's cattle with a running iron on the King Ranch in Texas and shot them both dead as he'd been instructed. Having killed two rustlers, he got off Scot-free.

Dad was impressed by how Fermin sat a horse, as if he were a natural part of the animal. He was covered with scars from knife fights he'd had in Denver bars and alleys. After going to Denver one fall, Fermin didn't return to the Harper Ranch. Later, Dad learned that Fermin died, having been run over by a car after a knife fight on Larimer Street's skid row.

A black man, Andy, had helped us for one season. Jay, then a little kid, asked him, "How come you wash and wash and that black never comes off, Andy?" Mom refused to feed Andy on the back porch as he insisted, but forced him to eat with our family at her table where all men were fed. She told him, "Andy, I haven't time to dish up food and cart it to you on the back porch. You have to eat with the rest of us, whether you like it or not."

Later, from Texas and all grouch, Bud used a bullwhip on our cattle. Dad put a quick stop to that and to Bud's tenure as a hired man.

Marty, a dirty wild-appearing brute, took our car to town in order to get a drink of whiskey. Dad had the sheriff pick him up. Afterwards with wide glassy wino eyes he said, "I didn't mean no hurt. Just had to wet my whistle. You just fired the best goddamn man you ever had, Willard."

Dad just kept driving him to town, replying, "I know you're probably right."

I enjoyed a husky cowboy called Raymond, who worked for us one spring. He didn't know much about ranching, but he thought it was glamorous. When we moved cattle, he thought he was on the television show "Rawhide." Always referring to "riding the range," he made phony picture-show cowboy talk. He just knew rodeo reflected the true ranching business, too. Mom told him, "Any similarity between rodeo and the real livestock industry is small." She tried to set him straight, but he wouldn't listen.

Stiff in the hips, Raymond didn't move too swiftly. He wasn't crippled, but he was as slow as a snail and had a hard time getting going. At the end of a branding day at the Norris Place, Dad and Bob were roping cows that had long, grown-out feet and were trimming their hooves back to the size of a cow's regular hoof. One cow was wild as all get out. Dad roped her by the neck, Bob caught her heels dumping her, and they held her stretched out between their two horses. Raymond did the trimming and then took the ropes off. When he removed the last rope, she jumped to her feet and took him. She had a red ring around an eye, and two long horns, and she was fighting mad. There was a lot of cow there, and her ten hundred pounds went right after stiff Raymond. With the cow breathing down his neck, Raymond ran forty feet across the corral like an Olympic sprinter and dove between the poles of the fence. I had never seen anyone move that fast. After that we all called him "Rapid Raymond."

Another spring Dad made me help a goofy hired man build fence in the wet insect-infested meadow near the second railroad bridge. Earl J. Smather's favorite saying, which he used nearly every time he spun a tale, was "I'll tell you what's the flat smack dab goddamn truth." He told non-stop tales.

Earl wanted to finish a stretch of the fence in six-inch standing meadow water when it started raining. I headed for the wagon on high ground telling him, "I've got enough sense to come out of the rain, Earl."

"I'm finishin'!"

I watched him continue putting up the wire on the posts in the mist. He was bending over getting his pliers out of a bucket when lightning struck a quarter-mile up the fence, knocking him head over heels in the water, and he wasn't even touching the barbed wire fence. After that, he was afraid of lightning. Anytime rain clouds appeared close, he went in a dead run for shelter.

I also remember grizzled old Mac who never shaved much and looked after our cows and batched at the Norris Place one fall. Taking a bath one day in the kitchen, he was sitting naked, soaking his feet in the galvanized wash tub in front of the roaring hot cook stove when the neighbor lady, Florence Irvine, knocked on the door. Mac just yelled, "Come in!" and when she did, she received quite a shock. She was looking for help because her hired man was lying prone in her front yard. He was refusing to get up or leave after she had fired him. Later and with Mac's help she eventually forced the nitwit off of her place.

Running a ranch was a difficult task for a widow woman. Florence relied on Dad who advised her and sometimes sent us boys to help her. I knew that he didn't want to go himself. Her constant whining drove me to distraction since Mom never

Growing Up Wild

whined about anything. Florence played the poor widow-woman role to a "T".

Once Bob and I helped Florence along with her two sons, who fought like cats and dogs, the daughter Iris, and their half-witted hired man brand calves. When we arrived, we had to fix the corrals, build the fire, and get the cattle in from a bog of a meadow. Florence didn't have a horse that would turn a calf nor did she have a saddle for most of her horses. Bob rode bareback and half of us chased the cattle on foot. We succeeded in finally getting them in about noon, when branding should be about over. We had a long day with her whining, the boys' fighting, and our wrestling huge calves. Exhausted, Bob and I agreed that doing work Dad's way was wonderful. Once our hired man Kip got established on the Norris Place, he could help them. I didn't have to, much to my relief.

Kip was a great milker. To my delight, he seemed to totally enjoy milking. He worked for us for several years, running the Norris Ranch each summer and working at the Two-Bar the rest of the year. Kip who was competent and easy going, always slapped his knee when he laughed. And he laughed a lot. Whenever I saw him he was wearing a blue Levi work shirt and pants. He wore his straw hat properly turned down at the front, the brim over his eyes. Having class, he came as close to suiting Dad as anyone who ever had worked for us.

His wife, Charlotte, was a little uppity. She thought I was uncivilized and in need of reforming. I had constant clashes with Charlotte and her two daughters, Jannette and Joyce. I called Jannette who was thin, "Bones," to the horror of her mother. I clashed with Charlotte on everything from describing the fall aspen colors as "egg yolk covering the hills" to our shooting of dogs. When Larry once threw a wooden pistol and killed one of her chickens, she raked him over the coals. When complaining to Mom, everything that happened, she blamed on us. She used to lock up her pets saying, "I'm protecting them from you Richard boys." A bossy woman, she exerted her authority by banning me from her house for brief periods after I had yelled in disagreements with her.

With our viewpoints being as different as water and oil, I teased and battled Charlotte. Overall, she was good for me because her ideas were strong, and she had guts enough to fight for what she believed. After a year, we came to appreciate each other, giving some respect to each other's ideas, but the battles never ceased between us. As the years passed, I think we both looked forward to our hot conversations. If there was anything I loved better than fishing, it was debating something. Mom said that Charlotte would come down to my level in arguing over some issue. I didn't understand what Mom meant, but I sure enjoyed my battles with Charlotte.

Mom and Dad would not come to a kid's level and argue with us, and they also kept their distance from hired help, never allowing too close a relationship. Mom always said, "If you get too close, they are here all the time, almost moving in."

While Kip and Charlotte worked for us, we also had "Crazy Jim" Hunsinger as a single hired man. He lived in one room that had an outside door off the side of Kip's and Charlotte's log cookhouse. Everyone knew he wasn't right in the head. However, he was totally harmless. Yet, he huffed, puffed, and grunted all the time. With beady eyes set in a round white-whiskered face, he peered timidly outward. His bib overalls gave him the shape and posture of a giant blue beetle.

Since Dad couldn't get any other help that spring, "Crazy Jim " was it. He nearly drove Mom nuts, as he would huff, puff, grunt, and talk to himself at the table as we boys snickered. He'd never pass the food. When someone tried handing him a serving dish to pass to someone else, he either dipped some of the contents out with a spoon or ignored the passer.

In the middle of conversations he'd butt in with loud statements that had nothing to do with what was being said.

One morning when we were talking about going to school, Crazy Jim butted in and said, "Oh, God! How they hollered and laughed back in Illinois..."

He seldom looked up from his food. He'd just continue to shovel food in, grunting and puffing while muttering to himself. Because Mom wasn't amused, she wanted Dad to find someone else. But I thought Jim was a riot. One day he came in and asked, "Bob, did you see me up town last night?"

"No, Jim, I didn't."

"Well, you hadn't better of seen me up there, 'cuz I wasn't," said Jim, laughing wildly and rolling his eyes.

We used to lead him on just to hear the strange fellow talk. He'd talk the duration of an entire meal and never really say anything. Dad finally made me stop egging him on.

Kip could hear Crazy Jim talking through the thin door adjacent to their living room in the cookhouse.

"That's sure a nice fire."

"You dern betcha it is!"

"Sure was a hard day, wasn't it?"

"You bet, I'm kinda tired."

"Yeah, I guess it's time to go to bed."

"Let me bank the fire and you shut off the light."

"OK."

"You can shut off the light now."

"Now?"

"Uh huh."

"We'll see you in the morning."

"OK, goodnight."

"Goodnight," said Crazy Jim to himself.

Those conversations between Jim and Jim amused Kip, who would just howl when he repeated them to Mom and Dad as he delivered our half of the milk from the cow barn.

One day I was pairing up cows and calves in the meadow and driving each pair past the haystack where Jim was flanking hay onto a hayrack. Jim started talking to me as I rode past. I'd drive the cow and calf a quarter-mile beyond him and push them across the river. When I returned, Jim would still be talking and pitching hay like crazy, as if I had been right beside him the whole time.

He finally retired on Social Security, lived in Walden, and patrolled Main Street in his tattered bib overalls. He wore his baseball cap pulled down over his eyes, his white whiskers stuck out in all directions. Huffing, puffing and talking, Crazy Jim talked to anyone who'd listen, to those who wouldn't, and to himself. He was a real nuisance with whom I talked every time I saw him on the street. What was going to roll out of his mouth next was always a mystery.

Finally, he got himself in dutch. At first, he was stopping people on the street. Then he started cornering everyone and talking and talking. Strangers didn't like having a funny old man intrude on them. He then started showing tourists photographs.

"Want to see a picture of my grandson holding his own?" The pictures showed his little grandson urinating. Town folks finally decided to do something about him. The city fathers told Crazy Jim that he couldn't hang around on the street anymore.

Jim was funny, and I missed him. Although he may have been strange, he was totally happy, he never once became angry, and he never complained. Today, as an adult, I think when I got old and goofy, I'd rather be oblivious Crazy Jim than some bitter, crabby, eccentric old guy.

Married couples came and went rapidly during my boyhood years. Harry and his lazy wife, Fern, left in the middle of the night. A few days later the law was looking for them. That they weren't married either shocked Mom, who said, "I knew something was wrong with that outfit with her still in a bathrobe at ten o'clock in the mornings."

Rudy and Martha and their rat-sized dog "Snipper" also left suddenly. A few days later Dad noticed saddles were missing from our barn. They had quit the country, and Dad was really mad about the loss of his saddles.

The Vossler's, who were great help and clean, had good furniture as well as a good dog. Mom said that you could tell a lot about people by their dogs. Bad people never had good dogs and vice versa. When Larry and Jimmy kept locking Vossler's son in a rabbit hutch, his mother went wild trying to find him. Chewing tobacco that Larry and Jimmy gave the boy broke the camel's back. Shortly thereafter, the Vosslers quit and departed our ranch.

Dad's parade of workers included Bones Clark who, to our horror, openly goosed his wife in front of everyone, constantly teased us, and inflicted hard "Dutch rubs" and horrible iron like pinches. Jay loved working with Bones who was more interested in tinkering with cars and machinery than working with cattle. His daughter was the most dim-witted and unattractive of girls. I got a hard licking for using my big mouth to point out how stupid she was. Afterwards, when Dad told me, "Rosemary can't help it," I always remembered to think as I pleased, but not spout off in running down someone who couldn't help the way they were.

The Reeds, who came to work one damp spring, had at least eleven ratty unkempt kids. In stair-step order, they followed their mother about the cookhouse. Mrs. Reed was a gaunt worn-to-a-frazzle woman who appeared exhausted all the time. Judging from her sunken-in eyes circled with black rings, I thought she probably needed months of rest. They had literally nothing. They lived on beans and cornbread. Mattresses on the floors served as beds. I never saw them use sheets. The older boys wore their dad's worn-out shoes and shirts. Of all the people who ever worked for us, they were the most down and out. They never had an extra penny to improve themselves or their condition. Everything earned was used to keep that big family eating. Within six months they moved back to Arkansas. Dad was glad to be rid of them. Mom was furious that they had left the cookhouse with crayon markings on all the walls as high as the tiny kids could reach.

Even as a kid, I thought my parents should have helped these down and out families in more ways, but I had no grasp of how to do it. My parents in their Depression era thinking felt that giving them a job was enough, not wanting to get involved in their living arrangements. After seeing so many problem-ridden people as our hired help, my thinking to this day as an adult has grown into a great empathy and concern for the working poor.

Another timber worker, Tom Gray, sought a job from Dad one winter. He said he had four kids. When they came to move their belongings into the log cookhouse, however, kids just kept getting out of the car and truck. Dad didn't think they would ever stop coming. There were a total of eight. They weren't in as bad a shape as the Reeds had been.

The Grays worked for us during a long cold winter and one summer. Tom was an excellent hardworking man. He'd been a heavy drinker and a bad drunk for years. Because he wanted to get away from town and the bars, he decided to try ranching work. Unfortunately, we lived too close to Walden, and he ended up in the bars anyway. Late at night, his wife and kids were always making the trip uptown to get their dad out of the Elkhorn Bar. To pry him loose from the bar was almost impossible until it finally closed at 2:00 a.m.

Sadly, we watched the man's drinking continue to degrade his family. Although they were always broke and owed everyone, he still went to the bar. Mom hated it, yet he was never drunk on the job and worked very hard. Dad didn't have any excuse to let him go. In fact, Tom had more energy and talent after drinking all night than many people who worked for us did sober. After a year, he went back to timberwork, continued to drink, and eventually died of alcoholism.

Before they left, the two youngest Gray boys, Bruce and Ed, were playing with the hatchet in the woodpile beside the cookhouse. They were about five and seven years old. Bruce, the older, told Ed if he put his hand on the block he'd cut off one of his fingers. Ed did, and Bruce cut it off with one swift whack. Mom and Norma Gray rushed Ed to the doctor in town, but it was a clean cut and nothing could be done to save his trigger finger

Their high-school-aged son, Dave, who was about as ornery as we were, battled us in rock and coal fights in the shop when he came to fill their coal buckets. When I'd shoot arrows so close to him that they stuck in the wood beside his hands, he'd retreat from the coalhouse. Then his mother would come fill the bucket without us bothering her, causing us to feel terribly guilty.

We used to throw rocks at the outhouse when Dave was inside. And, he'd fling rocks back when he came out. Once when we threw rocks at the outhouse, Mrs. Gray, not Dave, came from inside. Because Dad was disturbed by that incident, we stopped throwing rocks at the outhouse.

Later, Larry chased Joan Gray to her cookhouse door and shot an arrow at her, pinning her hair to the doorjamb. Norma Gray opened the door, unpinned Joan's hair, and broke Larry's arrow. When Dad heard about that occurrence, he took away Larry's bow and arrows.

As an adult looking back on that incident and others, we boys were clearly clueless, thoughtless, and stupid about what could have resulted from our antics. Our youthful mistakes clearly often ended in unusual good luck, something that could not be counted on in our futures.

The Doves worked for us and Dad said, "I have to set stakes to see that Mervin move." It was wintertime, and the work was feeding cattle. If he took most of the day for a half day's work, who cared? Dad did care, however, about the dozen relatives who soon moved in with them in the other house. As I listened to the folk's disapproval, I took it upon myself to drive the Doves out. Jimmy and I threw rocks at some of the kids, who were packed into the log cookhouse. Of course, the folks were not home when slow, plodding Mervin Dove chased us. When we sought refuge back in our house, he tried to break the sunroom door down in order to get at us. After we had told the folks, Dad used the event as an excuse to let the "slow-motion man" and all his relatives go. After the Doves departure, I had to help feed the cattle on the weekends. From that time on, I was very careful about who I helped run off.

Our next man was really different. Eddie Van worked on the run, knew cattle, and even had some livestock of his own. From a family of pioneer North Park ranchers, Eddie knew exactly how to do the jobs assigned to him. To work with someone so ambitious and fun loving was wonderful. Eddie impressed me by treating everything on the Two-Bar as if it were his own. Unfortunately, he decided that working on a ranch didn't provide him the opportunity to get ahead and accumulate more cattle. He moved to La Porte where he started a sheet-rocking business. I felt that Dad should have made Eddie a great deal to get him to stay. But Dad didn't do things my way.

When it came to ranch work, Bob seemed to be Dad's favorite. He and Bob were always off doing something with the cattle, while Jay was busy working on cars or machinery. Although I felt left out at times, I enjoyed the rivers and chasing wild things more than doing any work.

I did, however, get a lot of pleasure out of helping on the ranch even as an unpaid family member, always seeking praise and approval from Dad. He rarely gave any compliments or kudos. Trying to earn some recognition from him kept most of us working at our best.

Growing Up Wild

Each fall, Dad purchased steers that had to be branded, dehorned, and vaccinated. We boys were all required to help sort and run these new wild critters through our thirty-foot log chute into the red squeeze chute. I tried to find a way of getting out of the work in the cold, but my brothers or Mom would always expose my faked illnesses.

Jay Richard, the oldest, who loved mechanical things. Illustration by David Hartman

During what seemed to be a forever-cold afternoon, we kept animals ready for the hired man, Jay, and Dad who did the contact work. We kept poles between the animals to prevent them from piling up, turning around, or backing out of the chute. To keep from getting kicked, we climbed above them on the pole rails. None of us enjoyed the work and we bickered as everyone tried to boss. Our job required us to poke the animals, to twist their tails, and to kick them in order to get them to move up to the next set of poles which we then slid in behind them.

Eventually, each animal, after seeing an opening ahead, went for it. Its efforts were in vain; at the end of the chute it was caught by the shoulders and squeezed and held in place. We did the work amid bawling and crapping animals under the hot iron and cruel horn nippers. Cattle manure covered the chute, our poles, and my boot overshoes. We warmed our hands and bodies at the branding fire whenever we could. Although working in the cold was uncomfortable for us, Dad always selected such a day to keep the cattle from bleeding too much. When the last critter was let out of the squeeze chute, it was always a helping day that I was happy to see pass. Piles of horns three-to-five inches deep littered the ground there. The faces of Dad and the hired man who had done the dehorning were bloody red from the spray.

Dad who paid men to work, often said "Never send a boy to do a man's job." By hiring grownups as helpers, he spared my boyhood, letting me be a kid, calling on me only when I was really needed, or when he was short-handed.

But I never had any choice when sick animals needed doctoring. Day or night, Dad expected me to help. Sometimes when I was really young, I got wind of what was going on, and I hid. If Dad knew I hid on purpose, he punished me.

Although butchering, in Dad's view, was an all-hands helping activity, there were seldom enough knives to go around. Larry hated butchering and ran off a few times. Then Larry started holding his breath and passing out so that Dad would send him to the house. Soon Dad paid his passing out little heed, putting him to work when he came to.

With all my heart I wanted to, but I was never trusted to shoot the animal with the .22 rifle. In his mind only Dad could do that correctly. The job for us younger boys was to hold a leg of the dead animal, while an older brother, Dad, or the hired man skinned that part.

I also hated having to help Dad kill chickens. He'd have me catch them in the hen house. Then while I held them across a wide, wood block, he would whack off their heads with the big double-bitted ax. Something about the killing got to me. I always turned my head, and never watched. Helping Mom pick and dress the chickens for cooking, however, was a job I liked because the insides were not messy, but interesting.

Late each spring when the sheep-shearing crew appeared, I was ecstatic. They set up in the big red barn as we arranged panels and organized our sheep to have their fleeces removed by the chattering electric-clipper blades. Bent over, men worked on downed sheep using skeleton-like jointed steel arms with clippers at their ends. The sharp-bladed clippers were like hands hanging from a turning shaft along the overhead. I could never figure out why sheep were so totally passive when they were being sheared. A horse, in contrast, would have gone wild amid all the noises.

We boys got to tie the fleeces, pick up tags which were stray chunks of wool, and do the sacking after each white and naked sheep was released. I loved being surrounded by the pleasing odor of wool. Perhaps since these were the Richard brothers' sheep, I enjoyed it even more.

The joy of sheep shearing time was a pleasant throwback to the huge operations we had enjoyed on the grasslands in eastern Colorado when I was a little kid. In North Park with our few hundred sheep, the shearing was a one-day operation, still there was something special in seeing men in all their varied shapes and styles work for us.

With Dad and the hired help, I spent time fencing, irrigating, and feeding cattle. I learned the work ethics of men—the how-to of doing a job and doing it well. The hired men who made work fun and adventurous showed me how a good attitude could make any task endurable.

I was usually torn between work and doing what I wanted. For sure, I knew I never wanted to be a cowboy or anyone's hired hand. I didn't like anyone to tell me what to do. I wanted to run something myself as Dad did.

Since North Park was my people's land, as a kid I dreamed of carrying on the family line, running the Two-Bar, and owning it myself one day. Here my great-grandparents, grandparents, and parents had dreamed and worked the land which had once belonged to the Ute Indians. My mind often focused on The Point of Rocks across the meadows where our two rivers met. Over the years I had stood on that sandstone outcrop where Clovis People had probably stood and watched giant mammoths graze, where Utes had spied on buffalo wallowing, where Jap and Jay Monroe had watched their horses fight flies, and where Dad and Mom had counted Hereford cattle eating waist-high grasses. Thoughts of this place and of my people's history took my breath away.

I knew that eventually I had to improve myself and somehow learn enough to be more than just a ranch helper. Having seen so many helpers lives going nowhere, a better future was what I craved.

Chapter 13

GETTIN'

"That's a dandy!"

Any direction I scanned on the ranch landscape triggered memories of my boyhood adventures with animals. These events burned into my college age mind. Not a group of willows, stretch of river, or outcrop of yellowed sandstone escaped some wildlife encounters, making me the animal lover I had up grown to be. Sitting there thinking and observing caused me to realize how lucky I had been, becoming totally comfortable with anything that had walked, creeped, or crawled in my mountain empire.

I had grabbed wild things and never worried an instant about getting diseases, fleas, or the creeping crud from any of them. I poured water by the buckets from our irrigation ditches down gopher holes. Using leather gloves to keep them from biting me, I'd grab the soaked rodents when they surfaced. I stuffed them into a gunnysack, and after they had dried off and I had a keen look, I'd let them go back to their holes.

Using a wooden apple box propped up on a stick with string tied to it, I captured chipmunks and sparrows. I had earlier placed grain inside the box to attract them. From a hiding place my quick tug on the string would drop the box over them. I'd slip a sheet of cardboard along the ground under the box, and they were mine for a close examination and to show to my family and friends.

Down the ridge from the Two-Bar buildings where the road crossed the ditch, Dad once spotted a badger digging after a gopher. Dirt was flying until the badger heard us and retreated down its nearby hole. I piled off the jeep with my brothers and inspected the huge mound of dirt around the eight-inch opening, expecting that mean animal to charge out at any moment.

The hired man said, "We can wire him out."

"How?" asked Dad.

"Well, I'll show you. I've done it before," said the man as he uncoiled a ten-foot piece of barbed wire from the silvery roll in the wagon behind the jeep.

We boys gathered about the opening into which he thrust the wire down about six feet, tangled the barbs, and twisted them into the badger's hair.

"You kids stand away," ordered Dad.

"Here, help me pull him out!"

Dad and the man strained on the wire until eventually they had pulled the stubborn badger to the surface. Then all hell broke loose when the badger charged Dad and the hired man. They dropped the wire, and with hissing and snapping jaws, the badger put the hired man and Dad up on the hood of the jeep.

We kids scrambled up the hill toward the fence and threw rocks down at the badger. Finally it left, lost the wire from its hair, and under a hail of rocks waddled down the road to another burrow.

Then Dad asked the hired man, "What are you supposed to do with one once you wire him out?" The man just shook his head and laughed.

Dad allowed, and Mom encouraged, me to get animals across our 2,029-acre ranch. Nothing seemed to be off limits.

Most of the time wild things out-sensed me, out-witted me, and out-ran me. Seeing these animal abilities in action, I experienced first hand why people depended more on plants than on animals as food in the wilds.

Jimmy, Larry, Smokey, and I spent hours in the big pile of discarded poles and fence posts behind the north corral trying to capture cottontail rabbits and their young. Smokey's keen sense of smell would direct us, and we'd move the tangle of posts to find nests of young or hiding adults. We'd drop to our knees and try to grab one when it bolted as we removed the last posts. When we captured an adult rabbit, we carried it to the house and begged Mom to let us make a pet of it. One rabbit we were showing Mom had a host of fleas and ticks, which were crawling off the rabbit and onto Larry's arms. Mom shooed Larry out of her kitchen in a hurry saying, "Don't bring a lousy thing into my house again."

One summer I caught Colorado tick fever from a wood tick that had burrowed into my upper arm. I kept passing out from the illness. Finally, after I had endured a month of intermittent fevers, Dr. Morgan confined me to bed. For a week I gagged down a bunch of awful pills that helped me recover from the worst disease I ever got from an animal. We ranch people didn't pay a lot of attention to all the horrible diseases that were always around us. Probably our vast ignorance of these ailments and their many carriers was a good thing. Otherwise, our parents would have kept us locked in the house, limiting our exposure to animal blood, fleas, and bites. Although I had gotten tick fever and suffered so much, it didn't stop me in the least from continuing to enjoy capturing all kinds of wild things.

Jimmy, Larry, and I set steel traps around piles of rank cattle guts, left over after Dad butchered, to catch crows and magpies. We also set traps in mud around a drying hole filled with suckers in our big ditches. We caught adult birds worth a dime each and sadly a few barn cats and once a stray dog.

In winter, Larry and I set Indian snares for white-tailed jackrabbits on their hard-packed snow trails in the dense willows. We thought that selling the snared rabbits would be a great way to get money without much effort. We caught some rabbits, but coyotes or foxes had eaten most of them before we could collect them from the snares and sell them at the mink farm. That moneymaking idea turned out to be another failure.

Finally, like the great Shawnee Indians, I sought valuable animals with fur. I could sell the furs and get manufactured goods needed to be a better hunter and getter. Good arrow points, guns, and ammunition were expensive. I had to scheme to possess them.

When I was just twelve, furs brought a good price of up to seven dollars for prime large muskrat and over twenty-five dollars for each mink pelt. Bob, who bought the first steel jump traps, in early fall trapped along the Michigan River and caught several score of muskrats. When the river froze over, he sold the hides he had accumulated. After his first taste of the fur money, Bob wanted more. My eyes bugged out seeing his vast loot.

The next season I started trapping, too. I borrowed some traps from old Harold Rosenfield and purchased more with part of my haying wages.

"I was there first, and you can't trap on the Michigan," said Bob.

"Why can't I? You don't own the river," I answered in an attempt to stand up to my towering brother.

When he got wind of our territory dispute, Dad settled the argument. The Michigan was to be Bob's trapping territory, and the Illinois was to be mine. The land and the river below where the two streams met were open to both of us. I felt that

I had been rooked because he had more river and sloughs, but still I was younger.

Both of us started fall trapping close to our ranch buildings and gradually worked northward down the winding rivers. Although Dad had warned us not to start before the hides were totally prime, we each wanted to get ahead of the other in the race to riches, and foolishly trapped some unprimed animals. We also feared a cold winter could set in early and the ponds and river would freeze up, ending trapping.

Bob ran his traps on horseback; I did mine afoot. Getting up at four-thirty each morning, I donned my coat, hat, and gloves. Then, Smokey and I sneaked out together into a striking world few knew.

By venturing alone to the river, I developed a feeling of self-reliance. I didn't need anyone, just Smokey. I had to check my traps twice each day, because animals caught during the daylight could twist off their legs. That I hated! Leaving an animal too long in a steel leg hold trap was inhumane. I tried to overlook the cruelty, but deep in my heart I knew trapping seemed less than honorable.

In the dim light I picked up my gunnysack and headed toward the river. Buildings loomed as black objects and frost covered the cold earth. Each step I took scraped the frost from the gravel. Looking back, I could see dark footprints on a sheet of white frost. Smokey's and my breaths escaped from our mouths in small puffing explosions, floating up to the heavens.

I enjoyed moving on my own, instead of messing with a horse. Sitting in the saddle before sunrise was always cold on the seat of my pants. The horse could act up or buck, and the rider had to open gates. Horses were faster overall, but they were noisy and were a pain in the neck to worry about. At least, those were my arguments with Bob, my competitor, who was sold on running traps from horseback.

A little later but prior to dawn, Bob saddled his beast and headed down the opposite side of the ridge to run a trap line on the Michigan. His horse carried him rapidly from trap to trap. He dismounted only to reset sprung traps or pick up the trapped animals.

It was half light as I neared the river and searched for the first trap, which I found untouched, frozen over with ice. I moved along always hoping for the best while getting the unexpected.

The willowed Illinois River bottom where wild things abounded.

Magpies squawked, ducks quacked, and crows called, all sounds that comforted Smokey and me. At times, the coyotes howled and an old cow occasionally bawled far across the frosty meadows.

I hurried from trap to trap---resetting and re-baiting with parsnip chunks, which I jabbed onto a pointed willow stick, extending them over the traps. I watched to keep Smokey from stepping into the jaws of my traps. Like a Pawnee trapper, quiet and alert, I saw all with Smokey to help me.

With anticipation we approached each trap. It might be sprung or empty, have some fur, a foot, or an actual animal, which was alive, dead, or tangled in the tall grass. I hoped the captured animals drowned, since I made most of my trap sets for that eventuality when the water was deep enough. If the animal drowned, I didn't have to whack the victim to death.

Sometimes I had ducks in my traps, once a skunk, another time a cat. I gave freedom to a small muskrat caught only by the thin black tail. Another time a beautiful black-crowned night heron with its big orange eyes and long beak stood with one foot in the clamped jaws. We released all of the unintended captures unharmed, and I told them aloud, "Smokey and I are sorry. We don't want you."

Smokey once stepped into the steel jaws of an Oneida jump trap I'd set. His howling caused me to cry as I hurriedly released his toes, rubbed them, and soothed my big friend. Later on, I accidentally put my hand into a trap as I was setting it along a grassy muskrat slide. Such pain in two fingers caused me to pause and think about what I was doing. To set traps, which could capture animals other than those I wanted, seemed so cowardly. Yet, how was I to earn money?

On a frosty stream bank where I had two traps set along a cove, one of my traps had caught a great horned owl by a single claw. A muskrat in the other trap must have lured the hungry owl to land there. The huge pastel owl with its glowing yellow eyes frightened me. Its wings extended outward and forward in a wide arc. Because the feathers were fluffed, the owl appeared much larger than its actual size. Holding its head near the ground, it clicked and snapped its black beak in a terrifying manner and peered at me with unblinking huge yellow eyes.

Eventually, while I held it down with a stick so it wouldn't hurt itself, I depressed the spring on the trap. When I released the stick, the bird, not realizing it was free continued to threaten. Finally, it lifted off the ground and flew down the river. At that moment, I knew what silent hunters owls were. I watched the great bird lift into the air and leave without a sound coming to my ears. Although Smokey could probably hear it take off, I could not.

From five-dozen traps, I caught six muskrats, one owl, and had three sprung traps. Bob, who beat Smokey and me to the house, had eight muskrats.

After school I made another trap-run along the winding stream. The warmth of the late fall afternoon made this run a totally different trip. It was sunny and peaceful with a few big animals in sight among the barren, red-barked willows whose fallen leaves splashed the ground with yellows and browns. The ice had retreated from the river's edges and from the stagnant sloughs that clung to the stream as dead-water appendages.

Jimmy and Larry were with me, and we carried our bows. To see muskrats dive below the water's surface and swim into their underwater holes along the slumped brown riverbanks was thrilling, but failed to be good targets.

"Larry, there is a trap below the tall bank on that big bend. Would you check it while Jimmy and I cut across?"

"Yeah," he said as he dogtrotted off with the big blue dog at his side. At the next big bend he was coming to meet us when he jumped a jackrabbit out from humpy ground. Smokey was on it in a flash, but Larry scolded him off.

"No! Smokey, No!"

The big dog slunk back. Larry waved us over. Sensing something was wrong, Jimmy and I hurried toward him. The rabbit sat with its ears down, only a dozen feet away.

"Looks hurt to me--can't run much," observed Larry. All three of us eased closer. The rabbit didn't attempt to run again. A fist-sized patch of skin was missing along its left side, exposing ribs and its throbbing insides.

"What a mess. See the maggots," said Larry, "the wound has been there a while by the looks of it."

"Let's put the poor thing out of its misery like Mom would," muttered Jimmy. "That is just awful bein' eaten alive like that."

Our three hunting points stopped the rabbit's suffering in a split second. After we had washed our arrows in the Illinois River, we moved back to the trap line. Larry and Jimmy walked one bank while Smokey and I walked the other.

Late in the afternoon was splendid for checking the traps since everything was thawed during the day, and I was in no hurry. We peeled our eyes for muskrat trackings, tail draggings, and scat-droppings. The muskrats seemed to have specific mud-bar toilets where they walked and did their business. The rodents also slid down steep banks into the water on bent grasses. I placed traps at the base of these fun slides. Trails, holes, and dens were hot spots for my jump traps. I used bait only in places where there should be animals but no great spot to set a trap could be found. Most traps were adjusted each afternoon to compensate for the rise or fall of the water level in the stream. They couldn't be set too deep in the water or above it. A pointed "Y" willow branch was driven deeply into the streambed to anchor each two-foot trap chain, causing a trapped muskrat to eventually tire and drown. Drowned animals were much easier to skin since they had no head damage.

We sank sticks in the mud and lined them in a row to form a small fence across a slough's mouth. This fence allowed passage only across my sunken trap. We boys all looked for new trails and signs along the banks and coves.

We moved a good many traps and caught one muskrat during the afternoon run. Another tiny one which had been caught by its hair, stood its ground and snapped its yellow buck-teeth at us. We voted to let it go since we felt that taking such a brave little one would be unfair.

Larry and Jimmy went on ahead. I had to walk away from the river around an acre of dense, leafless willows where I paused and noticed how dry and lifeless the plants were. The seedpods of the iris rattled against my legs. The previous spring irrigation time in these iris clumps, green-headed Mallard ducks had nested and hatched nine fuzzy young. I watched the ground for the old nest.

"Yoowweee!" Larry's call pierced the air as he grabbed my shoulders from behind and knocked me off my feet.

"Are you trying to scare me to death?" I barked as my brothers rolled and laughed in the tall grass beside me.

"You didn't even hear us!" said Larry, all freckly faced and smiling. None of us made any effort to get up.

"Had we been Iroquois, you'd have lost your hair," Jimmy said laughing. I hadn't heard them rush ahead, cross the river, and hide in the willows.

"Let me go ahead and check the traps, Paul," said Jimmy, "I never get to see first when something's caught."

"All right, go ahead, but wait for us at the fence if we don't have anything else in the traps." We stayed and sat in the sunlit dry grass and talked.

"How long will it be before the traps get froze in?" asked Larry.

"Could be anytime. I would like another month or so. Trappin' gets tougher and tougher as the ice gets thick along the sloughs and banks. The muskrats stay under the ice. I wish it would stay this nice all fall."

"Can I help skin these out tonight?" asked Larry.

"I'll teach you, but cut pelts bring less money, you know."

"I don't understand this prime stuff."

I replied, "Well, as Ole Swan Nelsen told me, it's like the animals are gettin' ready for winter and their hair changes and locks hard to the hide which turns light inside. When the hide on the inside is dark, hair will pull out not being prime. Fur coats need hairs that won't come out, so the best price goes for the most prime hides."

"Why do those guys shoot them down at the duck ponds, if holes are so bad?" asked Larry.

"They say they hit 'em in the head with every shot, and another hole by the eyes and ears doesn't matter, but I think that's bunk. Who can hit anything in the head like that when it's swimming? I don't think they get a lot of the ones they kill either, in that cold water. They waste a lot of muskrats."

"I'd sure like to trap next year."

"If you could get some traps and stuck with it, we could have you trap the ponds and down on Post's place. You could sneak onto Hanson's too. But, with Bob and me both at it, there isn't much room."

Jimmy was dogtrotting far ahead. I warned Larry not to walk in my shadow and bring me bad luck. He crossed the river and we moved along scanning and resetting. After a couple of narrow river bends, we heard Jimmy's wild boy call.

We hurried and found him watching a big brownish muskrat standing with the trap and chain wrapped around a stake on a grassy point above the stream. The animal was tethered like a man about to be burned alive at the stake by the Ottawa Indians.

"Wow, Jimmy, it's a big one," yelled Larry as he inspected it, "Leg almost twisted off, too."

"Seven dollars, maybe," I said as I whacked it across the head with an inch-thick willow branch that sent it into twitching and a sudden death. When I released it from the trap, Jimmy held it up by the tail and did a little Indian dance in a circle as he stuffed it into the gunnysack. "I love it when we get somethin'."

Paul Willard Richard

Jimmy Richard, a boy always ready for adventure.
Illustration by David Hartman

"Especially when you get to find it first," said Larry, "Can I go ahead next?"

"Only if you promise we get another big one."

"Sure," he said as he headed down the stream.

Near the end of the trap line, Jimmy with his sharp eyes, spotted something sticking out of the rocks in the riverbed near Steamboat Rock. It was black and pointed. Working to remove it, we found an entire skull attached--a buffalo skull. We cleaned it off by removing the mud. Deep blackish green in color, the skull was nearly perfect.

We sat, talked, and wondered if perhaps a Ute Indian had killed it, or if sick, the buffalo had gone to the river to cool its fever and eventually died, when sometime later it had been covered with mud. How I wished we could have seen the exciting wildlife this buffalo had watched! To have been that wild with Indians all about, intrigued me.

In those free days of my youth, I wished to be a brave Indian instead of a white kid, fascinated with living before the coming of the white man. A life of being wild on the land, hunting, trapping, raiding, camping, and roaming freely appealed to me as a kid, staying with me all my adult life and to this very day. A love of nature and her natural Indian people eventually turned into much of my life's work.

Two of us carried the old buffalo skull, each holding one horn, while the other packed the sack with our muskrats across the pasture toward home. We walked across long hollows in the pasture. These were the buffalo wallows where seventy-five years before the shaggy beasts must have spent their lazy summer afternoons in mud or dust, fighting biting insects. We always thought about Indians when we crossed the wallows. I was proud to be carrying a real buffalo skull across this sacred place.

Most early mornings, I had to rush to get ready for school after I had run my morning trap line. Sometimes, by mid-morning, Mom would see groggy muskrats staggering about the shop. Having worked their way out of the gunnysacks, the muskrats would sit dazed in the doorway. At this sight, she'd close the shop door and call school. I had to dogtrot home at lunchtime and put the poor muskrats out of their misery. I couldn't understand why Mom wouldn't finish off those muskrats for me.

Each evening after I had done my homework, I skinned muskrats whose hides I hung in the large bunkhouse above the shop. After stretching them on bullet shaped boards, I hung the long rows of pelts on nails. As the pelts dried, I scraped them several times, to clean away fat and any tissue left after skinning. When they were fully dry I removed them from the stretchers, bundled them up, suspending them from the bunkhouse ceiling so mice couldn't get to them.

That November of 1948, Mom wanted to bet me a brand new bicycle against my fifty-two pelts that Tom Dewey would beat Harry Truman in the election. I just couldn't bet and risk losing all my hard-earned hides, so she could have a fur coat made. Instead, Dad later took my hides to a buyer at La Porte, Colorado, where the price I wanted was beaten down. The buyer gave Dad tips on how to better care for the skins. Bitter at the price, I took my money and planned to be more careful the next season, wishing I had taken Mom's bet since Truman had won.

The trapping contest between Bob and me came to a sudden end when he became a basketball star. Because he had to devote after school time and evenings to games and practices, he had no time for trapping. His life became all sports. Intending to do even more, I bought his pelt stretchers and traps.

The next season, Larry, Harry Rosenfield, and I took over Bob's territory and we trapped together hoping to do well enough to earn a ton of money. We set larger traps to catch coyotes, fox, and bobcat. When we built a fire over a big trap and put some bacon in the dying embers, we were using a trick Harry's dad said was a sure thing to get rid of human scent. But, we caught nothing. Harry's dad had also taught us to set traps for mink. We got four worth twenty bucks apiece.

As always, our plans to get filthy rich never quite materialized. Every year my extreme optimism set me up for a big let down. Usually, the price went down at selling time, our pelts were too small, were not prime enough, or weren't exactly what the fur buyer wanted. So, as Dad said, "It was a good introduction to the business world." I felt remorse at having killed and crippled so many animals for so little money.

Hunting, another ways of getting animals, provided meat for the family, not any cash for me. The folks, who gave me an allowance, would also sometimes help me with ammunition. I begged to do ranch jobs to enable me to earn enough for a box of .22 shells. It was hard sledding for a kid since shooting was expensive.

Making it all worthwhile was the praise I received for putting any kind of meat on our table. Mom always cooked my harvest and Dad said, "That's a dandy," or "This is sure good" regardless of the size or taste.

However, Dad was more interested in raising meat on the hoof than hunting for it, and he wouldn't expend vast energy to get wild meat by traipsing into the mountain backcountry when he could butcher a critter from our herd. Yet when a friend, a banker, or an oilman wanted to get a deer, Dad would become interested and take him to the "north end" for a young buck or two. His way of getting a deer required driving logging roads or waiting at game crossings for unwary animals. Dad was not one to hike and track down a deer or elk.

Although Dad never invited me on these easy deer hunts--maybe because there was some drinking involved--I thrilled at the sight of the bagged deer in the back of his pickup. With all my heart I wanted to shoot a deer just as Dad did. One fall he lined up a banker guest for an easy shot which killed two small bucks with a single bullet. Why Dad was more thrilled when his companions got a buck than when he did, I didn't understand. I was condemned to wait and watch.

Before each haying, Dad hunted Pitchpine Mountain behind the Norris Place. Too young for a big game rifle, I still went along on some of those hunts. Big bucks hung out in green timber during July when their antlers were tender with fuzzy soft velvet. Dad stationed someone on the south end of the long mountain with a rifle. The rest of us rode horseback through the pines covering the mountain's crest. We'd push big mule bucks toward the hidden rifleman ahead.

Usually we'd hear a couple of shots ring out and know that we'd have venison to feed the hay crew. One year after running a dozen big buck deer by Kip, who emptied his rifle missing them with all six shots, we had to do the drive twice.

"Buck fever for sure," Dad teased.

"But you should have seen the size of 'em."

"That should have made them easier to hit."

"Yeah, but I was so excited the rifle wouldn't hold still," laughed Kip. I was green with envy wanting such a chance.

Mac, our other hired man on the Norris Place, was cutting fence poles before haying when a nice, fat buck happened by. Knowing he had shot the deer out of season with one clean shot, he dressed it out placing it in the bottom of the wagon he was pulling. He covered it over carefully with fence posts and headed back to the ranch buildings. Near the bridge over Norris Creek, a game warden stopped in his green pickup and visited about beaver dams blocking Raspberry Creek. Finally the game warden backed away from the wagon and said, "Well, I guess you'd better get that wagon on home before it bleeds to death."

Then he climbed into his green, state pickup and drove off. Under the wagon, sure enough, Mac saw that a small pool of blood had dripped through the bottom boards.

Of course, as a kid, I didn't start out hunting such big animals and I had to use my bow and arrows. But, some day in the future I dreamed of hunting down giant bulls and bucks as well as bear, lions, and coyotes.

The hired man, while feeding cattle in our meadow told us he heard an animal scream like a lion in the willows. The next morning, we got our bows and searched along the edge of the meadow. Smokey discovered a set of huge cat tracks in the snow. We followed the tracks excitedly; they changed from walking to twenty-foot leaps as the cat increased speed. The cat's big tail made marks in the snow. The six-inch-wide tracks disappeared into the thick willows near the big head gates.

With steel tipped hunting arrows ready, Harry, Larry, and I talked of having a lion skin on the wall or flung over the bed in our shack. Yet, when the fresh tracks entered the several acres of tangled dense willows below the goat farm, we paused. If the big cat charged, how could we shoot in such a tangled mess? Our bravery waned, and we decided it had probably quit the country. We never entered the trees but were able to tell the tale of having tracked a huge cat. We all lusted to be great hunters.

The next spring we were flushing rabbits from the willows along a ditch at the Point Of Rocks. When one rabbit hesitated in an opening, I shot it with my arrow, pierced it in the middle, and pinned it to the ground. Hearing the horrible screams coming from the pinned rabbit made me sick in my heart, destroying my feelings about my archery feat. Harry clubbed it and stopped the screams. Then we stood looking at the silent rabbit and discussed whether we ought to be killing rabbits in a month without an "r" when we couldn't eat them. I was totally shaken. That experience changed my feelings about proving myself by killing animals which didn't harm us and which we couldn't eat. From then on the desire to kill just because I could, vanished.

Later Harry, my little brothers, and I launched a bow-and-arrow hunt along the Illinois River pasture with Smokey. Sage grouse were abundant among the clover stands in the bumpy ground. Flattening themselves between the grassy humps or behind the tall blue flag bunches, the birds crouched in low places. Since there were young ones among the birds, only a few would fly at a time. When we saw a few grouse fly, we spread out in a line with our arrows notched to bowstrings. Trying to detect the crouched grouse, we walked slowly along, while Smokey sneaked along with us. Often, he froze and pointed at the birds on the ground. Many flew. We usually wasted several arrows since sage grouse were tough to hit on the wing. When Harry shot one in the air, we were all surprised. Of all of those we spotted on the ground and shot arrows at, we killed three. I got two. We thought we'd done some fine hunting by shooting four sage grouse. Smokey had grabbed four others on the ground. Even though we finished the hunt with eight birds, we had to share half the glory with our blue dog. We marched proudly into Mom's kitchen and told of our harvest. I wasn't pleased when Jay said, "Smokey is still the best hunter in this outfit."

During high school, I got serious any time fresh deer signs appeared in mud along the creeks. Usually they were from does raising fawns in the willows. If we had actually killed a wet doe (one producing milk), the folks would have disapproved. They wanted no orphaned fawns from Richard hunting efforts. It was bucks only as Richard table meat. With steel-pointed arrows notched to taut bowstrings, we sneaked about in the willows after buck deer. Harry and I passed up sure hits on tan-colored female mule deer.

One day when Larry, Harry, and I arrowed a couple of young gadwall ducks near the old swimming hole in September, we were afraid to take them home. My parents had said, "North Park ducks taste like mud. Don't bring any home." We roasted them on willow branch spits over a big red-coaled fire in the dense willows.

"This really tastes good," remarked Larry as he ripped into the dark-meated breast of a quacker. I agreed, and concluded that our parents had not wanted us killing ducks out of season. We always called out of season poaching, "rancher season." North Park meadows and rivers produced thousands of ducks, but all of the ducks flew south when the ice all froze prior to the legal November bird-hunting season.

Wishing that Dad would take me hunting, I asked Harry, "Is your dad taking you huntin' this season?"

"Sure. But he's already killed a couple this summer up where he cuts mine props," answered Harry, "I don't see why he wants to buy a license and hunt with all those outsiders around."

I sadly said, "I don't know if Dad is goin' this year. Last fall he came across a hunter sitting against a tree and asked, 'Had any luck?' an the guy says, 'No, just a couple of sound shots and didn't hit 'em, which scared the heck out of Dad."

"Some of those guys get drunk and take sound shots blastin' everything," added Larry. "Mom says it's not safe to be in the woods during deer season."

"I'd love to go, even if I'm not old enough to hunt with a license," I said, knowing full well that Harry's dad let him carry a rifle and hunt beside him, the lucky dog.

"You heard about a guy who pulled into the game check station on Cameron Pass and checked his mule deer? He was surprised when the game wardens pointed out the steel horse shoes on its hoofs," said Larry, with a chuckle.

"Wasn't it last season that a man tied up his horse and hunted on foot around a mountain? Then he shot his own horse thinking it was a deer." asked Harry.

"Yes," replied Larry.

I added, "Down near Pueblo a man took his mother-in-law hunting. She was wearing a fur coat. He shot her in a snowstorm and said, 'I thought she was a bear.' "

We laughed as Harry added, "She could have been a real bear. At least he didn't tie her on the fender and put his bear tag on 'er."

I wished Harry's dad would take me, too. A real hunter, who used an old lever action 30-30 with open sights, old Harold drew blood and got deer, always with a head or neck shot. He said any other shots wasted meat.

One weekend that fall, I did go along on a hunt with the Rosenfields. I watched like a hawk how old Harold tracked and hunted. Coughing and hacking much of the time, he stopped often to smoke and listen. In fact, he listened and looked far more than he moved. He said, "You can't run down no deer, but a lot of idjits try." I hung on every word and bit of information the old hunter offered.

That next fall, David Hampton, a rancher's son on the other side of Walden, drove over in an old pickup and wanted me to show him where to get a deer. At school, I had earlier bragged that there were loads of bucks out at the Norris Place. Although Mom let me go with him, she didn't know that David had neither a drivers nor deer license. He had an old lever action .30-30 with a peep sight. I guided him to a sagebrush park surrounded by stark white aspen up on Raspberry Creek where Kip had told me bucks hung out.

We parked his pickup behind huge conglomerate rocks, slipped up between some red-trunked limber pines, and peered down. A buck and two does were browsing in the opening. David took the first eleven shots from about seventy-five yards never hitting or even scaring the big gray buck. He declared the gun wasn't shooting straight and put another half dozen shells into the magazine. I then shot four times and the deer never raised its head. David grabbed the rifle and finished off the ammo. The buck stayed silently eating before us embarrassed hunters. We left vowing never to tell about the seventeen shots we'd taken at a standing buck. I sure didn't want Dad or the Rosenfields to find out.

The next summer in July, Larry, Harry, and I went up on Pitchpine Mountain at the Norris Place. Harry, with his dad's .30-30 rifle, waited with Larry while I dogged the timber and pushed three little bucks by them. Harry killed one buck with a perfect shot. Proudly we dressed it out and hauled the little buck on a pole between us down to the ranch house where Harry's dad came to get us. It was the first buck for Harry, and were we ever proud!

Two weeks later Larry, Harry, and his cousin, Cookie, repeated the exact hunt with bows. In nearly the same spot as before, Harry made a heart shot on a two-point buck with an arrow. He was a true hunter.

Later the buttons nearly popped from my shirt when Dad offered me his .257 Roberts rifle for my first licensed deer hunt with Kip and a family friend, Clarence Douglass, from Denver.

I couldn't sleep and rose at 4:00 a.m., fixed jam sandwiches for our lunches, and scurried to get the horses ready under the one dull light in the horse barn. One horse spooked as I was leading it up the dark loading chute ramp into our two-ton Chevy truck. It knocked me down and stepped on me twice as it bolted crazily into the truck. I was in tears from the pain.

Not wanting to lose out on hunting, I ignored the throbbing in my thigh and arm. We talked about the planned hunt all the way to the Emigh Place which bordered our Norris Ranch. For twenty-one slow miles, the truck groaned along over the vacant dirt roads in the black night, then Kip backed it against a high bank in order to unload the horses. We waited.

Kip insisted that hunting on horseback was the way to get deer. He claimed a man could see much more from up on a tall horse. Finally we saw daylight enough to saddle up and to tie on our scabbards, ropes, and lunches. On the frosty October morning, we straddled the jittery animals. The leather chilled my rear, and ground fog blanketed the willow bottoms across the valley. The horses pranced nervously.

I was bringing up the rear as Kip and Clarence dropped down into the misty fog as if they had sunk into a gray ocean. In the willows over the soggy ground, the fog had lifted to about five feet, just enough to let us see ahead a bit.

Kip yelled, "There's a bear to the right. Get your guns! He's in the willows!"

Rolling off of my horse, I took the .257 Roberts with me smoothly. As soon as I hit the ground, my horse quit me, its hoofs pounding back up the sagebrush hill. I could see about a dozen feet ahead in the short willows.

"He's to your right; don't let him get away," Kip hollered. Moving through the branches, I finally had to get down on my hands and knees to slip below the tight arching tangles.

"A little more ahead. I keep losing him in the brush. He's coming your way, Paul." There on my hands and knees and unable to see ten feet or even to stand, terror struck. If my rifle misfired or if the shell was a dud or if I missed the charging bear, I'd never get off a second shot. I froze, unable to move.

Soon Kip's voice rose above the fog, "Hell, it's just a huge porcupine."

Half an hour later we had regained our composure, rounded up the horses, and crossed the valley into aspen mixed with lodgepole pines and sagebrush openings. Although lots of does greeted us, real deer hunters didn't concern themselves with them. We rode most of the day high up into the dense spruce and fir forest where I couldn't see forty feet. After we had lunch, we raced back to the foothills where we made drives on bunches of aspen. One of us rode ahead of a big clump and waited in rapt ambush, while the others rode through the cracking leaves to scare out big bucks. Alas, only small fawns and does fell into our sights all afternoon.

We worked lower and lower aspen groves toward the meadows to the south that faced Humpy Manville's Place far across the broad valley with Rabbit Ears Peak in the distance. Then we jumped a bunch of big bucks. As we bailed off our horses, the deer bounced and sank below the steep hill before we could fire. We mounted again. Far below, the deer broke into the open and raced across meadows between long chains of willows. We dismounted again. We blasted at them from long range until they were out of sight, and we were out of shells. We hit nothing, but the air reeked of gunpowder. My ears rang. I'd had fired my first five shots from the sleek .257 at eight bucks bearing sharp antlers.

We finally concluded that the distance had been much greater than we thought, as we had blasted thin air and wasted caps. Nevertheless, I was proud as punch at having gotten a shot at some big bucks. Buck fever held me tightly as I wanted a deer in the worst way.

That next week, while I was in school, Kip and Clarence hunted again, and each got a small buck. I again felt rooked. Would I ever get a buck? I thought that hunting from horseback, although fast and comfortable, was far too noisy. Most deer were out of range before I could get off of a horse. I wanted to sneak around, hunt on foot, and not fool with horses as Kip wanted.

The last weekend of that deer season, old Harold Rosenfield took Harry and me along to hunt in the north end where he claimed the deer were thick as fleas. It was my last chance for a buck. In his old green pickup, we bounced over miles of logging roads and finally stopped in a quiet clearing where cutting had taken place years earlier, leaving a ragged beat-up forest. There were thousands of tracks in the six-inch snow. Old Harold said the area was a crossover and that the deer were moving. Harry and I hunted together, sometimes separate, neither getting clean shots at bucks. Dozens of does and fawns crossed our paths.

Mid-morning, I stopped to do my business. There with my pants down and my rifle leaning on a log out of reach, I saw a bunch of does and two big bucks trot past within ten feet. By the time I struggled up and got the .257 Roberts, they were gone. Discouraged, I stood with my pants down and thought no buck would ever fall victim to such a dunce of a hunter.

I moved dejectedly to an old skid trail along which many years before logs had been dragged by horses to sawmills to make railroad ties. Eight-foot piles of gray slabs sat in hundred feet long rows. Dad had had old Harold haul some loads of them to the Two-Bar where he built high-board, slab fences and windbreaks around the corrals. I passed an early 1900's sawdust pile which showed where deer had churned white snow into orange-colored sawdust beneath as they crossed it. Skid trails branched out from the slab pile like a spider's web. I took a wide trail and walked soundlessly in the snowy softness.

After I had gone a few hundred yards, I watched three does bounce stiff-legged across the trail into my gun sights. I was ready this time. If I could just grow antlers on them, I wished, not lowering my rifle. Then came a buck following the does across the narrow trail. Making a snap shot, I didn't feel the 257 Roberts kick. The buck staggered as he zipped into the dense timber. With my heart pounding, I raced to the spot where a few red drops tinted the snow. I'd "drawn blood" as old Harold would always say.

Now to find the darned thing. I didn't know how badly it was hit. Soon the tracks that I was following joined a herd and left no more blood. After circling the last drop in the snow and unable to find any more drops, I raced back to find Harry or his dad. Harry and I returned, found the trail, and waited twenty minutes, as old Harold had always preached, for the buck to lie down and die. Back on the trail, we soon saw staggering and slipping tracks in the snow. Ahead, crumpled in the snow, was my first buck, a dandy.

Harry helped me dress it, and we saved the liver and heart. We wiped blood on each other's faces and gave our wild calls as blood brothers. Together we dragged the buck back to the pickup. I was happy as only a kid could be! Six points on one side and five on the other, but the shot in the flank wasn't perfect. When old Harold saw it and heard my tale, he grunted, "You done good." I felt eight feet tall when I showed the table meat to the family.

Other hunts to the sand hills and Pole and Independence Mountains followed. Although over the years I improved as a deer hunter, Harry was always better. He proved his skill on a late November trip to the Norris Place. We stayed in the cold rooms of the empty ranch house, heated canned goods on an old stove in an old dishpan. We took the jeep out, and for fun shot at jackrabbits in the headlight beams as we drove across the frozen meadows.

Hunting the next morning behind the ranch in the thick timber, we tried to kick out deer. A mountain lion ran past me in the thick brush in Harry's direction. I couldn't get a clear shot off, but Harry did. A cat scream followed, as the cat leaped and twisted in the air. It died as it fell. When I arrived, Harry was smiling that slight competent smile. We also got two deer that day. The *Denver Post* and State Wildlife Commission each gave a $50 reward for the cat. Harry was rolling in the dough, and I'd been part of getting a lion.

Two weeks later with nothing left to hunt, we went to try for a bear near the Crystal Mine. Although our bear tags were still good, there were no bear. We found elk tracks in the timber near Raspberry Creek above Livingston Park. Harry went on the fresh trail, while I cut ahead to a ridge just in case the elk went east. I climbed a steep moraine forty feet high to set up my ambush. The rocks and fallen trees forced me to put my rifle over my back by its sling so that I could climb up hand over hand.

When I reached the top and looked up, the sight stopped my heart. There, broadside, a monstrous seven-point bull elk thirty-feet away looked directly down at me. My hat and glasses flew off into the snow, as I ripped the rifle off my back. But the beautiful bull drifted away like a huge ghost before I could get a shot. I now truly had elk fever.

That next weekend Bob and Jay lured by my description of the big elk came back with me in snow up to the top of the jeep's wheels. There was still plenty of elk sign. We split up and hunted all afternoon solo. Jay and I, empty handed, met at 4:30 by the jeep as planned. We found no Bob. By 5:00 we were worried. After we fired three shots in the air with no answer, we set off on his tracks into the twilight. It became dark quickly, but we were blessed with a full moon that showed his tracks in the endless deep snow. We thought he might have broken a leg, fallen through the ice into a beaver pond, or gotten lost.

Terror shot through my body as we tracked Bob in the cold snow. Every few hundred yards, Jay or I yelled Bob's name and gave his boy call. It just echoed off the moraines or was absorbed by the snow as in vain as we trod along his trail. We knew that it would take hours to find him but had no alternative to tracking. The thought of losing a brother was sickening. Bob had to be in some trouble for him not to have met us as agreed back at the jeep. We hurried along in the soft snow among the black pine trees. Sorry for my constant contesting with him, I prayed for him to be safe. I vowed to be a better brother.

We used three shots again to no avail and eventually reached the moraine top overlooking deep Livingston Park. Still hollering at intervals, we descended into the vast valley. Before we reached the beaver dams, we heard his kid call answering us. It was the most welcome sound of my life. We found him safe, but tired.

Amid great relief and excitement, he related the details of his hunt. He'd been chasing a herd of elk, but he couldn't get a clear crack at them. They'd led him on and on into the dense timber on the south side of Livingston Park. Time had gotten away from him, as he expected to drop an elk at any moment. Suddenly, it was dark and he was a long way from the jeep. He hadn't heard our yells or shots down in the deep moraine valley, since he was much lower than we were.

When we climbed back up the rough moraines to the valley top, clouds blocked our guiding moon. Wandering in circles, we spent the next hours in darkness in heavy black timber without a flashlight. We knew the country, but in the jet blackness we stumbled and banged into trees in the bitter cold and deep snow. First Jay would lead, then Bob, and then I. We kept coming back to our old trails in the crusted snow. Since I'd never been lost in the dark before, I feared dying in the bitter cold. Although we talked of building a fire, we had no matches, and so kept moving along. Eventually, the moonlight returned in short flashes between racing clouds. We finally got our bearings, and exhausted, reached the jeep a half-mile away.

By some miracle the little jeep, up to its axels in crusted snow, started on that frigid, icy night. For once in my life, I was so tired that I couldn't talk. On that quiet thoughtful ride back home, I clearly remember sitting shoulder to shoulder between my older brothers in the tiny cold jeep. Getting big elk was far from my mind and not important as we drove back to the Two-Bar in that black and silent night.

Chapter 14

SCHOOLIN'

*"Coach, my dad won't sign your paycheck
if you don't play me in the game."*

My roving eyes soon fell on the highest hill in Walden where the school buildings stood tall and stark, reminding me of how exciting schooling had been for me. But my first encounters with the wonders of schooling were on Colorado's prairie as a little kid.

Back when I was five, I envied Jay coming back to our Great Depression era home from school with beautiful papers, books, and projects. After school we'd snack together on bread and butter topped with sugar, looking at his amazing treasures. Then Bob, too, was going with other kids to that place of magic and reading instead of picture looking as I did.

Mom and Dad spoke of school and teachers as the most important entities on earth. As I watched my brothers, I soon viewed school as the greatest place a kid could possibly be.

Hopewell School, outside of Limon, rose out of the flat, barren, short-grass prairie. It was a one-room school with an old pot-bellied stove and double desks in rows bonded to steel floor railings, where I finally joined my two older brothers. I was thrilled with my Big Chief tablet, ink well, pencil groove, and book storage space. Two outhouses and a small horse shelter stood behind the chalk white school. Sometimes riding

Paul Willard Richard

each way on old Croppie, we kids tied him in the little barn during the school day. A quarter of the students were Richards. The playground equipment consisted of an old set of wooden swings and a plank teeter-totter located in the dirt yard fenced with barbed wire to separate Hopewell from the surrounding cattle pastures.

There during recesses we played kick-the-can, hide-and-go-seek, red-rover, and ante-over the school building. I was in seventh heaven in this wondrous place.

Mrs. Vermillion, my teacher, was a red-faced, jolly, fully-rounded, gray-haired lady who reminded me of my grandmother in Brush, Colorado. I could tell that Mrs. Vermillion, who taught all eight grades, cared about me by the way she took care of me and kept me busy. A good teacher, she instructed us in the basic three "R's."

The only bad part about school was sharing a double desk with a girl. My brothers and the other boys teased me mercilessly about Donna, who was as cute as a bug's ear. Although I liked her, I didn't dare admit it.

Outside freedom came at recess and lunch times when we ate the egg and jelly sandwiches Mom had packed into black tin lunch pails. During those times, I often played hopscotch and marbles in the dirt with all the other grassland ranch kids.

Suffering through the Palmer method of penmanship with Jay and Bob, I made ovals and slants until my shoulders ached. My penmanship, however, never seemed to improve enough to suit my teacher. She wouldn't let me write with my left hand, as I wanted, but made me use my right. I wondered how Dad ever grew up to write left-handed.

Growing Up Wild

Young Richards at their one-room Hopewell School in 1942. Jay left of the teacher, Paul with goggles, and Bob on far right.

A huge picture of George Washington hung above the black slate blackboard. His puffy pink cheeks appeared to have red rouge on them. I wondered how such a strange appearing duck in a white wig could be the "father" of my country. On the wall hung a big flag to which we all pledged allegiance to our nation each morning.

During those Hopewell days, my country was deep in war. To support the war effort, we bought a few stamps each week to fill our little booklets. Eventually, we turned the small red booklets in for war bonds. I couldn't figure out who the enemy was, the Japs or the Krauts, or why Dad was so intent on listening, through all the static, to war news on our radio.

My thrill of going to school never wore off. I enjoyed most of all the books and adventure stories the teacher read aloud. Soon, I was reading to Larry at home.

Some of the Hopewell kids were wretchedly dressed with tattered clothing and had pig lard on biscuits or potato peelings for their lunches. One boy wore his father's run over and worn out shoes, which were many sizes too large. Since these kids didn't have enough to eat, Dad and other school board members helped arrange surplus government commodities for a school lunch program. One neighbor kid's father had committed suicide in the worst of the deep Depression. That family didn't have much of anything. Because of the free lunches, things became better for them--and for us. I became addicted to surplus hot prunes in powdered warm milk and sugar. We took turns fixing the school lunches on the old stove, helping Mrs. Vermillion.

Often, we came home from the Hopewell School to find that Mom had made oatmeal cookies, and on rare occasions, raised donuts, rolled in grainy sugar. School days were magic most of the time.

One boy at school was nicknamed "Haystack" because of his bushy hair. Having decided to impress the teacher and get rid of his hated nick-name, he used cow cream to slick down his unruly mop. The next day he arrived at school with every strand of his hair sealed in place in a new hairstyle. By late afternoon I smelled a strange odor coming from his head. The cream had soured, causing a reeking, offensive odor. The teacher had to scrub his head under the water pump in the schoolyard.

Weeks later I had a fight with him at school with my big brothers urging me on, he hit me on the head while I punched him in the belly before the teacher stopped us. I felt proud that I'd stood up to him when he'd called me "a four-eyed albino." Although I hadn't totally understood what he meant, I knew that it had to be awful.

Haystack's older brother was a much bigger problem. One day, Mrs. Vermillion kept him after school as punishment. A wild kid with a bad temper, he and Mrs. Vermillion got into an argument. He became so angry that he got the axe out of the wood box and chased her around and around the schoolroom as she screamed. Because the eight-grade boy had responded so violently to Mrs. Vermillion, she used milder techniques in her future dealings with him.

From our Jankee Place, one hill separated us from school, which was only a mile away. Often walking that distance, Bob and I were more concerned with the treats in our lunch buckets than with our studies. Jay, one of the oldest kids in the one-room school, was our leader, looking after us as we came and went to Hopewell day after day.

One day, George Nix, our neighbor, was having coffee with the folks. We boys were all ears around the table when he said, "A fella can twist the heads right off them dang burrowing owls by walking around and around 'em." Jay believed every word of the story and had wanted a close look at one of the little owls we passed on our walks to Hopewell.

The next evening Jay was late coming home from school, and Mom was beginning to worry when at long last he arrived. Dejected, he had spent several hours walking around and around burrowing owls trying to twist their heads off. He said that Mr. Nix had lied. Later I learned that because the owls move their heads back so quickly, almost without detection, they appear to be twisting their heads continuously around and around.

Jay had finished the eighth grade when we moved to North Park and began to attend the Jackson County Schools. In each of our classes there were more kids than there had been in the entire Hopewell School.

Both schools, elementary and high school, were located on a hill a few blocks east of the center of Walden and could easily be seen from our Two-Bar. My first day in Walden Elementary School was a terrifying experience. When I saw the throng of pupils in front of the two-story, white, green-roofed building, I didn't want to get out of the car. I remember saying to Mom, "I just can't go to school here. Look at all those kids!"

"You have to, and it's only a half-day today. Go ahead. It will be all right," she assured me. I felt like a nobody. Nothing in the classroom was familiar to me, and I didn't know anybody in my class. Besides, all the boys but one were bigger, too.

Mrs. Prime, my teacher, scared me to death. The opposite of my beloved Mrs. Vermillion, she was cross, never smiled, and didn't seem to care about me. I just knew I'd die in her overcrowded classroom with thirty-five third-grade students as witnesses. Because Mrs. Prime was so demanding, I stammered and couldn't read well in front of her. I guess she must have thought I was some kind of dummy, because the next thing I knew, she cast me off into the group of slow kids.

To my horror, I watched Mrs. Prime take the smallest boy, Dennis who talked too much, and tape his mouth shut. Because Dennis was always getting out of his seat, she also ran the straps of his bib overalls through the back of his desk, strapping him in his seat. As I approached school each day, I was mortified and sick to my stomach. I feared the old bat, Mrs. Prime.

My salvation arrived in a few weeks when they divided the class into two parts. Those students in the slow group, including me, were to get the new teacher, Mrs. Rudolph. Mrs. Prime didn't want any part of our "dumb group." Mrs. Rudolph, a crippled lady with a deformed left arm, seemed to be an improvement. To me she became an angel, who in caring about me lessened my fears. She gently guided me as I adjusted to the big school with all those kids.

When Jay was well into high school, Dad bought our first U. S. Army surplus jeep. At last, Jay had something to ram around in with the other boys, instead of having to borrow the folk's car for dates and special events. Since the jeep had four-wheel drive, Jay was able to get to school when other kids couldn't in North Park's deep snows. He would take us younger brothers to school, dump us off, and then make the rounds picking up his buddies. Jay made us younger brothers feel welcome in riding to and from school in the jeep, took pretty good care of us, and patiently waited for us when he had to.

I loved that little jeep and that ride to school. But to Dad, the jeep had other functions on the ranch. Those were always the top priority, keeping us walking a lot of the time. Our jeep was used when fixing fences, going places our pickup wouldn't, and freeing Dad from hooking up a horse team and wagon to go someplace quickly on the Two-Bar. The little Willy's pulled a rake in the hayfield and gave us speed in roaming the ranch to check on livestock or when zipping into nearby Walden. Dad only complained that it cost more for gas and repairs than a team and wagon.

After Jay graduated, Bob took over the jeep for two years. I had to wait until he left school to get my hands on the little handy machine that could get us to school fast on those cold wintry days.

Many of my school teachers were wonderful, caring people who left after only a year in North Park. I couldn't understand what Mom meant when she pointed out that my teachers needed more opportunities for cultural enrichment. I wondered what they could possibly need beyond the great hunting, fishing, and mountain beauty surrounding them. Other cultural matters were strangers to me as a ranch kid.

Each year the end of the school and the long bitter winter, a strange phenomenon occurred in North Park. Upset because of losing sports seasons, poor band performances, lack of teacher dedication, or poor discipline, a group of parents descended on the school board meetings. Always blaming the teachers and school officials instead of their kids or themselves, these vigilantes brought complaints. Some charges were: one teacher was an alleged homosexual; another teacher was drinking beer in the local bar; one teacher was a Mexican, which wasn't bad, except they wanted a smart Mexican in the classroom teaching their kids, not this dumb one. Some charges were sound; most were ridiculous. The usually female-dominated vigilante squad jammed the local school board meetings. Year after year, they confronted the board members, and forced them after hours of arguing back and forth to knuckle under to their demands.

Mom, in her frank and down to earth way, said it was the result of "cabin fever" since it occurred just prior to spring and at the end of the Park's long winters. Perhaps the confinement inside and close contact with husbands all winter gave some women a strong need to lash out. The best target, of course, was the school, not the husbands, but specific teachers not fitting an exact description of what a teacher should be. School board after school board suffered through these annual assault meetings up on the highest hill in little Walden.

Some good as well as some poor educators moved on after being verbally assaulted in public before the school board. It was difficult enough putting up with rural kids, many less than interested in schooling, their pranks, and the cold long winter. Our vigilante group was a final straw for many teachers.

To many ranchers, education was not as important as understanding cattle and ranching. So many a kid just limped along learning the basics of reading and writing. Many were killing time before starting into ranch work.

Since some of my brothers, and I were so interested in history and school, our folks purchased a beautiful, blue-jacketed set of The Books of Knowledge. We devoured them, especially enjoying the ancient history parts.

I carefully observed my teachers, and I admired them for what they knew and for their accomplishments. I never really thought I could go to college. Secretly, however, I dreamed that I was a teacher whose students would listen to my ideas and respect them. A ranch kid would never say aloud that he wanted to be a teacher. In my day, being a "School Marm" was not a manly thing for a ranch kid.

After three year in Walden, back in the summer after fifth grade, a wonderful event happened. Harold Rosenfield became my friend. I no longer felt like some little puppy yapping at the heels of Bob and older classmates, wanting their attention and friendship. Harry's family soon built a little house on our edge of town. Doing things at his place and the Two-Bar cemented our friendship. From then on, I had someone I could depend on besides my little brothers.

Mr. Jones was my sixth grade teacher and a very good one. He played more sports than my women teachers had and often took the time to throw balls with us behind the school. Knowing a man who could teach was a revelation. He stayed through my seventh grade and helped reinforce my secret idea to become a teacher.

Every day I still felt inferior when I stepped into the school building because of my weird eye. My left eye turned inward a bit, making it difficult to focus on the chalkboard. According to Dad, the turned-in eye condition was prevalent among our relatives back in Virginia. They had been nicknamed, "Cockeyed Richards." I felt like the most unlucky kid in the world since none of my brothers had the roving eye, or even wore glasses.

The eighth-grade teacher, Miss Able, a full-faced neophyte, plain-as-a-board, frumpy teacher had a double class of 7th and 8th graders. Because of the large number of pupils in the room, she had difficulty keeping order. To punish the boys she made us hold out our hands, palms up, then she'd whack us with her wooden ruler. We tried not to cry in front of everyone in the class. Thank goodness we had other teachers for some subjects who managed the classroom better.

When Miss Able wasn't looking, some of us were shooting hard, rolled-up pieces of paper with rubber bands around the classroom. The girls told on us. Miss Able made us stand facing the blackboard. She had us stand on our tiptoes and press our noses against the blackboard. A chalk ring was put around where our moist noses hit the board. We then had to stand fifteen minutes on our tiptoes with our noses in the circles. If we chewed gum, she made us stand in the corner with the gum stuck to our noses for fifteen minutes.

We boys were always in some kind of trouble with her. Yet she thought the girls were perfect. Miss Able had a "rat system" where the girls put a boy's name on the blackboard when he did something wrong that Miss Able didn't see. Yet she had no system for boys to rat on girls.

About once a week, Miss Able would flee the room to the principal's office while bawling. Then we were given a strong talking to by principal, Pete Lepponen. Usually, we shaped up for a few days, and then it would all happen again. Thank goodness that in the current age, the practices she used in her frustrations are taboo with kids.

In my P.E. classes, we played softball with the older high school boys. Bob was a super pitcher with a blazing fastball that seemed to rise. He struck everyone out with a vengeance. I wanted so to get a hit off of him to prove myself in front of the older boys. Although, wishfully, I thought he might just give me a good pitch to hit since I was his brother, he threw even harder to Harry and me and always struck us out.

Toward the end of my eight grade year when I was ready to face the challenges of high school with my ever faithful Harry at my side, I learned that Harry hadn't passed and would have to repeat the eighth grade. Since he and Miss Able didn't like each other, Harry hadn't tried very hard. Since she considered him stupid, he proved it to her.

Over that summer, I took it upon myself to help him pass the tests before the fall term so we could be in the same high school class together. Unmotivated, Harry gave up. I had not succeeded as his tutor, for apparently I had wanted him to pass and be in my class more than he did.

Growing Up Wild

I was fearful of entering high school without my mainstay, Harry. So, at five-feet-six, ninety-five pounds, I went into the world of bigger kids and more complicated situations. I was past the point of being able to say, "I'll get my big brothers to beat you up!" Jay was gone, Larry would help, but I couldn't count on Bob all the time.

As a freshman, I had to endure initiation as my older brothers had before me. A week was set aside to haze the high school newcomers. I had to wear my pants and shirt backward, wear two different colored socks, and wear two different kinds of shoes. One day I had to wear one of Mom's old dresses. Each day a big red "F" was painted on my forehead with dark red lipstick. If challenged by any senior, I had to snap a clothespin on my nose, put a shoebox on my head, and kneel when replying. I had to sing the school song if ordered to. Some of the big senior boys seemed to pick on Dennis and me since we were the shrimps of our freshman class.

The harassment went on all week with Friday the big day of the formal initiation. I worried and dreaded it, having no idea of what they might make me do.

We freshmen were paraded down the main street on Freshmen Friday. We were hauled in pickups to whitewash the big rock "J", for Jackson County High School, on the bluff north of Walden. Then each of us had to get a gallon of water from the Michigan River, walk on the highway to the Illinois River on the west side of town and dump the water in. After that, we were hauled in pickups to school for initiation in the school's gym.

Seniors ran the initiation with tenth, eleventh, twelfth grade students and teachers watching. We were told as a group that we had to eat a live earthworm, swallow a living goldfish, step into a bucket of broken glass, and step in a box of warm fresh cow manure. The steaming animal wastes, buckets of glass, worms and goldfish were shown to us nervous freshmen.

Although I didn't really think that they could actually do what they said, especially the bucket of glass, I wasn't sure.

When my turn finally came, blindfolded and barefooted, I was led alone into the gym. First, I had to tip my head back as they placed a strand of wet warm spaghetti into my mouth. Then, I had to swallow a warm sardine which had been substituted for a live goldfish. Next, my foot was shoved into a bucket of ice that did feel like glass. Just afterwards, my other foot was plopped down into a box of warm mud. Then I was permitted to remove the blindfold. The student body and faculty clapped and cheered. I was shown the spaghetti, sardine, ice and mud by the laughing seniors. My shoes were given back to me and I was allowed to sit on a chair to clean my foot with a towel. As I put on my shoes, I received an electric shock from a model-A coil that gave my body a strong jolt and sent me sky high. The spectators roared. Having survived the initiation, I was officially a Jackson County High School Wildcat, whatever kind of animal that was.

During the event a couple of freshmen girls fainted or had pretended to. One girl wet her pants. Those girls didn't have to finish. Thankfully the ordeal was finally over. An evening dance was held to make the freshman feel a part of school. I avoided the dance because I couldn't dance and was fearful a girl might ask me.

The ordeal my classmates and I endured in entering high school was scary since we were frightened stiff about what would happen to us. Seniors had made it sound as if they would half kill us. But we all wanted to be accepted into Jackson County High School. It turned out to be like an Indian Sundance, something to live through to become part of the village, something we could not avoid.

Looking back as an adult and an educator in the 2000s, I am horrified at the barbaric event we classmates were put through, seemingly with approval of the school and community. Perhaps it was the time and place where people had endured the same and thought, "we went through it, and so can they." Like many things in my growing up this hazing event, inflicted on young frightened kids, was something I never witnessed again in any other public school. As a career teacher, I shudder, just remembering it, and am happy such things are now forbidden.

To many people in my valley, school wasn't as important as it was to my parents. Mom was always upset when the opening of school was postponed because there had been a wet haying season. The rancher-dominated school board always voted to delay school so kids could help finish the hay harvest. Dad always thought it was silly to close school the first days of October deer hunting season. However, we kids didn't object to days off.

My dad wanted us to behave in school, and we tried to comply. However, he told stories of when he was in high school and how he and friends put a mule into the principal's office one Halloween. It was there overnight and made a real mess. He was suspended for it. Also, he was once caught after putting Limburger cheese on the furnace and stinking up the school. Another Halloween, he roped an outhouse and pulled it over on its door with a man inside. The man was so large that he couldn't crawl out either of the holes. Dad was afraid to let him out and left the man inside all night. So we understood that with Dad it was, "Do as I say," rather than "Do as I've done."

As small kids, Halloweens were judged by the quality of the treats people provided. If they didn't reach the standards we kids had in mind, or if we had a grudge of some type against the party, we tricked. First we learned to rat-tat-tat on windowpanes. With a notched thread spool slipped over a nail and pulled by a stout string, which made the spool rotate on the glass, we'd scare them. Then we'd soap house and car windows, dump over trash barrels, and even topple outhouses.

Paul Willard Richard

Eventually, in high school, we used the little jeep and a log chain to topple deeply-anchored privies.

Each school morning as a freshman, I made the sack lunches for all the brothers, eating mine in the little gym while some older kids danced to the music provided by the school's shiny jukebox. I was alone and much too shy to learn to dance or even when I knew how, to ask a girl. So I sat and watched some of the other kids drink pop and enjoy what I yearned to do. Without Harry, I was incredibly lonely.

Bob, a deadly shot, made the basketball team. I didn't go out for basketball because I couldn't compete with Bob and I didn't want others to compare us. It was a case of "Big Brother itis," so I just kept playing basketball in our barn by myself. I was proud to have Bob as the top scorer on the team for our school. I did everything possible to promote my brother, who was the first star athlete in the family. I bragged to everyone about him, went to all his games, and talked basketball with him by the hours. He liked the way I relived the games and kept track of his scoring and rebounds. That year, as a tenth grader, he became a Gore League All-Star, one of the youngest players to do so.

I felt somehow, someday, someway, I would measure up to what my brothers had done in the little high school. I followed Bob around, doing his bidding, and trying to earn his acceptance during the years we were in high school together. My treating him as if he were some hero, worked well.

Finally when Bob, the big basketball star, graduated from high school, I took over the jeep and got to drive my two little brothers to school.

Between spring and the start of my junior year in the fall, a miracle took place. I grew from five-six to five-eleven in height and went from ninety-six to one hundred fifty pounds in weight. My worries of being a "runt", as Bob's friends had always called me, were over. At last, I was as big as or bigger than the other guys in my class, and I began to interact more with my classmates. However, I still felt most comfortable at the rivers with Harry, who was now serious about school, although one class behind me.

Our social studies teacher, Mr. Stewart, didn't treat boys very well. He liked the girls, causing us boys to resent him. So one dark night we drove the jeep near his house in town. We had filled a paper sack full of fresh cow manure, lit it afire on his porch, banged on his front door, and raced away like the wind. Mr. Stewart saw the fire, ran back into the house for water, and put it out, instead of stomping on it as we had hoped.

Being full of the dickens, I sought out opportunities to prove I had some guts. Our second-floor math room had two doors. I peeked through one of the doors during lunch hour and saw the teacher helping one of her pet students. This teacher who had big breasts, liked certain boys. We suspected that they were her secret lovers. I picked up a chalky eraser and tossed it at the kid. Instead of hitting the kid, as I had intended, in horror I watched that eraser hit the teacher on one of her huge boobs. She was wearing a black dress and chalk powdered her. I ducked out and started down the hall, as screams emitted from the math room. Instead of fleeing the scene of my crime, I innocently reversed my direction and headed back toward the math classroom when the principal and others bolted from his office and joined me.

Although I never tossed anything in the direction of a teacher again, Harry and I once flushed big firecrackers down the toilets. As blood brothers, we kept our silence about that as the principal questioned our class.

One day after school, Larry and Jimmy put a garden hose into the open window of the Harris car, turned on the water, and ran. They were getting Mr. Harris back because the man had called the law on them without actually seeing that they had been the actual villains. The car didn't fill with water as they expected since the water leaked from the doors and trunk as fast as it ran in. Afraid to go back and shut off the water for fear of being seen, they finally called the Harris house saying, "Is Red there?"

Mr. Harris replied, "Red who?"

"Red Pepper. Doesn't that burn you up? Oh, here's another thing that'll burn you up; a flood has visited your car. Check it out, and be careful next time who you blame and call the town cops about. We never broke your windows."

Each winter, since Dad now headed the county school board, Mom invited teachers to the Two-Bar for supper. Seeing the teachers away from school gave me insights into teachers. I wanted so badly to impress them, but I feared failure in their classes since they now knew the folks socially. Not wanting to let myself down, I worked harder in school. While the teachers and Mom expected me to do well, I sometimes in my heart just wanted to play sports and goof around.

Lo and behold, the year after Bob graduated, I made the basketball team. I played on the B-team. I lived and died basketball in the winters of those next two years. I felt liberated since I no longer had Bob around to live up to.

Early in my senior year, the new coach, Sam, demoted me from the A-team back to the B-team hoping I'd quit basketball. I responded with a 33-point game, showing the fans and my coach that I didn't belong on the B-team. I had earned my spot back on the varsity again.

Basketball in Walden was a big deal in every sense of the word. Since there was no TV in those days, the entire community supported the team. Stores closed when the games were played out of town. Fans in long caravans of cars followed the county snowplows that cleared the roads for away games. The snowplows met us again on our return trip for the single-file drive along snow-walled half tunnels back to frigid Walden.

The coach's job was secure, providing that his team won more games than they lost, and if he didn't upset school board members by not playing their sons enough. Nearly all the ranching people considered sports as terribly important, a bit more so than folks in Walden.

I wanted to be a part of it with all my being and never worked harder at anything. I was a loyal part of a team of Les, Junior, Karl, Dogface, John, Fred, Ken, Warren, Bob, and Dick. We wanted to win at all cost, as if we were in a war of survival. Like the Blackfeet, we sent out scouts to study the other warriors' battles and learn their weaknesses. The coach helped us study other players' habits and moves as Tecumseh did in the 1790s when he spied on and learned about the frontiersmen in Kentucky before launching a raid.

Everyone at school talked about sportsmanship, and at the end of each game we were to circle around and give a stomping cheer to the other team. I hated having to do that cheer and detested the cheerleaders chanting in the losing moments of our losing game, "Whether we win or whether we lose, we're Wildcats just the same." But, the coach would say to the team, "If winning isn't important, why keep score?"

Most of our team considered the cheerleaders to be a bunch of showoffs that didn't know or appreciate the pure game. Basking in their own glory while riding on our efforts, the cheerleaders took the game too lightly in our minds.

Each player had his opportunity for personal stardom by being "high point man," "top rebounder," "top guard, "most steals," or "best foul shooter." These honors, in our local paper, were proudly wore just as the Cheyenne long before wore scalps and showed captured horses following a battle. To help bring tribal victory, we competed for these top honors. Instead of a victory and scalp dance, we gathered in the Roundup Cafe booths, in cars, and in school halls, and for days we relived and reviewed our efforts. Then, planned the next game.

Our team letter jackets of blue and gold were decorated with our tribal symbol, gold balls and silver bars reflected our tenure and team membership. As top dogs in our village, we showed off quietly and strutted about in subtle dignity. Our community knew who their warriors were and respected our battles of honor.

Both Bob and I used to tell our coaches, kidding of course, "Coach, my dad won't sign your paycheck this month if you don't play me in the ballgame tonight." Dad never knew about our playful threats, and the coaches never thought them very funny. Today, I cringe thinking back on how the coaches must have felt.

While at home, Mom would say, "You're too wrapped up in this basketball. It's not that important in the long run." I couldn't see her viewpoint. What did she know about the game? And, besides, I wanted her and Dad to see that they had two sons who could play basketball. I even wore the same 77 numbers that Bob had worn. But I was never half the player.

On one team trip, with basketball dominating my thoughts, I was jolted into a great sadness. We ranch kids didn't get out of our home county often. Between Granby and Kremmling, I saw thousands of starving deer along the highway. Their bodies littered the railroad tracks since many were too weak to avoid the train on its daily runs to Denver. I suddenly realized that Mom was right and other things mattered, such as the poor deer and how I was not doing much with Harry during basketball season.

My senior year we played in the district games and upset Kremmling who had beaten us twice by wide margins during the regular season. By some act of God, I suddenly scored thirteen points in the third quarter. Having battled for two years to show the coaches my worth, I started the final playoff game as a six-foot senior. All I wanted was to start a big game, just once. And there I was a ranch kid with all the townspeople, kids, and my parents looking on and screaming the cheer, "Paul, Paul, he's our man. If he can't do it, John can..." in a massive vibrating gym as the championship game started. We lost the game by two points in a heartbreaker, ending our season, but giving me a lifetime of memories.

Bob even finally recognized me for making the starting lineup and for playing well. In my heart, I knew I'd done well with my limited abilities, poor eyesight, and all. As part of a winning team, I'd shown the folks I could play.

Earlier that fall, I'd played on the school's first football team. Speedy Harry didn't like the game and wouldn't come out despite my coaxing. But Larry's roughhouse nature was perfect for football. The playing field was located in our meadow below the house at the edge of Walden. Mom watched from her living room window on the hill. During the first game in our school's history, when someone called time out, we all ran for the sidelines to talk with the coach, as we had done in basketball. How green we were at football. I played every game, and we lost them all.

I had great fun that spring when Harry and I pitched our team to the state playoffs in baseball. Having thrown rocks all those years on the Two-Bar had finally paid off in pitching skills. I had won my third sport letter to equal Bob's achievements.

We had other dubious family achievements. At lunch one day when Jay was in high school, he put our jeep into four-wheel drive and skillfully eased it up the cement steps and inside the school lobby. There wasn't more than half an inch clearance on each side of the doors. His classmates admired the feat. But the principal was less than impressed and told Jay to back it out at once before it fell through the floor. Bob put the same jeep inside the school when he was a junior, as did I, to the dismay of the principal, Mr. Voris. When Larry did the feat as a 10th grader, the new principal called Dad who was still president of the school board.

Jimmy drove the jeep to school a bit during his freshman year in high school. He wasn't old enough to really drive it legally. He did manage to squeeze the jeep into the school lobby much to the horror of the principal. It was a clean sweep with all five Richard boys.

I didn't seem to realize that there were other things going on in the world outside of sports. When I was a senior, Mom said in disgust, "If anyone opened your head, a danged baseball would roll out. That's all I hear."

Although I was our class's yearbook editor, I left the entire job to my yearbook staff. The yearbook turned out to be the poorest in a decade since other people had to finish it at the last minute. My name was on it as editor, causing me painful shame since I'd dropped the ball in helping my classmates.

My last two years in high school in Walden were delightful. I had jeeped around, learned a lot about not putting all my energy into one thing, and played sports. In Jackson County High School, I was a big bug in a small puddle. I totally enjoyed myself, I stuck with other ranch kids in a pinch, and I felt like I was somebody.

Chancy Mankin ran the local drug store hangout below the Odd Fellows Lodge on Walden's Main Street. He had put up with Richard kids' pranks for years. One day he met Mom in the grocery store and said, "You know, Edith, at times I just never would have believed it could happen, but all your wild sons have survived and are growing up to be pretty good."

Maybe I ran wild and got away with more mischief since Dad was president of the local school board. However, Jay, Bob, and I all felt ten feet tall when Dad handed us our diplomas at high school graduation. Jimmy and Larry graduated later. We all made it--all five of us actually graduated from the high school on the hill. Over the years of our schooling, poor Mom and Dad had put up with a lot. Mom had no gray hair, but Dad sure did.

Chapter 15

EXERTIN'

"I doubt if you can lick your upper lip!"

Time was flying by as I continued revisiting the past rather than trying to find a way to save the ranch. My mind was flooded with the pleasures and pains of my years of trying to grow up and learn to take care of myself. Being on sacred ranch ground again, stunned my mind. There were so many facets to my ranch kid past to remember. I drifted away to my naive youth.

Since I'd been raised in an all boy ranch family, I had to learn about girls. Although some of the lessons came at unexpected times, I learned to exert myself in dealing with the creatures who tried to run things at school. A ranch boy couldn't be a wimp and let them totally lead our class.

At the termination of the seventh grade, we had an end-of-school picnic down by the sandstone bluffs in a willowed meadow on the Homer Hampton Ranch south of town. There in the willows we ate hotdogs roasted over a bonfire and played games along the Illinois River. I was in my element as things soon evolved into a boy-against-girl skirmish. I led a small, boys' band with Harry. When we blasted the girls with dry cow pies, they ran away in a scattering stampede. One of the girls struck a tree stump snag with her knee and fell. Paula Berry then accused me of intentionally hitting her in the right knee with a branch. I pleaded my case to the teachers, who seemed inclined to take Paula's side; they wouldn't listen to 7th grade rowdy boys. They said the matter would be dealt with later at school.

With cow pie assaults over, we turned to Mary Jo. She was rather mature, wrote love notes, and carried them with her. The boys, trying to get these at all costs, planned an attack in the willows. They dragged Mary Jo to the turf and searched her purse and pockets as she fought like crazy. No love notes. Determined to find the spicy notes, I noticed a bulge under her sweater at the belt and assumed it to be her wallet. As she sat up, I grabbed her sweater just as the teachers and all the girls were approaching to break up the what-ever-was-going-on attack. There was the billfold, but before I could grab it, Mary Jo rolled and twisted away. I stood aghast holding one end of her sweater which was now up around her neck and revealed her large bare breasts. Everyone fell silent for a moment. Then I released my grip, allowing Mary Jo to cover herself.

Teachers yelled, girls cried, and Mary Jo, who was older and more mature than the rest of the girls, called me a "four-eyed sex maniac" in front of everyone, as I stood with the snickering boys.

Back at school, I had to face the principal, ancient Miss Osier. In her office, she stared at me with beady eyes below purple tinted hair and sucked in wrinkled lips. Recently, she had spanked an eighth grade boy, who, when she finished, took away her yardstick and broke it in half. He was expelled.

After what seemed an eternity she said, "Explain yourself, young man." Those words came from the narrow lined mouth I feared.

"I didn't mean to do it. We were all after her wallet," I said, cringing.

"How dare you take hold of any girl's clothing."

"I was only trying to get at her wallet. All the boys wanted it. Then she just twisted almost out of her shirt. Honest, I didn't mean it to happen." I could tell by the look on her face that she wasn't buying my story.

"If this wasn't the last day of school, you'd have a lot of time to make up for this and for hitting Paula."

"I didn't do that," I protested. "I didn't hit her."

"Be that as it may, young man. You should have had enough sense not to be in the middle of it. You know better, being from a good family. I'm calling your mother to come to take you home. I'll let her deal with it, and you can have all summer to think about changing your ways," she said as reached for the heavy black phone.

Mom came to school. Miss Osier and Mom spoke privately in her office as I waited nervously outside, sinking into a hard chair and wanting to die. On the way home to the Two-Bar, in silence, Mom never said one word about the situation nor would she listen to anything from me. She stopped me when I tried to talk about it saying, "No more." Her message was that I'd better watch what I did around girls, because she expected better.

Later, I heard Mom telling Dad that Mrs. Berry, all in a huff, had told her, "Paul is the meanest boy in that school, and you have to pay the doctor bills for damage to my daughter's knee." But, to my relief, my folks never had to pay anything.

Soon after that, Dad hired a destitute new man with a tribe of dirty, downtrodden kids, who all slept on filthy stained mattresses on the bare cold floors of our cookhouse. Their ragged clothes were stuffed into cardboard boxes shoved into the dim corners. The kids raced about the house, uncontrolled. Mom was put out at having such a bunch around and put up with them because help, according to Dad, was hard to find. We boys played with them some, but we soon stopped because most were younger and girls to boot. The girls took to tagging after us around the Two-Bar. When the newness had worn off, we employed all kinds of deception in ditching them so that we could do boy things.

One afternoon I was shooting my bow and sinking arrow shafts deep into my target on the backside of our big hay pile. One of the older girls, April, came to watch. She was a sixth grader and a year behind me in school.

"Paul, will you teach me how to shoot the bow?"

I was shocked that a girl wanted to shoot a bow. April's request made me uneasy. "Maybe sometime later," I replied.

"How come you don't want to play with me anymore?"

I was really on the spot and replied, "I'm just trying to improve my aim so I can get some fish once we turn the ditch on."

"You just think I'm no fun because I'm a girl," she said, hitting the nail squarely on the head.

I stammered in answering, "No, I just don't play with girls much because we have boys in our family."

"I like you a lot. Do you like me?"

"Sure," I replied. But I could feel uneasiness welling up in me, as I fired my arrows at a faster rate and never looked at April.

She moved closer saying, "I want you for my boyfriend. Would you like to kiss me?"

I gasped, "Maybe," as I wanted to sink into the ground. When she stepped toward me, I turned on my heels.

Changing my mind, "No!" I shouted over my shoulder, as I headed for the river. I never wanted her to know that I had no idea what to do. I'd never kissed any girl.

For the next weeks, I avoided seeing her at school and on the ranch. I kept my distance from her as if she had the bubonic plague. I was saved when her father got a better job and they suddenly moved to a timber camp in the south end. Mom was delighted to be rid of the "outfit" as she called them, and I was relieved to never have to look again into those blue-green eyes of the hired man's daughter.

Paul Richard, the story teller, who loved wild things and became a biologist. Illustration by David Hartman

Bob and I once peeked at another hired man's daughter as she got undressed in the cookhouse, seeing nothing but her underwear. We stopped peeking after two boys in the grade between us got caught being "Peeping Toms." The town marshal had followed their tracks in the light snow directly to their houses and caught them. They had to apologize to the girl and her parents. I would have just died if my parents had to deal with that.

Dad never mentioned sex to any of his sons. He just wasn't the kind of man to line up his sons behind the bunkhouse and give us a "birds and bees" talk. He must have expected us to figure things out by observing the animals on the Two-Bar. We all saw what cattle, sheep, horses, dogs, chickens, hogs, and other critters did that produced their young. Mom was much the same. However, they both were big on treating women with total respect and wouldn't tolerate bad talk about other people or their mates. So I was raised in almost total ignorance of girls my age, but most kids my age were in the same boat.

Later, Dad had hired a skinny, strange guy who worked on a rake in haying for about a week when a horribly fat woman driving a big wreck of a car suddenly appeared. Claiming to be his wife, she wanted to sleep in our bunkhouse. Dad said, "Not in my bunkhouse with other men around." She stayed that night in the beat-up car in the yard. Mom told Dad, "This can't keep going on."

It was raining and the car was parked behind the bunkhouse that afternoon. One of the haymen said, "Guess what's going on in that car behind the shop?" There were no windows on the west side of our bunkhouse on the second floor. But there was a double sash window in the shop on the ground level. I rushed there with Bob and climbed onto the shop workbench, peeking out of the top smudged window and into the old jalopy. We saw a gross couple of half-naked people rocking the vehicle, doing the likes of which we'd never seen before.

Love and sex stuff seemed to be all around me as I hit the eight grade. That fall in our high school shop class, some older boys used a lathe to grind out a foot-long wooden statue of a male sex organ, mounted it on a small board, and pulled a pad of steel wool over it after having glued it to the wooden base. After study hall, they sneaked in and placed it on the desk of Miss Able, my eighth-grade teacher. We boys snickered as we waited. Prancing in to teach us, she picked up the object and asked, "What is this?" holding it up to the class. Then her face instantly turned stark white as she slowly lowered it and dropped it into the wastebasket. She headed upstairs for the principal's office. Furious and red-faced, Mr. Lepponen grilled all of us boys about the item, pacing back and forth in front of us with the thing in one hand. Of course, the girls had first been sent to another room by the principal.

As I entered high school, I hadn't a hope of getting dates with girls. Still small, blond, shy, and four-eyed, I lacked money, transportation, and nice clothes. In addition, I had little experience with girls. I lacked confidence and feared rejection as much as I feared hell itself. So I had my crushes from afar, lusted a little in my heart, and questioned if I'd ever have a girlfriend. Because I also questioned whether I really wanted to give up all I'd have to in order to romance a girl, I went after sports.

One of my high school classmates went to the Laramie First Street red-light district to see the ladies of the night. He contracted VD and had to take shots of penicillin from Doctor Morgan. Word around school among the boys was, "Bruce has the clap." Had it been me, I would have died a slow death. What would Mom or Dad have said?

With other ranch kids and school chums, I started hanging around after school in the Roundup Cafe on the north end of Main Street before heading home to do my chores. The cafe had a long counter, tall stools, a soda fountain, and a grill at the far end. Booths bordered the opposite wall, except in front where there were pinball machines. A jukebox rested against the far end of the counter and in front of the hamburger grill. All the booths, counters, and walls were done in light, knotty pine. A heater grid in the far end of the floor was where we kids stood to warm up and melt the snow off our overshoes on those cold winter days.

Our Roundup was a lively place. Kids were coming in and out, the jukebox was playing Patti Page, Eddie Arnold, and Doris Day songs, the pinball machines were usually ringing, and the students were giggling, yelling, and loudly gabbing.

For those with jeeps or cars, the contest was to see who could park the closest to the front door of the Roundup. Hamburgers, chocolate cokes, and tin roofs were the treats of the times. In the evenings and on weekends, we relived ballgames, gossiped, dreamed, and schemed in those knotty pine booths. Boys met there for trips, to pick up dates, for car races, and for fights. An unfancy place, kids felt at home there and most adults didn't.

To show whose vehicles were fastest, boys and girls my age jammed into cars and raced from the city limits four miles to Brownlee's silver-colored oil storage tank. North of town, the test hill was rutted and scarred where we proved whose jeep, car, or truck could best power-climb. In the old Roundup Cafe, we proved ourselves in pinball, story telling, and teasing. In my high school Walden days, parking was being in a car holding hands and talking while "making-out" was actually kissing a girl.

I loved our little jeep and gave it a tough time, too, but I never parked with girls in the cold ranch vehicle. I would roar off the little hill in front of the county sheds where the snow plows and trucks turned around. The snow was always packed down, making the hill icy and slick. I would cramp the little jeep short and spin clear around at least five times. Then I would crank the jeep around and spin it the other direction. Harry and my brothers loved cutting these doughnuts in the ice as much as I did. Sometimes when I was in high school other jeeps would join us. Once we had five sets of headlights spinning around like tops in the dark night.

However, our parents never knew of the jeep spins. Bob once turned it over with six kids inside, but none were injured.

Dad never uttered a cross word, but said, "Take it to the garage uptown and have Vern fix it."

After I graduated from driving horses, our one old tractor, our jeep, and our family car around our five acre ranch yard's circle drive, I finally got to drive by myself and soon learned that cars were killers. That happened when Dale Chadwick rolled his car on the community-building curve. When we heard of the wreck, we raced out of The Roundup and drove to the nearby scene on the south edge of town. Dale's car had gone end over end six times. I saw Dale dead on the curve. Some of the first to arrive on the scene, we saw the other guy with him lying in the barrow pit. We saw him die in the grass as he gasped for air. None of us knew what to do as the town marshal finally arrived and hovered over the victims. Beer bottles littered the scene. A stream of blood two feet wide from Dale's body had ran clear across the highway on that steep curve. Seeing someone I knew in a bloody mess was awful. I felt numb standing around the scene and ended up puking in the grass. Looking back, that event should have stopped me from taking risks and doing the unwise. However, some of we mountain boys seemed to take forever to learn the obvious.

To impress buddies and girls, we did some real stupid things in cars in North Park. A bunch of us, including Harry and I, were in a couple of cars looking for something interesting to do. We heard there were some cute girls at the 4-H Camp near Gould in the south end. We were wearing old black hillbilly hats--the ones that hang down. We pulled into their camp and started talking with the girls. No adults were there, just this one older guy, maybe a college kid.

Maybe we cussed too much--and we probably looked like a bunch of thugs in our silly hats, but pretty soon this young guy came over, pulled down on us with a rifle, and told us, "Hit the road." I really gave the guy a lot of lip. Then I cussed him out before we left. I told him, "We'll see how tough you are without a gun if you ever come to Walden." Mine was foolish tough ranch talk in front of the big crowd of camp girls and my six buddies.

Finally, under gun-point, we retreated into our cars and pulled out on to the road in front of the 4H Camp. Maybe three hundred feet away, Les Powell pulled up beside the road and said, "Let's shoot cans." We all piled out with our rifles and started blasting beer cans we easily found in the barrow pits.

Instantly, the watching crowd of girls back at the 4-H Camp ran for cover as if they were under fire. They hid behind buildings and hugged the ground. To see them hit the dirt and hide behind every log and tree was funny for a moment. Knowing that they would probably call the law pretty soon, we roared off for Gould. We didn't want to meet Sheriff Woodruff on the road and took the Rand cutoff to Walden so we could miss him.

We were all sitting in The Roundup by the time Woodruff strolled in and gave us the once over with his cold steel eyes. He told us that we were in big trouble for shooting up the 4-H Camp. Then he told us not to leave town. Since we hadn't really shot at the camp, I was not worried.

Later, Judge John Price held a hearing on the incident in the county courthouse. The camp officials presented a good case, but they couldn't prove that we actually shot in their direction. In giving his statement, Harry said, "If I'd been shootin' at 'em, there would have been a bunch 'em dead."

At the end the Hearing the Judge really read us all the riot act and warned us about trespassing, cussing, and shooting in the wrong places. But that never slowed us down much from our "horsing around."

Later I was stopped in the jeep for running a stop sign. The Town Marshal, Ross, asked, "What does the word 'stop' on that sign mean to you, Mr. Richard?"

I said, "Spin Tires On Pavement," and roared off, hitting the nearby Two-Bar's rough pasture where his police car couldn't follow. I had played cat and mouse with him before and enjoyed our chases. I didn't dare do such things with sheriff Woodruff.

Surrounded by comforting mountains, my high school friends and I considered ourselves top dogs. Our rivals were the log choppers who bordered us to the north by Fox Park. Others rivals were in the south Gould area. We considered guys from Steamboat Springs, Granby, and Middle Park as outsiders and undesirables. Wyoming types from Encampment and Saratoga were not our favorites, either. Laramie football types didn't please us when we met during dances at Wood's Landing.

It was time of local territories when fights were common and expected. Places like Wood's Landing were roadside slaughterhouses. I had to be prepared to defend myself there. Log choppers, football guys, and North Parkers ranch guys never mixed well during wild Saturday night dances where lots of heavy drinking was taking place. There had always been boy conflicts as I grew up, including bare fisted battles between we Richard boy.

Once Mom told me that she had heard my name yelled on Walden's Main Street just as she finished with her grocery shopping. A boy riding by on a bicycle shouted to another kid across the street. "Hey, there's going to be a fight."

"Where?"

"Up at the light plant."

"Who's fightin'?"

"That Zangari kid and one of those Richards, Paul, I think."

"Wow, I don't want to miss that."

I had a big scrap with the tough Italian kid from Denver. Although I won the fight, I had sore ribs and knots on my head afterwards. Mom didn't seem too interested in the fight, but she listened to the whole story.

We school kids exerted ourselves fighting. Word spread when a boy was called out. Kids gathered at the city light plant lawn since fighting at school was against the rules. While the stately, white cinderblock building generated electricity for the town of Walden, we boys fought. On the light plant's soft grass, we didn't get hurt as much as in fights at nearby rocky vacant lots. Usually, we fought bare fisted, by rounds, and had older boys in charge. There were clear winners and losers. The fights were fair, for in my Walden no one tolerated two-against-one, big-against-little, or older-against-younger situations. Nobody kicked a downed scrapper either.

In my ranch family, fighting among us boys seemed to erupt at frequent intervals. Usually, the fights lasted only a short time and the reason for the fight soon was forgotten. Fighting was expected of ranchers' sons. In fact, if a boy in our culture didn't fight, people looked at him askance and wondered what was wrong with him or if he might be a sissy.

Although my Dad never bragged about fighting anyone, he listened to the heavyweight boxing matches, probably the only sport in which he expressed a personal interest.

Mom didn't approve of our boxing or fighting inside her house. Things usually got broken. So we boxed with boxing gloves by rounds in the barn with each other and with the neighbor kids. Most of the fights ended when someone became tired, got bested, became mad, or just quit. If I wanted to box and was tougher or older, I had to take it easy on my opponent. If I didn't, I'd end up shadow boxing alone.

Although some town folks told me fighting was entirely wrong, I saw it as a good way to develop the ability to defend myself. I felt a confidence in knowing what fighting was all about, how to do it, and in realizing that nobody could entirely dominate me. I said that no matter how tough or big someone was or how badly I got beaten, my opponent would at least know he had been in a fight. Our youthful saying was, "He may give me my lunch, but I'll always get a sandwich off him during the scrap."

So we Richard brothers fought in barns, in alleys, in drug stores, in schools, in pool halls, and in hay meadows, in sagebrush flats, in back yards, in foot-deep snow and in gravel pits at night before dim car headlights. When it had to be, we were still Richards, and the outcome was a matter of pride. Let it never be said that a ranching Richard chickened out or was mean or dirty. As an adult today, I shake my head and wonder how fighting could have been as it was since most of the tiffs could have been settled in easier ways.

Larry, the most fight-prone and toughest of our tribe loved to fight. Having started fighting with other kids at an early age, he had that stubborn streak essential to being a good scrapper. In grade school, he licked most of the kids in his class. "The bigger they came, the harder they fell." From then on he ruled the roost and held his position, and often fought bigger kids older than he was. In high school, many boys were on his side, and even sought his protection. Fast as blazes, he punched extremely hard. Because he knew how to fight, he had great confidence. And, he didn't know the meaning of fear.

As tough as Larry was, however, he couldn't best me when we got in a tiff. I could always best him, or he'd back down. For some reason, and lucky for me, he could never really hit me squarely. His blows would be half-hearted and glancing. Larry just couldn't clean up on me like he did other fighters.

I couldn't bluff Bob. He would haul off and let me have it whenever he pleased and as often as he pleased. I usually gave him a wide berth. Once I attacked him after he really hurt me. I hit him in the knee with a big rock in revenge. Totally ashamed of myself, I watched him cringe in pain, and immediately apologized. After that, however, he stopped using me as his personal punching bag.

My big fights were mainly with strangers or with schoolmates. I seldom became friends with someone I'd fought. Yet one case, after the fight with Tony Zangari, was the exception as we became friends afterwards. Our fight at the light plant had gone twelve endless bruising rounds before the stocky Italian decided it was time to give up. Was I ever glad he did!

Other times I had to decide whether something was worth fighting for or not. Although my high school chums and I swore, "No girl is worth fighting over," strangely, most of the fights I saw in high school had a girl's affection as an entangling factor.

Once I saw an outsider hurting a waitress in our Round-Up Cafe. This blonde guy, about six-one, was twisting the arm of our longtime neighbor, Hope Waldron. Although he was probably just messing around, I didn't like it from an outsider. My comment to him about being "real tough with women" was accepted as a challenge. The fight was on. Up the main street for a block we fought. We finally ended up in front of the Park Theater where the town marshal pulled me off him. I think we both had had enough. My right hand was numb from missing the guy and hitting a car's hubcap when we were on the ground. From my appearance—the knees torn out of my pants, my ribs sore, my lips cut, and my hands with the bark knocked off the knuckles—it was hard to tell if I had taught him a lesson.

After that fight and a few others in which I'd been super fast and aggressive, my school chums started calling me "Dempsey." In the hall at school, I flew off the handle, decked a kid, and broke his glasses. Instantly, I felt rotten about it. Then later a kid slapped me in what he thought was a fun political debate. My temper went, and I knocked him over a table in study hall. Those actions both earned me time after school to reflect on my quick temper.

After I called him out for saying something seedy about my brother, Bob, Tip Eaton fought me to a standstill. Although there was no crowd or brothers around to cheer me on, he and I battled in a graveled lot and fought down the street. I'd numbed my hand hitting his forehead and couldn't do much. Then after I hit a gas pump with a wild swing, I couldn't use my hand at all. Exhausted, at my suggestion, he too was willing to call it a draw. With that result, neither of us lost face. We never finished the fight, and he never again said evil things about my brother.

At the end of my junior year an older boy in school called me a name, reflecting on Mom. Well, defending one's mother was a high priority, even if the guy hadn't really meant to be offensive. Hot tempered as I was, I wanted to fight. When I called him out, he said, "Don't let your mouth overload your ass."

I snapped back, "Don't sweat it. Just be there. I doubt you can lick your upper lip." All afternoon in school I wondered whether I'd made a mistake to challenge him since he was bigger. Besides, I'd never seen him fight.

The battle, held by rounds at the light plant, was a barefisted affair witnessed by a huge crowd. With my brothers and Harry urging me on, I thought I was really tough. But the rounds seemed endless, and my opponent was much more of a challenge than I'd expected. Eventually, my arms felt like dead logs. It's tough to continue battling, knowing you're whipped. Although accepting defeat was not easy for a ranch kid, I knew when the better fighter had beaten me. I learned a good lesson in humility by having Paul Broughton stomp a mud hole in me and walk it dry. I remembered Dad having told me earlier, "Don't get too big for your britches; there's always someone tougher."

With my pride hurt, I had a heap more insight about toughness after getting soundly whipped. It took the desire to start fights right out of me. From then on, mine was not the role of predator but one of a strong, swift, defensive attack when I knew fighting was the only way out. I felt a little better when the toughest kid in my class said, "At least you have endurance and guts, Paul."

Over that summer, I had grown like a spring calf as I shot up six inches and put on forty pounds. I got some body hair, too. Sports, and not girls, were still in my heart most of the time.

I continued playing sports, adventuring at the river, hanging out at The Roundup, and avoiding the social scene with girls. Watching from a distance showed me that I wasn't ready for the time and effort a relationship with a real girlfriend entailed. Even if I had wanted to date a girl in my class, it was impossible in my mind. There were far too many things to do on the Two-Bar, the Norris Place, and North Park's wide-open spaces, all more fun than being with girls. So, I never dated anyone until the end of my senior year.

As I neared the end of high school, our tight local clan was slowly eroding. North Parkers were traveling more, mixing less in town, and isolating themselves in front of new television sets, getting the one channel out of Cheyenne, Wyoming. Roads were now better paved and maintained in winter. Improved cars carried people away from our mountain bowl through the mountains and out into the big world of Laramie, Fort Collins, or even Denver in hours rather than taking all day.

My brothers and I had messed around and pulled all kinds of misdeeds, many of which didn't show much "horse sense." We seemed to have been slow to learn. However, if we hadn't exerted ourselves in fighting, in driving, and in dealing with girls and local authorities, perhaps our capabilities would have remained unknown to us. There had been great security in belonging to a rural community as I grew up. My small town, which was always protective of its youth, allowed me freedom to make costly and valuable mistakes.

As an adult, I now realize an "old boy" protective safety net had been in place in my mountain ranch setting, protecting us while allowing vast freedom for mistakes and hopeful corrections during my growing years. My rural community was far more lenient than city boys today face in their exerting, learning, experimenting, and trying to grow up to become men.

Chapter 16

WINTERIN'

"I can't stand to see him suffer anymore."

From my vantage point against the buck and pole fence, I could see the surrounding snow-capped mountain peaks above the evergreen forests in every direction, causing me to turn my mind back to the everlasting and nasty winters that dominated my growing up. Mom always quoted my great-grandmother, Lindy Monroe, when describing the seasons in North Park saying, "This darned country has nine months of winter and three months late in the fall." The Utes had named the mountains I could see to the south over tiny Walden, The Never No Summer Range, supporting my Mother and great-grandmother's feelings. Yet, as a boy, I never felt the same as those strong ranch women did about the long winters that shortened all our other seasons.

I could see Mom's point when our meadows turned golden brown in late August. Before the month ended, traces of white showed on the high peaks to the west. By early September, willows and aspens decorated the low foothills with splendid yellows and oranges, and by late October snow usually stripped them bare of their brightly colored leaves. As fall gave way to the North Park winter, nothing green growing remained except for the evergreen forests.

I viewed my kid winters as a time to build snow caves, to have snowball fights, and to plan raids with the Rosenfields for the next summer. I also thought of the puzzles I'd assemble on the living room card table when it was too cold for outside venturing.

Before every winter set in, however, it was time to sell our cattle. Each fall Dad gathered steers and some tail-end heifers, hoping to sell them at home instead of taking them to a market out of North Park. He kept the best heifers as replacements for our own cowherd. He bartered for the best price with cattle buyers who arrived in fancy cars and inspected our herds along the two rivers. They never sat a horse.

Many a fall afternoon my older brothers and I saddled our horses and pushed the steers to a meadow from which cattle buyers could get a good look. When they passed by to inspect our herd, I felt ten feet tall in my old Heiser saddle. These were Richard cattle.

Dad, who considered our cattle equal to the finest in the Park, had one year won a red ribbon at the National Western Stock Show in Denver with his fed yearling steers, proving their quality. He wanted our cattle to bring at least the same price as our neighbors' had brought. If the price offered wasn't what others had gotten, we loaded our steers and heifers on the train and sold them in Denver or Omaha stockyards.

Since it was the one big income time, our livelihood depended on the price. Like most ranchers with bank loans and mortgages, Dad took the earnings to Denver and paid the interest on our bank loan and on the Two-Bar mortgage. Then he took out new loans to finance us through the next year.

After the yearling cattle were sold, I knew winter was close at hand. The frosts were heavier each morning. Days shortened, nights lengthened, and the cold winds penetrated me, whistling around the corners of our ranch buildings. On the surrounding mountains, snow appeared at increasingly lower elevations until at last it reached us at 8,100 feet. The first snow at the ranch was usually light and gave a friendly warning of what lay ahead until May.

I knew we lived in one of the biggest "snow holes" in Colorado, and Dad said jokingly each winter, "This may be the year the Park snows clear full to the top." Winter weather kept us home attending livestock. It was a time of three-and-four buckle overshoes, chopper mittens, heavy coats, and warm hats along with long-john underwear. We made fast trips to the two-holed outhouse. During most of my growing up winters, I was warm on only one side at a time--the one closest to the wood cook stove or kerosene heating stove. Although I wore most of the clothes I owned, I was usually chilled. My hands seemed to be always cold as my red blood showed through my pale skin.

The approach of Christmas excited me. How I planned, waited, yearned, and, along with my brothers, counted the days! In October, each of us let the folks know what we wanted as a big gifts--Jimmy, a sled; Larry, two new pairs of boxing gloves; Bob, a bicycle; and Jay new ice skates. I wanted a 45-pound pull bow. Although we provided Mom with exact details and catalogue numbers, we were never assured of these items. Whether we had been good enough or whether the folks felt the gifts were right, were the determining factors.

My best behavior was in the months prior to Christmas as I buttered up Mom. Knowing that the folks would usually get us a couple of smaller gifts kept me dropping hints. By early December, we boys had nearly worn out the pages of the tattered catalogues and our wants were clearly known. We knew it was fruitless to get greedy, and the folks let us know quickly when a request was "out of line."

We brothers also drew names to give five-dollar gifts to each other. Of course, we all had to figure what to get our parents, too. They provided us with ten dollars each. In addition, we boys made lists of what we wanted and exchanged them. We soon learned who had our name. We lobbied, threatened, and bribed that brother for what we wanted. "I won't get you anything, or what you want, if you don't..."

Around the first of December, Dad took all of us who could cram into the cab of the pickup to the west side mountain foothills. There we tramped in the deep snow until we found the right tree---the kind he wanted---a Douglas fir with soft flat needles. We'd cut and drag the tree back to the pickup and mount it in the bay window of the ranch house. We'd decorate the tree with bulbs, tinsel, and popcorn strings and place an angel on the tiptop. Then we would spend hours on the floor looking at our tree, poking packages, and dreaming.

As the holiday tension built, I would dip into my magpie money, haying wages, and saved allowance to buy more and more gifts. I exchanged names at school with classmates, and the teachers gave me something, too.

One year, Larry, Jimmy, and I went together and purchased a musical powder box for Mom and a pair of wool-lined driving gloves for Dad. We excitedly played the music over and over in the basement without knowing that Mom could hear it clearly up in her kitchen.

Because we were super-snoopers, our parents had to lock unwrapped gifts in the trunk of the car where we couldn't possibly get to them. We even went so far as to snoop into Mom's shipping receipts from Wards and Sears. We subjected the packages under the tree to squeezing, shaking, pinching, and having small holes poked into them.

Once when I was snooping for packing slips in Mom's jewelry box, I found a letter from Evelyn Monroe, who was asking to come and live on the ranch with us. She promised that there would be no problems and that she would be a good grandmother. Although there was no envelope with a return address showing where she was, the date was recent. I was afraid to ask Mom about it because she'd know I'd been snooping. Now I had a secret--a living grandmother. But, much later I would learn more about my grandmother and where she was living.

By Christmas Eve, because we were so keyed up, Mom and Dad allowed us each to open one gift, except the major one, under the tree. We had popcorn and cocoa before we went to bed. Since we couldn't sleep, we'd keep peeking into the living room at the lighted tree to see if any new gifts were out. Eventually, morning came and new packages and special gifts were always there. Not once did I ever see Santa or my folks put out the gifts.

We dressed hurriedly and sat waiting at the tree for everyone. The youngest boy started playing Santa, and we opened the gifts one at a time until the tree was bare. There was always some final surprise gift somewhere in the room, the house, or the barn for a boy who had given up on getting what he wanted.

After Dad quickly milked the cows, we started off breakfast with a traditional fresh sugar-topped grapefruit. We played with our toys and games while Dad and the men fed the cattle. The men returned early for a big Christmas dinner of turkey with oyster dressing, pumpkin pie, Dad's favorite rolls, mashed potatoes, Mom's favorite of marshmallow-covered sweet potatoes, and all the relishes including cranberry sauce, which I loved. When we were all full, she brought out the fudge and other candy and nuts.

We tried our new gifts, played board games together and worked puzzles far into the cold dark night. As much as I was pleased by how much Mom enjoyed her music box, even more so I was thrilled with my new forty-five-pound pull bow.

That 1948 Christmas, Croppie, our long time old horse, was in trouble. Although his teeth had been filed down, his hay-grinding ability couldn't be improved. In the increasing cold, his strength was ebbing. He was deathly thin, showing his ribs through his thick hair. A week before Christmas, Dad led him into a stack pen on the Illinois to let him have all the hay he wanted. It was a tribute to the old horse, for no other horse was ever allowed to eat in a haystack. Croppie was grained daily, but he steadily went down hill. Soon it became obvious that our old friend would not see another winter. While feeding the cattle, Dad and Jay visited him each day during Christmas vacation. The rifle hung in the scabbard on the sled, but Dad couldn't do what had to be done to an old friend who had once saved his life.

Our companion for years, the short-eared horse had been a topic of conversation. Each of us had learned to ride on his steady back, trusting his surefootedness. No horse had ever been more faithful or reliable. Croppie, who had done it all from being a good cow horse to a gentle kids' horse, had finally earned retirement.

It was a cloudy dank cold afternoon of Christmas Day when Jay approached Mom.

"Mom, I'm going to take the gun and go down and see Croppie. If he isn't better, I'm just going to shoot him. I can't stand to see him suffer anymore."

"It would probably be a good idea, Jay. I don't think your Dad has the heart to do it. Maybe he just hopes Croppie will make it."

"He was my first horse," said Jay tearfully as he walked out of the door with the rifle under his arm. Jay let me join him.

As we walked down the ridge in the soft snow and bitter cold, we thought about the old horse we'd grown up with. We had loved him and cussed him at times, but we didn't want to see him suffer. Most of all we didn't want to shoot one of our best friends.

Upon reaching the haystack, we couldn't see the old horse. Jay levered a shell into the chamber of the .32-20 Rifle and with tears walked around the haystack. There in the snow lay the old horse, cold and still. He had died during the night. We both wept. In silence, we followed our tracks in the snow back home. I went to bed early that night, seeming to have lost the Christmas cheer.

Mightily loved Croppie, the boys' first old, gentle horse – trustworthy and surefooted.

Cattle were fed daily during December as winter had set in solidly with bitter cold. On New Year's Day, it looked as if a storm were coming. When the gusty winds started blowing from the west, the weaning calves in the corral jumped sideways, kicked up their heels, and greeted the new year of 1949. On the six-foot-high manure pile, our workhorses romped and played like colts against an ashen sky to the west. At supper Dad remarked, "There's been a ring around the moon and the livestock was sure bucking this afternoon. Sure to be a weather change."

By this time of year, we were always ready for winter. But this one was a bitter surprise even for those living in Colorado's biggest snow hole. As dawn ushered in three feet of new-fallen snow, the mercury dipped many degrees below zero. Although I appreciated our new inside bathroom, Dad still preferred the outhouse. I couldn't understand why.

I strained, listening to static riddled radio reports telling about the weather conditions on the plains of Colorado with frozen animals standing upright in fence corners in a completely snowbound state. Twenty-five thousand ranchers and farmers were suddenly isolated for weeks on the plains. It was the exact kind of storm that Dad had feared when we lived with our sheep bands near Limon.

What a way to start the new year of 1949! Dozens of people had been frozen in their cars after being trapped on the state's highways. Thirty-nine died as the storms lasted days and days on the windy plains of eastern Colorado. Reports kept coming in of tragedy where people and livestock had been unprepared. Cattle stood in the prairie howling winds and starved. People had no way to feed them in the deep blowing snow. Over the next two months, at least twenty-five percent of Colorado cattle and sheep on the flat prairie died. Three more big storms followed the New Year's four-day blast and kept an icy lock on our west.

Our cattle were fed every day. Dad saw to that as snow piled deeper. It was too cold for a crust to form on top of the three feet of snow. The wooden runners of our big feed sled settled nearly to the ground in the sand-like snow. Workhorses had to be rested often on the way to the feed grounds. When soft snow piled up under the front sled bobs, the men sometimes had to shovel it out. For a few days, light winds moved the deep snow back and forth, shifting it like great sand dunes across sagebrush and meadows.

It continued to snow as my brothers and I waded and struggled to school though the shifting sea of white.

Snow piled deeper and deeper. Soon we could see only the backs of the giant feed team above the five-foot deep snow. Hefty workhorses lunged and heaved as they tried to pull the sled through the thick white snow. Since Dad and the men couldn't see anything except white, they often had difficulty finding haystacks or our cattle that stood humped up on feed grounds in the bitter cold.

Soon the winds came stronger. The wind blew like the furies of hell, piling up snow until it covered haystacks with ten-foot high drifts. If a buried haystack were found in the blinding ground blizzards, the feed sled was pulled over the fence and beside the top of the stack.

Mom, to my amazement, kept us all home from school a few days because of the terrible weather. I was thrilled to read and play board games with my brothers on the huge dining room table that had been handed down for three Richard generations. Winter had us trapped in our mountain bowl with no way out.

In our isolation, the worst happened when I got a toothache that aspirin didn't help. Since there was no way to get to a dentist outside North Park, Dad found a dentist, of sorts in town. Reluctantly, Mom took me to his office on our feed sled pulled by the horses in the dank cold. It was old Dr. Mac Cartney, the town soak. Mom had to gather him up from the Corral Bar. In the dentist chair for my first time, I faced the old rank-smelling man who appeared to have slept for weeks in his rumpled clothing. Muttering to me about my two decayed molars, he had me keep my eyed closed and my mouth open. In a flash he yanked out my two teeth, hurling them to the far corners of his office. I heard them bounce on the hardwood floor. He never bothered to pick them up or give them to me as dentists were supposed to. Mom was indignant about his not using Novocain, but he just muttered to himself and headed back to the bar with her money. I said I hated dentists, cried most of the way home, and swore to brush my teeth every day. I heard Mom tell Dad that she hated living in such a cold snow hole where she couldn't get a kid to a decent dentist.

But we were winter locked with cattle to feed. Scooping snow from the top of each buried haystack to get at the hay was backbreaking work in the winds. One man shoveled snow, while the other flanked hay onto the sled. Keeping hay on the sled was also difficult. Sometimes the wind blew pitchforks of it across the meadow and scattered it in the whiteness.

When they were flanking hay, Dad and the hired men worked without their coats, even at forty below zero. Their Scotch caps, frosty breaths, and chopper mittens could be seen in the whiteness as they moved hay. The winter work wore out both men and horses as they battled wind and cold to fill the fifteen-foot-long sled with rich green food for the cattle.

Horses with frost-covered faces, long hair, and shaggy bodies stood with arched backs against the cold while the sled was loaded. The horses stood with their heads pressed together for protection from the stinging winds. Once the load, or jag, of hay was on the feed sled, the horses lunged and struggled to move it from haystack to the feed ground. Even though the horses were stopped and rested often, they played out easily. It was a hard winter for the horses even with Dad's switching teams every other day. Dad wouldn't let me or my brothers help feed in the horrid cold. "It isn't a place for kids," he said.

Feed grounds on our open meadows became nearly impossible to use. Either hay blew away, or the blowing snow soon drifted over it. Dad finally moved the feed grounds to the tallest willows which would give some protection. The hay wasn't scattered by the winds as much. However, it meant freighting hay a longer distance, but there was no choice. That frigid winter some North Park ranchers fed their cattle at night, hoping the winds would be calmer. We were lucky that our ranch was protected by the tall west ridge and had big willows. Yet the constant winds shifted the deep snow daily. The winds blew hard every day from January seventh until the middle of February.

While Dad and the hired men were battling to feed the cattle each day, we kids fought our way to and from school in the deepening drifts. Jay's old jeep wouldn't run, and even if it had, it couldn't have gotten through the five feet of snow on the level. One morning on the way to school in the wintry blast, we noticed a thermometer on the Red and White Grocery Store in Walden. It read minus forty-two degrees Fahrenheit at 8:30 a.m. The wind was howling. Before facing the cold blast and struggling on, we crowded into the store doorway for a few minutes.

Walking was difficult, and we couldn't see in the blowing snow. No motorized vehicles moved at the ranch, and few moved in Walden. Our best defense against that cutting wind and blinding snow was walking backward. After we had faced the storm and walked a few yards, we then turned our backs to it and walked backwards. Then we turned forward into the stinging, wind-driven snow again. Those windy months, I walked backwards as much as forward. The folks worried about our coming and going to school when they couldn't see our barn across the yard. However, we had our special places along the way to school to get out of the wind. We took breaks behind fences, in doorways, and at Rosenfield's house.

When visibility was impossible, Dad came with the feed sled to pick us up a few times after school. I remember seeing four black horses with shaggy long hair covered with snow standing in front of school. Frost and snow were clinging to the face hair, frosty steam belched from their nostrils, giving them the appearance of creatures from a prehistoric age.

Dad's face and the hired man's face were dark and leathery brown from snow and windburn. At times we couldn't see a thing as we forged through the drifts in town. The main ranch gate was fifteen feet high, and the snowdrift was within three feet of the top when we passed around it. We were hunched together on the sled with our backs to the whipping wind. It was a relief when we reached the red barn and got out of the wind. We'd leap from the sled and struggle in the thigh-deep snow to reach the house. We'd walk over the yard fence, step down, and stoop to get into our porch below. With tall snow banks surrounding it, home was warm security.

Soon Dad came into the house. He put the pitchforks in the kitchen corner and laid the horses' bridles on the pile of coal black overshoes. In such weather, he didn't put a frozen bit in a horse's mouth or want to work using a frozen pitchfork handle. A horse's wet tongue could stick to the bit and a frozen fork handle could snap.

Before supper we did chores. Larry and Jimmy brought wood and coal in for the cook stove. Jay got oil for the heating stoves. Bob pumped water in the big corral. Larry took care of the 4-H sheep and calves. Jimmy and I fed the chickens and gathered the few eggs. After we had shoveled the snow out of the chicken house, we tended to the rabbit hutches. We dug them out and got hot water from the house for the rabbits and for Mom's chickens so they could drink before it quickly froze. Dad milked the cows and fed them hay; he grained and hayed the workhorses. The hired man fed the sheep and helped Bob and Jay feed the calves in a swirling world of white snow and bitter cold.

At the supper table we enjoyed plenty of good conversation about the rough snowy day and school. There was a certain feeling of safety in spite of so much snow and cold about us. While the seemingly never-ending winds blew, we played cards, did homework, played with Smokey, listened to the radio, and talked of trapping in the spring.

Each morning Dad checked the thermometer attached to the north side of the house; first he had to scrape off the thick window ice to see out. Ten, twenty, twenty-five, forty, forty-five, thirty-seven, and forty-one below-zero temperatures continued as the forever winter dragged along.

The wind, which finally ceased on the twenty-third of February that winter of '49, had blown every day for over six long bitter weeks, as storm after storm gripped the Park. The quiet was haunting without the house's continual creaking. We dug out. Within a week the county cleared our road. To avoid the fifteen-foot drift under our ranch gate, the snowplow operator plowed around it in the sagebrush.

The storms had taken a heavy toll. Mule deer had been stranded on sagebrush hilltops northeast of Walden, and the low sage surrounding them was buried under deep drifts. The poor deer stood and died. Nearly sixty percent of the deer in Jackson County perished by starvation.

I rode with Dad in the pickup and saw hundreds of live deer, just skin and bones, along the highway toward Wyoming. The deer, too weak to get out of the road, would stand with a dazed stare in their soft eyes. Dead ones littered the roadsides. Town dogs killed many in the deep snow because the dogs were able to walk on the crust, while a deer's sharp hooves sank to the bottom and slowed them.

Some of the deer died because the Game and Fish Commission, in an effort to save them, decided to drop alfalfa hay by airplanes to the starving deer on their isolated hilltops. Dehydrated and starving, the deer gobbled up the hay. Since they couldn't digest it, they soon died of hay impaction of the digestive tract. The misguided help was like suddenly giving a starving man a six-course meal.

In the spring, over five thousand dead deer were stacked in long piles and burned with gasoline. That winter ended the great deer population in North Park because the state game managers never again allowed eight to ten thousand deer to populate North Park.

That awful winter some of our neighbors were snowed in for three or more months. The Florence Irvine family didn't get to town until May. Worst of all, the Manvilles, who had wintered in Greeley, had forty head of cows starve and die in the willows along the road to the Norris Ranch. They had become isolated from the main herd. Manville's hired man was alone and had not bothered to count the cattle he was supposed to feed. Dad was outraged, saying, "You can't depend on hired help to look out for your interests."

One cold day that winter when Larry and I were cutting out guns from boards in the cold shop, he dared me to lick the anvil. Stupidly I did, and my tongue stuck fast. I panicked like some rabbit and in freeing myself tore skin off. He said, "You're as stupid as one of those starving deer and can't figure out another way to do something. You could have spit down your tongue, or I could have gotten some hot water and freed you."

"My sore tongue won't hurt nearly as much as you will when I catch you and pound the tar out of you." Larry ran like a rabbit out of the shop, but I cursed myself every day it took for my tongue to heal.

There were more jackrabbits than we had ever seen. Deep snow buried their food and sent throngs from the sagebrush flats to our meadows and along the rivers. On snowshoes after school, we began hunting them. Harry Rosenfield, Larry, and I would head for the haystacks. Pulling our toboggan and walking on snowshoes, we hunted for the big white jackrabbits, which sold for eighteen cents each.

As we approached each drifted-over stack pen, the rabbits ran to escape in the thigh-deep soft snow. They'd flounder around the haystack, we'd circle the stacks, and blast them with our .22 rifles as they ran wildly. Bogged down and in deep snow, some of them were unable to avoid our bullets. One time one panicked rabbit stopped and froze in place just on the toe of my snowshoe. Being out of shells, I took a swing at the animal, worth eighteen cents, with the butt of my rifle. I missed and broke the toe of my snowshoe. Later Dad told me, "A rifle's supposed to be shot, not used as a club," and had no sympathy with my snowshoe plight. Old Harold Rosenfield fixed the snowshoe for me.

After we had loaded the snow-white rabbits aboard our toboggan, we made the long drag home. Those winter evenings I went to bed early, tired, and with visions of cash and how to spend it dancing in my head. We sold the rabbits, piles of rabbits that we stacked up like cord wood in the log shop, but I only made enough money to pay for my ammunition. I had shot at every rabbit I saw, missing most. There was a lot of space around a gangly, long-eared, white-tailed rabbit running on white snow. By killing the rabbits, we had saved our cattle a little hay that the dead rabbits would have consumed. Dad approved of our rabbit hunting, telling us that twenty-eight rabbits could eat as much as one cow during the winter.

He also encouraged us to keep the rabbits out of the corral feed racks. Over the railroad track from the west as the sun was sinking each evening, the snow-white rabbits made for the green delicious Richard hay. Although we killed large numbers of them, they still came until it was too dark for us to shoot at them.

Abundant coyotes stayed near the haystacks where the rabbits congregated. I once went along with the men just to see the coyotes that stayed some distance from the sled and haystacks. I never got a shot at them with my arrows.

As winter wore on, the coyotes became more brave and challenged Smokey. Smokey could whip one or two in a good coyote-dog fight. But, when a pack ganged up on him, Smokey would get bested and run to the men. The coyotes became so brave that they kept Smokey under or up on the sled most of the time. He would race out a few feet and challenge them with a growl and sharp barks. When they reacted and came after him, he'd race to safety and bark at them from under the feed sled. Dad didn't have any reason to shoot coyotes, for they were helping control the hordes of white-tailed jackrabbits, eating his hay.

Winter winds had deposited hard drifts ten-feet high behind the ranch house. It was a distance of about two hundred feet down the steep grade on hard-packed snow. What a temptation for kids. We used our metal runner sleds, or we nailed a small board on one ski and would sit on it and ride down. Sometimes we slid down steeper parts of the hill on pieces of cardboard; the first person held up the front edge of the cardboard and everyone else piled on behind. Someone would get us started, and down we'd slide to that eventual pile-up at the base of the slope. We would crash, roll in the snow, laugh, wash one another's faces, and move into snowball fighting.

In late winter, we always made a trip across the Illinois River to the big ridge high above our secret owl caves in the sandstone outcrops. With Smokey and our toboggan, we each grabbed a long icicle from the porch and sucked on it as we headed west over the crusted deep snow. Climbing the big ridge was a real chore. It rose several hundred vertical feet above the rivers and meadows, and the winds blew over it directly from the west, dropping loads of snow, forming a dome-like cap drift. Over the cap drift we'd go on the toboggan, sitting one behind another, and sometimes having Smokey aboard. The seven-hundred-foot slide brought fears and freezing tears to my eyes. Somehow we avoided hitting the willows below and glided far across the river onto the white Illinois pasture. After a few trips up and down, we headed for home.

Then, because Smokey's long hair collected balls of ice as he struggled through the sea of snow, we had to stop often and break the ice balls with our knives.

We forged on crossing the Michigan River ice and headed for the railroad tracks where the train's snowplow had cleared a path. Unexpectedly, we happened upon a set of animal tracks as large as saucers with at least ten-feet between each set. We followed the tracks until we saw where a long tail had hit the soft snow. That mark told us immediately that we were trailing a mountain lion. We quickly went home, not wanting to encounter a hungry big cat while we were weaponless, except for our always present hunting knives.

We seize every opportunity for some fun in the depths of winter. Jay became a wonderful ice skater who took long graceful strides and made beautiful abrupt turns, inspiring me to skate, too. I used figure skates as Jay did, but Bob, however, swore hockey skates were what a real man should use; to him figure skates were for girls.

We boys often made weekend ice-skating trips together. We started on the Illinois River, donned our skates, tying our shoelaces together, and hanging our shoes around our shoulders. We skated north between finger-like snowdrifts reaching outward from the riverbanks. Where drifts totally covered the ice, we simply walked over the snow on our skates. Sometimes ice blocked the water underneath the river ice, forcing water up onto the surface. This liquid overflow made us walk on our skates around the watery surface until we reached hard ice again. There were many different kinds of ice along the river, depending on wind direction and tree protection. There were places where the river current was swiftest that never froze thick. I knew the river well, avoiding those thin areas. I had to think all of the time as I read the ice, the drifts, and the banks remembering how currents moved when the creeks were open in the summer.

I saw rabbits, coyotes, and birds while enjoying the variety of snowdrift shapes and deep blue-green ice along the miles of willow-protected rivers. Much of the time we were hidden in a world of our own, protected by huge drifts on each side. We were so busy with our own skating that we often forgot the dangers along our rivers.

When we reached the point where the two rivers met, we had our lunches. Then we skated back south up the Michigan River toward home. Jay was in the lead and Bob was far ahead, neither wanting to be slowed down by little brothers who skated at a slower pace. Larry and Jimmy who stayed together always brought up the rear.

As I glided by a dense stand of thick willows, Bob's head appeared in the corner of my eye just above the icy surface. Standing chest deep in cold water, he was unable to crawl out of the hole into which he'd crashed.

"Help me out of here," he pleaded.

"You bet," I replied trying to get close to the hole he was in, but the ice cracked under my skates when I got near him.

He yelled, "Hurry, I'm freezing."

"What should I do? Every time I get close, the ice tries to break under me."

"Lay down flat and crawl. That might work," he yelled in panic.

Eventually, I was able to get a hand to him, trying to tow him out onto the frozen surface. Several times, big chunks broke off under him until I was able to get him over to stronger ice out of the underlying current. His face, I remember, was half blue from the cold. He rapidly froze into a stiff man in his winter coat, as we moved on the Michigan River ice to the railroad bridge below the ranch house. I was half pulling and half pushing him as he continued to freeze stiff. There, I used my warm fingers to thaw his skate laces and change him into his icy shoes. He couldn't bend or reach his ice skates or feet. He tottered home leaning on me, walking as best he could as if wearing two stiff stovepipes on his legs. He was half frozen when we reached the house, barely able to talk, but Mom sprung into action warming him with warn water, blankets, and her hot cook stove.

That awful wintry event has always stuck in my mind. Later we all realized that if he had stayed much longer in the ice cold river water, it could have been the end of him since there was no way out except with help. If I had not spotted him, he would have eventually gotten hypothermia and been washed under the river's ice. That thought scared us into staying closer together when we skated, reaffirming Mom's feelings that our rivers were dangerous places.

We held less dangerous Two-Bar skating parties and invited town kids, holding them where we knew the ice was thick. We lit a big willow branch fire and cooked hot dogs, and played hockey games with willow branches instead of real hockey sticks. We used a tin can as a puck. Our parties were held in the secluded trees where adults couldn't see and winds wouldn't bother our orange blazing fire. We spent lots of time snowballing, building snow forts, and standing about the fire talking about our great athletic skills and skating ability. Although none of us were very good skaters, we had races to test our speed and as always we bragged a lot.

These winter parties were loads of fun until Jay and Bob started inviting girls. Then everything changed. They spent time trying to impress the girls totally forgetting about us younger brothers. Because I knew they didn't want me around, I stayed away.

I had earlier worked with Bob to make our barn hayloft a winter basketball court, and we agreed it would be girl free. We cleared away the hay between the baskets and had ball games around the upright beams on the wooden floor. We had to shoot short or flat shots because of down-hanging rafters. Bob, who practiced more than anyone, developed a perfect flat jump shot. In high school games, people always remarked how his flat shooting lacked arch.

Each of our long winters, some of our Norris Place baled hay was piled behind the chicken house. A huge pile of hay, twelve feet high, forty feet wide, and over two hundred feet long was a great temptation. By moving and rearranging bales, we constructed a series of tunnels and compartments in the big hay pile. Dad didn't like our playing in his bales. So we worked in secret on the west end away from his view. We had chambers, meeting rooms, and passageways deep in the hay. It was a secluded place where we could escape the winter, plan, and horse around in dim flashlight beams.

Snowballing was an art befitting our strong arms, since we missed throwing the rocks that were now under North Park's winter snow. We molded snowballs around coal and froze some overnight into ice balls that we intended to use on the hired man's son we hated. He had earlier used these weapons on us. With regular snowballs, we made other sudden attacks on each other around building corners. Some attacks were organized skirmishes from behind snow forts that we had built from giant chunks of crusted snow. Snowball wars were constant once enough warmth was present for us to mold snow. No one was safe from our volleys except Mom and Dad.

Our Sunday evening meals in the 1950's were often chili and sandwiches, a relief from the constant beef, potatoes, and gravy, our usual fare. After we had eaten, we'd head for the barn and play basketball in the awful cold. We often played in jersey gloves, hats, and heavy coats. Breath erupted from our faces in clouds as we dribbled and shot baskets until bedtime.

When we came through the snow back to the log house, half frozen, Mom sometimes had popcorn and hot cocoa waiting for us. We visited and told stories until past bedtime when we had to brace ourselves to enter the cold, unheated bedrooms. There, we crawled under piles of blankets and produced our own heat until dawn. When I was curled up on my knees heating up my bed I had my best thinking time, seldom thinking that our winters were as bad as they really were in comparison to other places in Colorado.

Early in April of 1949, the river ice started weakening. The watering holes enlarged until Dad feared cattle would fall into the holes and drown. He spent long afternoons at the river, watching the cattle drink and saving drowning cows with his rope and trusty Brown Shorty. Finally, he closed the gate leading to the watering hole and ended drinking for the day. Water-hole problems were a sure sign of ice break up.

By winter's end, the cattle no longer bunched about the feed sled eager for hay. Instead, they scattered across the snow-spotted meadows and looked for green grass. They had to be called to the feed grounds. Dad would yell, "Here boss, here boss," until they reluctantly ambled in to eat. Our old cows were as tired of eating hay as Dad and the men were of feeding it.

The cows were now big with calves and had to walk farther to their feed grounds, as Dad kept shifting from one feeding ground to another. Lots of walking made calving easier for cows, or so Dad contended.

I never forgot that bad winter of 1949. And for years when we drove to the Norris Ranch at Manville Lane, I saw the tangled dead willows that had been chewed stark white by their starving cattle. Skulls and piles of white bleached cow bones littered the ground, sending chills up my spine.

As a boy, cold winters had been a routine since those wind filled months never changed much. Those nasty winters were simply a part of our ranch life when we boys had to make our own kid fun. We were totally accepting of our lot.

Our winters seemed eternal at times and limited my freedom. After seven months of barren cold, I was ready for the change to spring. Those long winters made me appreciative of having something to do away from the Two-Bar. I often thanked God for school in the dead of icy North Park winter. As time passed and I finished high school, changes in thinking about my world, about my winters, and about my life were happening.

Chapter 17

CHANGIN'

"Never call us farmers; it's the ultimate insult."

I sat befuddled as I looked at the historic ranch house that held my parents who were about to change everything. Change was something I dreaded. My life was a steady security because of this home base that had always been there and to which I could always return. Then suddenly, I recalled that earlier big change in my ranch family that had left me dumbstruck.

Fall was always a time of big seasonal changes. As autumn was heavy upon the land, each day the sun was retreating farther south. The morning sky appeared a cloudless blue. Through the crystal sky I could see the stars earlier each evening and with unusual detail. It was as if the heavenly distance was lessening.

In the cool mornings, haymen buttoned their jackets tightly and hunched over as they rode to our hay fields. Frost had taken its toll; cold-blooded insects had no protection. Gone were the busy horse flies and ambitious mosquitoes. The mountains surrounding the Two-Bar came nearer in the cloudless clear days, showing features unnoticed before, here a canyon, there rocky outcrops. The peaks took on deeper hues of blues and purples; shadows lengthened. At sunset the fading rays set the peaks and sky ablaze in dazzling oranges.

That September day Smokey, who had always been a part of us, was in his usual spot beside the plunger, sleeping now and again in the autumn sun. He would wake to watch the activity of the haying crew and to check the members of his family as we rode by on hay moving machines. Lately he had been tortured by the seizures older dogs endure. During these mild fits he was disoriented and pitiful. It pained me to see him sometimes snap uncontrollably and froth at his mouth.

Dad watched the old dog wake up in the grass beside the truck. It was the good dog's fifteenth haying season with us. Smokey's ears perked up as he rose, stretched, and ambled toward the bright green haystack. There he stood for a long time alone, watching his family members riding by on noisy machines, moving hay piles across the green meadow. Now every action was too fast for an old dog whose hearing was failing. He was seemingly apart from what he'd once been right in the middle of in following the boy's horse teams and chasing wild things they spooked.

As the afternoon was warming up, he again checked the river bottom willows and the bluffs where he had roamed. Then Smokey sauntered back from the stacker and moved under the truck bed to seek some shade. There he fell asleep, without Dad having seen him return. After pushing up a load of hay, the big truck rumbled backwards over Smokey. Instantly, Dad knew something was not right. Leaping from the truck, he found Smokey under it and totally still. Shaken and silent, Dad sadly laid his body under a willow east of the stack pen. He didn't know what to do and stood for a long time in his grief thinking of how to break the news to everyone.

He soon waved his arms calling everyone into the slide, stopping the haying operation. We gathered around Smokey under the willow. Sobs and cries came from young men who hadn't cried in years. They turned their backs, muttered, put their hand in their pockets, and walked about trying to control themselves before returning to the prone Smokey.

At the end of that haying day everyone stood in silence as a boy dug deeply into the Two-Bar's chocolate soil and buried Smokey under the willows near the head gates where so often we'd fished by hand while he barked in the trees at wild things. With him we had eaten gooseberries under the willows and run up and down the nearby ditches chasing trout. We had often helped him to catch small ducks in the nearby slough. It was a fitting place for the old dog to rest, for here he would always be a part of the ranch where he'd roamed free all his days. With a horrible sadness and a dry lump in our throats, we left the good blue dog behind as the sun was setting in a brilliant blaze to the west.

Dad broke the news to Mon who in tears fell into a chair and sobbed for a long time. All of us were heartbroken having lost a family member who had always been our pride and steady companion. Little was said around the supper table that dank night.

Losing Smokey hit me like a ton of bricks. I was at a loss, not knowing how to control my grief. In the moonlight, I finally fled down to the Illinois River and sat on the bank going over all the old dog had meant to me. How he had saved us from the mad cow, and the thousands of great times we roamed together. All of us had had special moments with our steady friend who was more of a person to us than a pet. I knew how lucky I was growing up with such a friend, but the loss was just too much. It was several months before I could think of Smokey without having tears and feeling lonely.

Words could not express the grief. It was unthinkable that Smokey was gone from the family. No dog ever gave more. Besides being a total friend, he had taught me the absolute value of giving in order to be happy. Even today, decades later, I always tear up when thinking of my Smokey. He was so much more than a dog.

His death caused me to see that change came to the Richards as it came to all people. It was perhaps the beginning of the end of my boyhood. I started questioning values and wondering about the future, instead of living and assuming all would remain constant.

Why had I enjoyed such luxury of wild freedom growing up? Perhaps it went back to my parents and how they had grown up. A profound influence upon my Dad was the treatment of his own father by his grandfather, Benjamin Franklin Richard, way back in Strasburg, Virginia.

Ben F. Richard had eleven kids he worked hard and paid little. Expecting sons to work because he fed and sheltered them, the old man worked them as his own father had worked the slaves in the 1860s before emancipation. One day his eldest son, Charlie, ran away from Ben Richard's cruelties and came west. Charlie's father, who mistreated all his children, had never let Charlie be a boy.

Determined not to raise his own sons as such slaves, Charlie Richard raised Willard and his three other Richard boys in an unusually tolerant manner in Brush, Colorado. Most of their rearing he left to his gentle wife, Dora, who never spanked them. The parents allowed the boys a great deal of freedom, since as a kid Charlie had had so little himself. Willard Richard, in turn, continued the same tradition. He allowed abundant freedom and space where boys could be boys. My father and his three younger brothers each had families of all boys. We had male family traditions with historic exploits to uphold. Plus, we had the freedom from work unlike what Charlie Richard, our grandfather had experienced.

My mother made double sure of our freedom. An only child, she had grown up lonely and restricted. Had she not been able to escape each winter to school in town, to attend boarding schools, and to stay with her grandmother on the Two-Bar, her childhood could have been unlivable. Mom swore that she would never raise her kids in such isolation and loneliness if she could help it. Edith Richard wanted us to have the freedom to make mistakes, to grow, to learn, and to enjoy childhood.

My mom and dad benefited from negative learning, knowing what not to do. Heeding the past and their own growing up experiences, they used "horse sense" in not limiting my ideas and freedom.

I could see changes in our ranch life that bothered me. We had always had such good times gathering around the wood and oil heating stoves in our underwear and talking each morning while we got into our warmed up clothes. Now, with central heat, we didn't. I missed the visiting and story telling when we had all gathered around the oil lamps, the galvanized bathtub on Saturday nights, and our one old radio. The more new things we had to make life easier, the less closeness we had in being together. I missed hauling buckets of water with Larry and Jimmy. We had carried two big heavy buckets between the three of us, the same for coal. Not being together as much gave me an empty feeling. Sometimes I hated the electric lights, the running water, the central heat, and the television that had replaced our life of closeness. I knew the changes were better for the folks, but sometimes I was sad about leaving the old ways. Yet I had to look ahead.

My ranch-boy thinking was made up of the rural wisdoms of my day. I believed these ideas, tried to believe them, and experimented with them, because I was, after all, a ranching Richard.

To no one were we inferior. In our large family we were supposedly equal. We could hold our heads high and not take a back seat to anyone at anytime. Sure, there were people with more skills, more education, more creativity, and more money and land. However, just being ranch people made us equal to all. And we violently objected when someone treated us as inferiors. Because our ancestors had been some of the first settlers in the valley, we were proud and equal to every other pioneer family and their descendants.

Since we knew we were equal, we also knew that our rights were the same as those of everyone else. No one had better treat us unfairly or try to take our rights away. Other people were equal, but they couldn't be better or have more rights.

In North Park, there was a "class" of people more equal and more privileged than the ordinary citizen. We ranch people controlled power in the government, schools, and on most boards. Although most ranchers felt that everyone had rights, ranchers and descendant of ranchers were a tad bit better. Being born into a ranch family gave special privileges that interloping timber workers, miners, merchants, or technical people--no matter how talented or well educated--could not enjoy. Even when these ranch descendants were somewhere else, they carried the stamp of somehow being "taller in the saddle." Without a doubt, because people in ranching owned most of the deeded land, they were privileged in North Park, extending their influence into the small town and beyond.

I was a part of that select group. A rancher related to early pioneers had more status. The year your ancestors arrived in the Park was important in ranch circles, whether it was 1879 or 1886. What one's grandparents and great-grandparents had done among other ranching people had special influence. A ranch-linked person won out over anyone else for a county job, position, or award, as privilege prevailed. The power structure sustained the rancher's sense of being special and belonging. The ranchers might profess equality for all, but they practiced otherwise. After all, ranchers had settled the basin after the Utes were removed.

A defensive lot, North Park ranchers were inclined to look down on others before others could look down on them. Once a non-ranching person proved to be no threat, the ranchers became less condescending. Always feeling somewhat superior, the ranchers in showdowns with non-ranchers voted the ranching viewpoint and usually conformed to other ranchers' wishes. There was unspoken pressure to stick together and to retain landowner power.

We feared outsiders and newcomers a bit. Suspicion of them was natural, perhaps as a holdover from the days when "slick" outsiders took advantage and sold ranch settlers liquid medicines that would supposedly cure anything. "Place a basic trust in other ranchers and things will work out," was the philosophy in a showdown or election in my North Park.

Be a rancher and be strong. A man on horseback was much better than a man who walked or worked in the dirt or earned a living in other ways. This view was similar to that held by the Ute Indians, who had roamed the mountains and plains on horses and had refused to become farmers.

Never call us farmers; it was the ultimate insult. Nothing was as important as ranching. Many ranch people believed ranching inside North Park was the only worthwhile activity on earth. People couldn't be engaged in anything more meaningful. From this provincial viewpoint, my feelings of self-centeredness and haughty intolerant pride grew as a kid.

If someone from outside the Park or the ranching community had done something that a rancher hadn't done and talked about it, the provincial rancher's view considered it bragging. Conversely, if a rancher in North Park had done the same thing, then the achievement was great, and everyone should know about it.

Ranch thinking was comfortable; ranching was "King of the Park." So we Richard kids grew up with great pride and with a self-centered view of our worthy endeavors. My parents' efforts to guide me in my youth toward a somewhat wider viewpoint went against the North Park rancher attitude that surrounded me. So I grew up feeling that ranching was sacred and that North Park was the only place despite my parent's efforts to have me see beyond the surrounding mountains.

Riding horseback helped me to develop independence. On a saddle horse, I could range far and wide, see more from that height, and control my direction off roads or trails. I had a feeling of being able to do as I damn well pleased exactly whenever I wanted. My independence didn't limit the rights of others or go against the law. But overall, I controlled others in my youthful mind. Other people didn't control me or any other Richard.

As I began to grow up and to try to find my own way, I began to test these rancher's creeds. Was it true that I was equal and had the same rights, while at the same time was superior because I had pioneer ranching ancestors? Was I really that special and privileged? Such questions troubled me as I matured enough to learn to shave. I gradually sorted out what I believed. My beliefs continued to change a little because of my experiences with four brothers who were all different, yet much the same.

Changing and modifying my thinking was painful. Mom and Dad, who were great readers, tried to give me ideas and kept up with what happened outside North Park. The news was on the radio and our new TV every day. The folks belonged to book clubs, always took magazines, and read the daily *Denver Post* and our local paper.

My parents knew that I would have to leave home someday and that I would probably move to a less provincial world. There, in that new environment, I would have to reconsider my beliefs, discard them, or alter them. My parents felt that I should expand beyond North Park and the Two-Bar and knew I'd need to be able to adjust to life in the big world. I often resisted thinking about the future. In the end, each of my brothers had adjusted differently to the big world. In some cases, the apple fell close to the tree, and in other cases far, far away.

As the first Richard to eventually head for college, I took an explosive and scary leap into new thinking and new ideas. My concepts of rural life were shaken to their very roots. I soon found out that I wasn't nearly as important and special in the big world of educated urban people. I learned that the world could go on nicely without me and without my sacred ranching.

After my first year of college and on a visit back home came the first hint that change was evolving rapidly at the Two-Bar. On the border of our ranch lived an old-timer whose ideas hadn't changed much since he was born in the Park in 1880. Dad told me about a visit he had paid this old-timer that summer before they actually listed the Two-Bar for sale. My dad seemed to think his visit to Linsdy at his log cabin was very important. Totally out of character, Dad gave me an exact blow by blow repeat of the entire conversation.

Dad told me that he had guided his pickup through the cattle guard on the east side of the ranch to what we called "the goat farm," since it was on a dry and rocky bluff. Ahead, he could see the squat log cabin that rested on the brow of the hill. Below it and several hundred feet to the west stretched the ranch's lush meadows and the two rivers. In his final years, Linsdy Coe lived alone as an old-age pensioner overlooking the Two-Bar Ranch from his bluff.

An old rusty colored dog stood on the flagstone porch and gave grunting barks as Dad stepped from the pickup. Because it was a warm July morning, the cabin's door was wide open.

"Come in, Willard," said Linsdy, getting to his feet and pushing the screen door open. He extended his age-spotted hand.

"Was on my way to check water in the Queen Ditch. Since I was so close, decided to come by, Linsdy."

"Anything special on your mind besides these big mosquitoes?"

"No, not really."

"I have some coffee and a pan of my best sourdough biscuits here, Willard. I'm eatin' kinda late. Want some?" asked the thin, white-haired man, turning to the small iron cook stove and reaching for the coffee pot.

"Darned if I won't just oblige you, Linsdy."

Sitting at the small table beside the sliding sash window, they ate biscuits covered with jam and gulped black boiled coffee. Flies buzzed in the corners of the windows while mosquitoes danced outside on each pane.

"Dandy view from here."

"Damn right! I spy on everything you Richards do down on that old Two-Bar Place," replied Linsdy.

"Snow's sure goin' off fast this summer on the mountains. Glad we're about finished irrigating."

Linsdy pointed to the snowcapped peaks to the west and said, "Back in that Fryingpan Basin country, that snow never melts. I've never in my eighty-one years seen it free of drifts, even in late August."

"Yeah, but I don't get any water from that west side drainage. It's south snow that counts," said Dad, noticing the small radio, tiny bed, and large supply of food the old man had hoarded. He didn't have a refrigerator, but there were several cream cans of water in the corner along with his broom and rifle.

"Wish I had some of that good water running up here. This well is no darned good. Bagby brings me a few cans of town water each time he comes to look after his horses. Can't drive, you know, too damned old! Like it a big sight better here than in town, by grab. I just don't fit in with town people anymore."

"You were just born too late. Most of your breed have come and gone, Linsdy. Riders like you just don't exist anymore. Least I can't hire one."

"In my heyday, I could ride with the best of 'em, Willard. We rode this whole country from here into Encampment and down to Kremmling. Those were the days. No people like that now," said Linsdy, as he gazed into his coffee cup, letting his mind drift.

"I just heard there are nearly twenty-three hundred people in the Park."

"It was a better place in 1882 when there weren't two hundred of us and we were meat hunters over on the Canadian. I grew up there huntin' and ridin', you know? There were just jillions of antelope and sage hens all over the place. Now I never see an antelope. It's a damn shame, Willard!"

"Yes."

"Now the damn tourists, fishermen, hunters, backbiters, and outside riffraff have ruined this great country. A man can't go anyplace without seein' people, people, people..." muttered Linsdy as he walked over for another cup of coffee. His shoes had no laces and Dad had never seen him with socks on.

"Yep."

"When we first came to this country, we could have made most of it into one big ranch and kept all these tourists out. That's if we'd had a little money. Just seems like all my life I just worked for my month's wages and dreamed of ownin' a big ranch with lots of cattle," said the old man, standing and pulling up his baggy pants over his long-handled underwear. White hairs on his thin chest poked above the top of his faded red underwear. Also a few hairs protruded out of the buttonholes on the left side where it was unbuttoned.

"Maybe a ranch isn't what it once was. You may not have missed too much not havin' one to worry about."

"For damn sure I don't like the way you young guys use all that new fangled machinery, Willard. I notice you got one of those balers now and have trucks, jeeps, and all that clankin' stuff on your place. Last year, you was broke down and stuck more 'n you hayed. I watched you. Bet it cost a hell of a lot more in the long run than usin' horses. I think you people are dead wrong gettin' away from horses," raved Linsdy as he slammed his hand down on the red-checkered oilcloth covering the table.

"You're just getting cranky. Horses are sure less expensive, but we can't find anyone like you to drive 'em anymore, Linsdy. Without my own boys, we'd had to go to machinery a long time sooner."

"If you looked, you'd find some."

"Maybe so, but I can't spend time runnin' around lookin'. It's real hard finding a man who can drive a team and wants to work, and I can't take the time to teach a man to work horses."

"That's what gets me now, tourists and outside people a-comin' in who just don't want to hit a lick of work. I don't cater to the way people spend all their time just runnin' around. I don't like what I see. Everybody has to do everything and go every place. Just runnin' around so much, there's no time to spend with anyone. Seems like so many of them just don't care about anybody but themselves. If I were God, sure as hell, I'd take their cars away, make 'em stay home. It'd be better."

"Linsdy, they'd be running around on horses then like you and I did!"

"I think it would still keep 'em closer to home, more where they belong."

"Well, my boys run around a lot. Takes lots of gas, too."

"They sure are growin' up fast. Summer last, they came by and we visited a long spell. I see 'em running around and fishin' in the ditches, but they don't come up like they could."

"I'll tell "em to come hear some of your tales. They enjoy it."

"Good! I don't much favor bein' alone all the time."

"Most of them are pretty grown up now. This past Thanksgiving Edith and I were alone. First holiday since we were married."

"Did you enjoy it?"

"Was a little lonesome. But we'd better get used to it. They'll all be heading out on their own."

"Are they still goin' to school?"

"Last year was Jimmy's final year of high school. He's the last one. We always felt if we could get them through high school, our duty was over. If they wanted more education, then it was up to them."

"Sone of 'em in college. Wish I had done it."

"In your day nobody up here went. You didn't need schooling like now. World was simpler."

"Why didn't you go?"

"You mean to college?" asked Willard.

"Yes."

"Now I wish I had. Sure would have helped me givin' speeches and I might have run for public office. I would like to have run, but the lack of schoolin' and givin' speeches held me back. I could have gone, too. Instead, I got into the cattle business and got married. Then the roof fell in--that Depression," said Willard.

"Those hard times nearly sent me under, too. Lost my little ranch. If I hadn't been a good hunter, sometimes we'd have gone hungry."

"We had a hard time in eastern Colorado, but we got by all right. I think the real harm it did was to my thinking."

"What do you mean?"

"Well, Linsdy, it ruined us money-wise and made me too fearful. After going through something like that all those years, we didn't take chances. When a man spends years of doin' without and hardly has enough to eat and no money, it's hard later to risk anything big. My mind was always back in the hard times of Depression, instead of on the future. When things got a little better, I was cautious and feared going under again."

"Willard, I had that same problem not seein' far enough ahead or thinkin' big."

"Exactly. Edith and I should have bought more land here when we could. But we had that old lack of trust in banks and the fear of takin' a chance. The old Depression seemed to be just over our shoulders all the time. We were afraid, and it was a mistake."

"My mistake was spendin' too much time lookin' for gold, drinkin', and gettin' so old. You know, Willard, I'm just so Goddamn old."

"Naw, you're not."

"I've seen my better days, for sure."

"Guess we all have. Ranchin' for us is getting harder. With the boys gone mostly, it's hard getting anyone you can depend on. Besides this is a young man's country. When you're over fifty, it's less fun. A lot more hard work."

"Those winters really bite as time goes on. I can remember when it didn't bother me at all. Now that wind gets clean to my bones. I know what you mean."

"Times are changing and we can survive now with the boys about raised. Both Edith and I would like to winter somewhere else or ranch where the summer and winter are the same length."

"You're not thinking of sellin' out, are you?"

"We talk about it. When someone comes along to offer us more than the place is worth, I'll sell."

"Then what would you do?"

"Probably deal in cattle. I never wanted to be a slave to a ranch, but I do like cattle trading. I found out over the years that I was never a rancher at heart, Linsdy."

"You could have fooled me."

"We never really owned this ranch. It owned us."

"That is by damn the truth about the things."

"Say, I've got to check that water. Anything you want me to bring by?"

"Maybe a little water from the fountain of youth and a bigger old-age-pension check. I just hate wastin' my time away, awaitin' to push up daisies."

"Much obliged for the biscuits and coffee. See you later," Dad said as he walked out the door to his pickup. The pioneer cowboy was standing in his cabin doorway swatting mosquitoes with one hand and petting his dog with the other.

A few months later in his living room, Dad told me that story, quote by quote, he finished by saying, "I never want to be old and alone like that, just waiting to die." I could tell he had given the matter a lot of thought.

"You won't have to with the five sons you have," I said.

I think Dad wanted me to know how his conversation at the goat farm had sparked him to finally settle on selling out. Being in a talking mood, rare for him, he continued right on about our ranch and life on the Two-Bar. He seemed to be clearing his mind more than having a dialogue with me. I listened intently to my ranching father.

"That conversation with Linsdy Coe got me to thinkin'," said Dad. "I'm proud of this ranch. A lot of years have gone into getting it back in shape. Sure was a mess when we took it over. Most of the fences are new or rebuilt from the old buck and poles we had. Head gates are right now, and the dams stay in the rivers, too. The ditches are in real fine shape and carry water like they should. Our corrals and buildings are like I want 'em, and things work. I'd hate to start it all over now. When we first moved here, it seemed as if everything needed doin' at once. It works well as a unit with the heifer pasture at La Rand, the Norris Place, and now the Davis Place we added. If all the parts were joined, it would sure be easier and save a lot of gas and riding, but they aren't.

"Lots of things I don't like about this place. It's hard to irrigate and the ground is rough to hay with all the buffalo holes and sloughs. It's too close to town and dogs. But on the other hand, we can get to town easily for parts or what we need. That saves time. Best thing has been the ease of getting you boys to school. No battling bad roads like lots of people in the Park do.

"It's been an ideal place for you boys. Close enough to enjoy town and school while having roaming room here. We, at least, gave you things to keep busy and out of trouble some of the time. If it hadn't been for the room here, I don't see how we'd ever have raised you. Some of you would have been in trouble all the time.

"We haven't made a lot of money here. Thinking back on my gabbing with Linsdy, if I'd taken more chances and bought the Simpson Place and done a few things like that, we would have been better off now. But then, it could have all gone sour. Nobody knows the future. We tried our best. That's enough."

He squinted at me. "I've made a lot of mistakes with you guys. Maybe I should have pushed you more into ranching and worked you harder. Maybe you would have been less trouble, but we wanted you to have some ideas of your own, too. Perhaps we should have let you in on more of the decisions, but I didn't really know how to do that. Had we, maybe things would have meant more to you. It's been real hard talking to you about a lot of things. It's not that I'm not happy with you; it's just that uneasy feeling about your future. If we'd been tougher on you and cracked down on everything you did, maybe we would have had bigger problems. We always assumed you had good sense and could figure out what was right after you got in and out of a mess. You usually have been good help, too."

I was uneasy with his talking, wondering what he was getting at.

"Your mother doesn't enjoy the confines of North Park that much. She hates the isolation and the long winters. I'm amazed how that woman can hide her feelings and keep everything going. What a worker she's been all these years! Guess I need to show my appreciation better. Maybe she's as tired of this as I am. Haying is coming and she has to work her socks off seven days a week. I have to work and worry, but it's different for her than me.

"We both dread haying and winter. We are seriously considering selling out. Seems silly doing something that gets just a little harder all the time. Should we do something we both worry ourselves sick about? We're too busy to enjoy life, and the ranch is less and less fun when you boys aren't around."

Because I didn't know what to say, I just sat silently shocked, waiting for my father to continue.

"It's quicker using our jeep and truck to fix fence and haul a few cattle someplace instead of driving a team and wagon or going horseback. Some people on the west side are even using these new motorcycles to check on and chase cattle around. I don't approve! Horseback is the way to work cattle. I guess it all saves time, but all of it is sure more expensive. I haven't liked giving up the horses to this expensive machinery that costs way too much to keep running. But your mother sure loves her bathroom, her washer and dryer, her running water, and getting rid of that ole slop bucket. She loves that electric stove. Things will sure be easier ranching in the future than how we did things in the past, but it's now really expensive to operate.

"All you kids can't ranch. It takes this whole thing to make us a living. There just isn't room. It's been enough helping Bob get a start. No one can make a go of it up here in the ranchin' business without a start from parents or without marrying into a ranch deal these days. There just aren't start-from-scratch self-made-ranchers in this country anymore. Maybe in homestead times, but not now. It's too expensive. We couldn't help more than one of you. Don't know if Bob can make it, even with our help and his in-laws. We just can't turn everything over to him, either. Your mother and I have to live and everything we have is invested right here. We're thinking of listing the place and selling."

Bob Richard who ended up as the ranching son in
North Park. Illustration by David Hartman

I was speechless. I didn't want to go against my proud father without thinking the sale idea through. He seemed to be justifying selling and discouraging me from ever trying to ranch because of the expense involved. He never asked me or any of my brothers what we thought about their decision, a decision that changed everything.

Over time I wrestled with the decision. I had different ideas with their plan, disagreed, and developed negative thoughts about the pending sale. Still I couldn't express these feelings to my dad without undermining him.

How could they even think of selling the land I loved and had grown up on? Our swimming hole, the rocks, our camps, the rivers, and the meadow willows where we had our raids and battles just couldn't be sold. Every bend on the rivers, every outcrop of rocks, and every bunch of trees were special and held fond memories. I needed them to be a Richard. Somehow, the entire ranch had to be there as something I could go back to and touch. I needed something to identify with, to tell me who I'd been and from where I'd come. Home couldn't be sold. How could we ever sell part of ourselves and the soil containing the bones of Smokey?

What would become of our place in the community? Everyone knew us. Our father had a great reputation as an honest man, a good neighbor, and an excellent cattleman. How detached I'd be without my roots. The ranch had always been my escape in times of trouble. Just knowing it was ours kept me strong, and having something special which others didn't have made me feel blessed. An extension of me, the ranch was the cornerstone of my beliefs about myself.

But how could I object? It was, after all, my parents' ranch. I had watched other ranchers whose kids had stayed at home and had eventually taken over spreads from their parents. Too often, the parents moved away, left everything behind, and ended up with less than they needed to live a good life in their twilight years.

I struggled with these feelings. Sometimes I openly protested as potential buyers came to inspect the home place. Secretly, I hoped nobody could buy our ranch. I continued to feel hostile about giving up the land where my great-grandfather had ridden, had worked, and had grazed cattle and sheep. I didn't want to lose my place in history. I wanted to retain my heritage and keep the land I had learned so much from. What would become of me without the home I'd known?

For over a year, the ranch was listed. Continuing to attend college, I adjusted to the idea that one day the ranch might no longer be ours.

Waiting for the sale of the ranch was painful, and I often coped by casting the ranch situation from my mind, feeling helpless. I hoped it would never be sold or that the folks would change their minds about selling it. I even convinced myself that they had listed it at too high a price for anyone to be able to buy it. I wanted to have my cake and eat it, too, with both a career and the Two-Bar staying in the family.

But now, the sale had actually come. Was I too late in dealing with this hated change? Did I make a grave mistake in going off to college, thinking that a brother would eventually take over the ranch? The Two-Bar would no longer be my ace in the hole, my refuge, a place to retreat to if things went bad. Was I just being selfish in my thinking? Despite gradually knowing what was happening, news of the folks accepting an offer came like an earthquake to my life. Now, feeling totally disarmed, I actually had to face my parents in the big ranch house.

Chapter 18

REALIZIN'

"Had the dog run faster it might have caught the rabbit."

I crossed the ranch yard, now vacant of Smokey's ever-present greetings. Without the big blue dog's wagging short tail and his constant brushing against my legs, all seemed amiss. No longer could I postpone it. I would face not memories but reality with Mom and Dad in the ranch house. I hadn't come up with any new plan for saving my boyhood haunts. All I'd done was relive moments.

The screen door banged behind me as I at last entered the Two-Bar kitchen. The folks were sitting in the living room surrounded by glistening hardwood floors dotted with bright Navajo throw rugs.

"Saw your car parked out by the barn and wondered where you'd gone. The river is too high for fishing yet," said Dad, looking at me with his clear blue eyes.

"I just walked around a while to stretch my legs; long drive up from Greeley."

"Did you have lunch?" asked Mom.

"I brought something along and ate it just before I got here," I said, "but sure wouldn't turn down a cup of your coffee."

"Let's go to the kitchen, and I'll get some. How about you, Willard?"

"Sure."

"I suppose you were shocked that we actually sold." said Mom. "You sounded stunned on the phone."

"Guess I was. Didn't think you'd ever sell when it came right down to it."

"This Nebraska bird has more money than sense and really wanted it. First guy with enough money. Wants to make it a showplace for registered Herefords, so he says. And we won't have to face another winter," said Dad happily.

"I am delighted to be getting off a ranch after all these years," said Mom "It's going to be nice with no hay crew to cook for this summer."

"Where'll you go and what'll you do?"

"Plan to rent a house in town and stay until we get all the cattle arranged on shares. Then move someplace lower. Don't know for sure," said Dad.

I was amazed that they didn't have more specific plans. Perhaps it had happened too fast and being asked to give possession in one month had caught them flatfooted. "How can I help?"

"You can lend a hand when we actually try to move all this accumulated junk," laughed Mom. "Most of it will go to Bob out on the Flineau Place. Good thing, too, since we'd never have room in town."

Dad added, "I don't plan to ranch again, just run cattle without owning a ranch. Ranch without a ranch and all its grief, if that's possible!"

"I know you don't like it, but it's all said and done since we signed the contract," said Mom.

"You're better off with an education than ranching anyway. It'll be a better life, better future," said Dad. They had always gently guided me away from ranching.

"I'm glad you think so. I'd be happy with both. If I'd known you were really going to give up home, I might have wanted to help you run it instead of going off to college."

Scowling a little, Mom said, "I don't know how that could have worked."

"I will come home and ranch right now. You can retire to somewhere warmer."

"Yes, but that would limit us both. This place doesn't bring in enough to support two families," she replied. "And after that Depression, we don't want to scrimp and scrape like that again."

"I wouldn't require much, and you could live as you wished."

"Neither one of us would be happy scrimping that way. It is too expensive ranching in this country. Get your education first, then see," added Dad.

"I just wish I could move up here now. I've got my fifty cows," I replied.

"If you ranched here, this place would own you as much as it did your mother and me all these years," Dad said.

"I'd like to try it and teach here in Walden. That might work."

"Nonsense!" Mom said in a raised tone, "It won't, and I'm glad you can't. We have been all through this before, and it's water under the bridge now, Paul. It's a signed contract, and we can't back out even if we wanted to." After a quiet pause, Mom moved our conversation to other topics.

Later, Dad left in his yellow Chevy pickup to visit a neighbor about pasture for the cattle for the coming summer since they wouldn't have the Two-Bar.

In the kitchen, I asked Mom, "I've never understood why you always disliked this ranch and North Park so much when we kids found it the greatest place?"

"I suppose, Paul, it's because I'm no kid, and how I was raised up here was lots different from the way you were. My childhood was miserable and it sticks with me."

"I know that, Mom, but you must have enjoyed some of it. You always talked so much about your dad and what you did."

"I never would have moved back up here again if it hadn't been for needing schooling for you boys. The location of this darned ranch was perfect. At the time your dad was really crazy about cattle ranching here, too," she said, "But we have learned North Park is for the birds, and the snow birds at that."

"Well, I won't dispute what you say, but I think your negative feelings on the matter have a lot to do with sellin' out."

"Oh yes, Paul, I've always complained about a ranch as long as we have been here, and you know how I've cussed cold North Park, too. That didn't keep us from staying here all these years, did it? There is so much about all of this you don't know. Other things have developed since you have been away in college these past years. You don't understand."

"Try me!"

"I've been thinking about this talk with you, and the best I can do is give you a copy of my daily log for the last years to read. It'll tell you some things that might help you understand." She went into her bedroom and soon handed me two soft red books entitled The Silent Secretary, her notes for the past two years.

"I usually don't let people read these; this is different. When you get back to Greeley, sit down and read 'em. Promise?"

"I promise."

Later, back in my college town of Greeley, my eyes scanned her entries. All were written with sharp blue ink in her perfect penmanship.

EDITH'S LOG - 1960

January:

1/1   Awful cold--snowy. Heck of a way to start a New Year!

1/7   Letter from Mama in the State Hospital--begging again to come live here. Will it ever end? 27 years there--W. has been great about her in this all these years.

1/8   To National Western Stock Show in Denver, cold but fun for a week. Did some good shopping. Nice to get away from home. Willard to our banker and saw livestock people at the commission companies. Good Time.

1/19 Willard exhausted after feeding today. Very cold!

1/21 Wrote Mama telling her I have no way to take care of her so she gets what she needs.

1/22 Bob here talking to W. about how to get more cows.

1/25 Jimmy working part time at Cooper Motors and staying here now. Runs nights with his girlfriends and buddies.

1/26 Paul called--enjoying classes. Jay in from the oil field--roads awful.

1/28 Hate having W out in this. Washed!

1/31 Willard played out today. Shouldn't have fed. Ironed.

February:

2/1 Coyotes in the yard this morning--after my chickens, I suppose. Deep snow. Maybe a foot last night.

2/9 Wedding anniversary. Locked up on the ranch--tied to cattle. Wish we were in warm California to celebrate--can't be done.

2/11 Willard really played out. Slept most of the evening in his chair. The bitter cold really is hard on him.

2/15 Should have another hired man so W. doesn't have to go out in this. He won't hear of it.

2/16 Jimmy helped feed today. Great for W. to have a day off. He went to his school board meeting.

2/18 Larry called. Horrible windy and drifting. W. rode the horse to town for some things for me.

2/23 Jay snowed in on the east side at the oilfield. Six more inches last night.

2/25 Hired man quitting at the end of the month. W. can't do this alone. Worry, worry!

2/27 Sunny day--awfully cold.

2/29 Hired man leaving tomorrow. W. found someone to help for a week or so.

March:

3/1 Larry lost his job at Convair in Cheyenne. Cutbacks, he says. Will be home tomorrow. Willard to his Soil Conservation Service meeting.

3/3 New hired man can't feed all these cattle. Worthless and hopeless. Larry helped today.

3/5 Larry headed to Oklahoma to look for a job.

3/8 Bob helping W. feed after he fired the hired man.

3/10 Larry back. Told W. he'd help feed until we got someone. Days getting longer.

3/11 Saw Ruth Johnson today on the street. Had the gall to ask about Mama. The old bat knows exactly how my folks were cheated out of the ranch, and Mama's situation. She is the limit! I hate living up here!

3/14 W. picked up a hired man to feed. Good thing too, Larry has a job offer on the railroad in Laramie; starts tomorrow.

3/15 Hired man sick. W. fed alone.

3/18 Paul up on spring break. Not spring here. He and Bob helped W. feed.

3/20 W. looking at hired man from the Bighorn--has some cattle. Will come the first of the month.

3/25 Paul back to college. Bill Donalson helping feed until the first of the month. W. really tired. Some melting.

3/30 New man moving into the other house. Downright warm for North Park.

3/31 Bill left today. Was good help--nice kid. New man, Jim Loutham, all moved in. Really melted off. W. not feeling well and saw the doctor. Dr. Morgan told W.--slow down.

April:

4/1 Finally bit-the-bullet and listed this place for sale with Van Schaat in Denver. Asking $200,000--may take forever. W. plans to keep all the cattle if we find a buyer. How he loves them.

4/2 Saw first green grass today, but had to look hard.

4/10 Another letter from Pueblo--this time she wants me to come see how much better she is and how she changed. Same old story. I've protected my family all these years from her. Didn't want them around that awful problem. Will write the psychiatrist about her again.

4/11 Bob here helping W. pull calves. Needs a big break. Willard will sell him cows on credit. I'm staying out of it.

May:

5/1 Saw C. Burr on the street today. Hate that man so for helping steal my folk's ranch. Difficult being civil--but was! Willard to draft board meeting this afternoon.

5/14 Last cow calved today. Still have thirty heifers to go. Good crop this year. W. plans to cull the herd this fall to replace older cows he'll let Bob have.

5/20 Another looker at the ranch—no sale.

5/29 W. says hay looks good this year. He went to the North Park Draft Board meeting this afternoon. He's been on that thing forever.

June:

6/1 Paul not going to summer school. Moved into the other house here to help, needs college money.

6/2 Letter from the doctor--just as I figured, Mama's still not fit for family life and needs the care of an institution.

6/3 C. Burr approached W. about buying the LaRand pasture. He's the last person on earth I'd sell it to after he stole the rest of my Dad's adjoining ranch.

6/14 Jimmy in a bad car wreck up by Westview Cafe, but unhurt. Larry here after fighting and drinking--sleeping it off. Neither very interested in ranching.

6/15 Mosquitoes out in force.

July:

7/10 Ditches shut off for haying.

7/20 Started mowing today

7/22 Jimmy mowing, W. bossing and raking, Bob running the new bailer, Paul tailing the bailer, Jay at the oil field, Larry in Laramie, and me cooking. Away we go.

7/30 1200 bales today, and not a workhorse in the fields. Really sad. How I always loved them.

7/31 My dad's hay ranch would have run rings around this one and all our rough ground. Dirty shame to have lost the best hay ranch up here. Only 600 bales today.

August:

8/1 Helping Bob hay the Fuller Place since he has no equipment At least I don't have to do the cooking alone.

8/31 Haying done for another year except a little soft ground. They will get that later. All men gone tonight. Freedom!

September:

9/1 Bob buying the older cows and some others W. is culling. Wants W. to finance him--not easy since we owe the bank.

9/14 Saw Mama today. Nothing changed--can still put on the good act--looked so very old. I know what I've done is best--it still hurts having her there. Why did she always hate me--not want me? Doctors once said these mental things come on in the early 20s. Sure did with her, and my Dad and I had really tried to endure it.

9/15 W. off looking for cattle to buy for Iowa feeder from the neighbors.

9/23 My birthday--53. W. wants to take me up town to eat tonight. Also, gave me a box of candy--still knows my love of chocolate.

9/24 Paul talked Jimmy into going to college in Greeley. We will pay for it.

October:

10/1 Visited Lucy Mason. She understands the whole story of my life and how it feels to lose a ranch and parents in one feld-swoop. Great friend.

10/15 Sold our steers at 25 cents per pound. To Denver to settle up with the bank.

10/16 Just met the bills this last year and no headway on the FLB loan. Would be tiny now if we hadn't sent both boys to Wentworth those four years. W. borrowed for the next year. Feel like we are getting nowhere fast. But its ranching and loads better than in hard Depression times.

10/17 W. off again, buying cattle for the feeders from Iowa. Loves the dickering with ranchers on price more than the commissions he gets.

10/20 Bob elk hunting with his father-in-law on the west side. Paul up hunting with a bunch of professors and Jimmy behind the Norris Place.

10/26 W. let Bob put his cows at the Norris Place, but says there is little grass there and doesn't see why he's doing it. Guess he has to have some place to go with them.

November:

11/1 Heifers sold for 24 cents to Mr. Hinkhouse an Iowa cattle buyer. Draft sent to the bank. Wish we had never paid uncle Brush that money in the ranch settlement, we might now own this place free and clear.

11/25 Bob's father-in-law let him bring his cows to the Bergquist place since he was out of feed at the Norris Place.

11/26 W. at the stockyards shipping several rancher's cattle to the Iowa feeders, including ours.

December:

12/1 Started feeding cattle today. Late for us. W. promised to get enough help so he doesn't do much.

12/4 W. birthday--also my Dad's. Baked a cake thinking of them both--two good ranchers who love animals and treated them right. How my boys would have enjoyed my Dad if they had the chance. Sad he died before they could!

12/10 Big snow--calves sick. Willard worn out doctoring them. He hired Paul to help feed during his Christmas vacation. Still thinks at times that he would like to ranch--has only fifty cows.

12/23 Paul back to Greeley for two days. All gifts and cards done--just in time.

12/25 Christmas alone with W. First time since 1928. Still snowing and blowing. Shouldn't live in this icebox.

12/28 Road closed to town. W. exhausted after helping feed in this cold. I'm insisting he get someone else to help when Paul leaves.

12/30 Doctor says W. should stop smoking and slow down with bad arm--he is 55. Glad it came from someone other than me--the broken record.

12/31 Jimmy's college grades rotten. Shouldn't have let Paul talk us into it.

After reading the first year's entries and remembering that I had been busy in my separate world for several years, I sat back and gave some deep thought to how little I knew of the true day to day situation my parents had faced. College had shielded me from much of the inner workings on the Two-Bar.

1961

January:
1/1   Men watched football all afternoon. Had big dinner. Worried about W. and our New Year.
1/6   Mama writing to her old Park friends telling them that I'm keeping her in the state hospital for the insane against her will, and nothing is the matter with her. Needs their help to get out--all I can tell them--contact the doctors in Pueblo, yourself.
1/7   Paul back to Greeley. Need to get my husband off this ranch before I don't have one. He feels he has to have a hand in all the feeding. He can't sit in here and just watch! Men!!!

February:
2/1   February came in like a lion with lots of new snow.
2/9   W. is finally letting these two birds feed alone. I'm dumbfounded!
2/20 W. to his North Park Stock Grower Meeting as their new president.

March:
3/1   Jay burned in a gas explosion at the oil field. Now in Laramie hospital. He will be fine--lucky.

3/12 Jimmy's enjoying being a mechanic, but says he doesn't want to spend the rest of his life crawling in and out from under cars.

3/26 Paul's grades good this quarter.

3/30 Bob to take over the Flineau Place in May leasing it from Bergquists. Thought it would go this way once he got enough cows.

April:

4/1 Bob here--needs more cattle to make a living. We listened; he plans to get a night job at the sawmill.

4/15 First calf today. W. busy riding and getting ready for all the heifers to calve.

4/22 Word from the state hospital that Mama is being transferred to a nursing home in Brighton--no longer needs to be in Pueblo--but still needs custodial care.

4/23 Glad I protected my family all these years from Mama. They will never know the hell I went through growing up unwanted with an ill Mother.

4/25 Bob happy and moving to the Flineau Place today on the west side--lease deal. Bigger ranch and more hay, and with more cattle from us.

4/28 Heavenly Days! Ranch buyer here and we actually signed the contract. A miracle; now to tell everyone.

May:

5/2 May came in like lamb, and I can see the green grass— Spring at last.

5/10 Told all the boys we had sold. Bob happy, Jay happy for us, Paul shocked, Larry and Jimmy a bit upset. Jimmy said-- "You can't sell, this is the only home I've ever known." W. and I glad it's finally done.

5/12   Glad to be getting rid of this place while W. is still in one piece. Bob and W. working out a deal for all the ranch equipment. Jay here for lunch and all excited about his job running that oil field. He loves all those pipes, valves, lines, and motors--way beyond me--total Greek!

5/14   Paul coming up tomorrow.

    I sat a bit dazed after finishing the second year's diary, having never known so many details of my grandmother's insanity. Now I understood why Mom never talked in depth about her, nor would Dad. In ranching circles in those times, it was a disgrace having someone not right. A thousand questions raced through my mind, including, selfishly, whether I could be afflicted with the same mental condition. Was it genetic or acquired? No wonder Mom hated the country where some people might have blamed her for her own mother's continued confinement in Pueblo. I realized that Mom had carried a tremendous burden. Her mother who hadn't wanted her was not right mentally.

    To also learn about all the problems with the hired help surprised me, too. It must have been a big worry to the folks and a factor in the eventual sale. Bob's trying to get into ranching may have also pressured them into selling. Once free of the ranch, they probably figured they could help him more in his ranching.

    Dad's physical decline surprised me, too. Only Mom would have known about his condition because he never complained, ever. Having to feed four or five hundred cows in North Park was difficult enough for a sound young man. But Dad was dealing with a crippled left arm and poor lung capacity, as well as putting up with spotty hired help. It was enough to take the pleasure out of a long winter's work.

I had never fully seen all these contributing factors. And the hired help troubles had always been such a part of life on the Two-Bar, with people coming and going, that I took it for granted. To see them written down had a striking impact. I felt ashamed of myself for having questioned Mom and Dad's motives.

As a supposed adult, I vowed to change my attitude, be strong, and support them in their decision. If I'd chosen to ranch, and if I had been around to take more of the burdens off Dad, maybe things would have been different. But the folks hadn't encouraged me much either. It reminded me of a saying attributed to my grandfather "Had the dog run faster, it might have caught the rabbit?" Also, with Bob trying desperately to ranch, I hadn't seen any big opening for me. Since I had chosen to attend college, I was now clearly out of the ranching picture despite my fifty cows that all these years were run with Dad's.

When I visited that spring to help with all the moving, I clearly realized that the ranch was no longer going to be home for me. It was still a hard pill to swallow.

There was no sale of equipment or division of goods among us boys. Every wrench, wagon, tractor and workhorse was transferred to Bob on his father-in-law's ranch near Lake John on the west side. Since the folks never planned to hay again, they let all the equipment go where it was needed. Dad kept all of his cattle. By the first of June, the folks had rented a house in Walden.

When I saw Mom in the Two-Bar log house for the last time, she was waiting for the truck to take the last load of furniture. I could see her through the big picture window as she sat hunched over her small desk starting a fresh Silent Secretary journal for her new town life.

Mom and Dad seemed greatly relieved when Jay finally hauled away that final load. I heard Mom say to Dad, "If this old ranch could talk, what a tale it would tell about our years here."

"You bet, it was a good place for us all," he replied, and together they drove up the rutted road to Walden, leaving behind a way of life that had become a habit.

Their departure from the land was complete. The tensions were now gone. I was amazed to see how carefree and happy Mom and Dad were their first summer in town. They had a more active social life. On a ranch, there was always something that required their immediate attention, and that feeling of having to be home to look after things was now gone. Never before in their married lives had they been away from the constant demands of ranching life and milking cows.

In the house they were renting half-a-mile away from the Two-Bar's gate, early that July I had my talk with Mom. We sat amid all their familiar belongings, causing me to feel at home as if we were on the ranch instead of in tiny Walden.

Looking directly at my incredible Mom, I started the conversation, "I was shocked to read about your mother."

Becoming totally somber, she replied, "I suppose so. It's tortured me all my life."

Seeking more details I asked, "What caused her to be committed in the first place?"

"According to my grandmother she wasn't right, that second summer she returned to teach up here. Something had gone dreadfully wrong with her when she graduated from the University of Denver. And Lindy begged my dad not to marry her, but he wouldn't listen."

"What seemed wrong?"

"She stayed to herself, was sullen, and had lost her zest for life. Yet my dad couldn't see it, and he and I paid for it all our lives. My mother didn't have to be institutionalized until their ranch was stolen. That mess sent her clear over the edge. She wanted my Dad to commit her, telling him over and over, 'Something is dreadfully wrong with me, Jay.' "

Not satisfied, I pressed the point asking, "Exactly what was wrong with her?"

Giving me a blank look, she told me, "The doctors always told me she wasn't fit for family life. We never understood all that medical lingo. And, I wouldn't have her around you kids or Willard. She tried all her life to wreck my life, and I wasn't going to have her around my boys, ruining theirs. She never wanted me, even as a baby, and I'll never know why."

"You did a great job with us despite how you were treated."

"I was determined to make a home for you kids, to be here, and to keep an eye on you. Not have you be the waif I was."

"What will become of her?"

"They'll probably keep her in an institution. Believe me, you're better off never seeing her."

"Of four grandparents, I've seen only one, and only a few times. Never got to really know any of 'em."

Grinning, she said, "Too bad you never knew my dad, Jay; he was wonderful. What a heck of a life he had trying to deal with my mother. It's sad he died young, when you were two. Now she is living forever in that awful place."

"Every family has its problems."

With a determined look, she answered, "Well, this is one you don't ever have to deal with, Paul. I've seen to that, by not letting any of you know much about it. Not anything anyone can do anyway," she said with a sadness that caused me to change the subject.

"Sure is different not having the ranch. But they still let me fish down there."

Smiling confidently, she said, "You don't need a darned ranch to lean on, Paul. Willard and I both think you're smart and can do things beyond ranching."

At that moment, I suddenly realized my mother was exactly right. The ranch and my folks had done their jobs molding me. I found that it was my parents and brothers that I loved more than the ranch itself. It was time to move on. I had learned a way of life from the years on the Two-Bar with its variety of people and natural wonders. My growing up years were treasures I could carry with me and relive as often as my mind wished.

The last time I saw my beautiful, boyhood ranch, it showed some changed fences, bridges, and roads. The meadows, rivers, and pastures, however, remained unaltered. Most of the buildings of my boyhood were as they had been many years before. I felt blessed remembering the fun of exactly what had taken place on our ranch.

Now considering why I had been given such great freedom in growing up, my mind focused on my father and mother's upbringings. Mom's terrible childhood had made her want to give me wide freedom since she didn't have it herself as a child, her mother being unsupportive, negative, and not wanting her around. My father and his father had no good role models, all busy and absent livestock-tending fathers. Wisely, my dad never heavily controlled any of his son's lives, only concentrating on the big issues in our growing into manhood. In my case, that which was visited upon my parents was fortunately not inflicted upon my generation.

In time, I realized that the sale even brought relief to me. No ranch duties beckoned, only good feelings, fond memories, and deep roots tugged at me. That which I had gained from the ranch could never be sold. Its memories were at my core and the basis on which I could develop a larger identity.

Although I hadn't realized it, I'd really left the ranch before it left me. The love of my past, my selfishness, and my Two-Bar kid memories had clouded my thinking because I feared the future. As the years passed, everything became crystal clear.

I had lost nothing and gained everything from my growing years.

The Two-Bar experiences were solidly a part of my being, something I could build upon. This place was still mine, and in my heart, a part of me would always be a wild ranch boy of North Park.

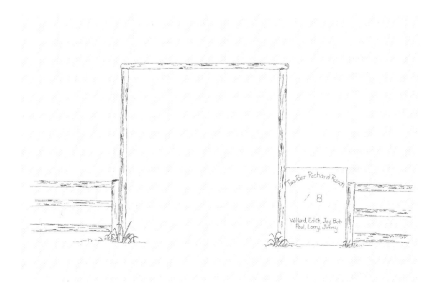

Two-Bar Ranch gate when the ranch was finally sold.
Illustration by David Hartman

ABOUT THE AUTHOR

The great-grandson, grandson, and son of North Park ranch people, Paul Willard Richard was raised in the days of working ranchers. He grew up wild and free at 8,100 feet elevation on the Two-Bar Ranch on the northwest edge of Walden, Colorado. His love of the ranch's rivers and outdoor life led him to eventually become a professor of biological science at the University of Northern Colorado in Greeley, Colorado. He taught junior high, high school, university, and adult students for thirty-two years. His heart has always been in the North Park he writes about. As a professor emeritus of the biological sciences from UNC, he lives and writes in Greeley, Colorado.